# The Complete Personal Bankruptcy Guide

### Edward A. Haman

Attorney at Law

**SPHINX® PUBLISHING**
AN IMPRINT OF SOURCEBOOKS, INC.®
NAPERVILLE, ILLINOIS
www.SphinxLegal.com

First Edition: 2006

Published by: **Sphinx® Publishing, An Imprint of Sourcebooks, Inc.®**

<u>Naperville Office</u>
P.O. Box 4410
Naperville, Illinois 60567-4410
630-961-3900
Fax: 630-961-2168
www.sourcebooks.com
www.SphinxLegal.com

This publication is designed to provide accurate and authoritative information in regard to the subject matter covered. It is sold with the understanding that the publisher is not engaged in rendering legal, accounting, or other professional service. If legal advice or other expert assistance is required, the services of a competent professional person should be sought.

*From a Declaration of Principles Jointly Adopted by a Committee of the American Bar Association and a Committee of Publishers and Associations*

**This product is not a substitute for legal advice.**

*Disclaimer required by Texas statutes.*

**Library of Congress Cataloging-in-Publication Data**
Haman, Edward A.
The complete personal bankruptcy guide / by Edward A. Haman.-- 1st ed.
p. cm.
Includes index.
ISBN-13: 978-1-57248-545-7 (pbk. : alk. paper)
ISBN-10: 1-57248-545-0 (pbk. : alk. paper)
1. Bankruptcy--United States--Popular works. I. Title.

KF1524.6.H358 2006
346.7307'8--dc22

2006000079

Printed and bound in the United States of America.
SB — 10 9 8 7 6 5 4 3 2 1

# Contents

# Using Self-Help Law Books

Before using a self-help law book, you should realize the advantages and disadvantages of doing your own legal work and understand the challenges and diligence that this requires.

**The Growing Trend**

Rest assured that you will not be the first or only person handling your own legal matter. For example, in some states, more than 75% of the people in divorces and other cases represent themselves. Because of the high cost of legal services, this is a major trend, and many courts are struggling to make it easier for people to represent themselves. However, some courts are not happy with people who do not use attorneys and refuse to help them in any way. For some, the attitude is, "Go to the law library and figure it out for yourself."

We write and publish self-help law books to give people an alternative to the often complicated and confusing legal books found in most law libraries. We have made the explanations of the law as simple and easy to understand as possible. Of course, unlike an attorney advising an individual client, we cannot cover every conceivable possibility.

**Cost/Value Analysis**

Whenever you shop for a product or service, you are faced with various levels of quality and price. In deciding what product or service to buy, you make a cost/value analysis on the basis of your willingness to pay and the quality you desire.

When buying a car, you decide whether you want transportation, comfort, status, or sex appeal. Accordingly, you decide among choices such as a Neon, a Lincoln, a Rolls Royce, or a Porsche. Before making a decision, you usually weigh the merits of each option against the cost.

When you get a headache, you can take a pain reliever (such as aspirin) or visit a medical specialist for a neurological examination. Given this choice, most people, of course, take a pain reliever, since it costs only pennies; whereas a medical examination costs hundreds of dollars and takes a lot of time. This is usually a logical choice because it is rare to need anything more than a pain reliever for a headache. But in some cases, a headache may indicate a brain tumor, and failing to see a specialist right away can result in complications. Should everyone with a headache go to a specialist? Of course not, but people treating their own illnesses must realize that they are betting, on the basis of their cost/value analysis of the situation, that they are taking the most logical option.

The same cost/value analysis must be made when deciding to do one's own legal work. Many legal situations are very straightforward, requiring a simple form and no complicated analysis. Anyone with a little intelligence and a book of instructions can handle the matter without outside help.

But there is always the chance that complications are involved that only an attorney would notice. To simplify the law into a book like this, several legal cases often must be condensed into a single sentence or paragraph. Otherwise, the book would be several hundred pages long and too complicated for most people. However, this simplification necessarily leaves out many details and nuances that would apply to special or unusual situations. Also, there are many ways to interpret most legal questions. Your case may come before a judge who disagrees with the analysis of our authors.

Therefore, in deciding to use a self-help law book and to do your own legal work, you must realize that you are making a cost/value analysis. You have decided that the money you will save in doing it yourself outweighs the chance that your case will not turn out to your satisfaction. Most people handling their own simple legal matters never have a problem, but occasionally people find that it ended up costing them more to have an attorney straighten out the situation than it would have if they had hired an attorney in the beginning. Keep this in mind while handling your case, and be sure to consult an attorney if you feel you might need further guidance.

**Local Rules**  The next thing to remember is that a book which covers the law for the entire nation, or even for an entire state, cannot possibly include every procedural difference of every jurisdiction. Whenever possible, we provide the exact form needed; however, in some areas, each county, or even each judge, may require unique forms and procedures. In our state books, our forms usually cover the majority of counties in the state or provide examples of the type of form that will be required. In our national books, our forms are sometimes even more general in nature but are designed to give a good idea of the type of form that will be needed in most locations. Nonetheless, keep in mind that your state, county, or judge may have a requirement, or use a form, that is not included in this book.

You should not necessarily expect to be able to get all of the information and resources you need solely from within the pages of this book. This book will serve as your guide, giving you specific information whenever possible and helping you to find out what else you will need to know. This is just like if you decided to build your own backyard deck. You might purchase a book on how to build decks. However, such a book would not include the building codes and permit requirements of every city, town, county, and township in the nation; nor would it include the lumber, nails, saws, hammers, and other materials and tools you would need to actually build the deck. You would use the book as your guide, and then do some work and research involving such matters as whether you need a permit of some kind, what type and grade of wood is available in your area, whether to use hand tools or power tools, and how to use those tools.

Before using the forms in a book like this, you should check with your court clerk to see if there are any local rules of which you should be aware or local forms you will need to use. Often, such forms will require the same information as the forms in the book but are merely laid out differently or use slightly different language. They will sometimes require additional information.

Besides being subject to local rules and practices, the law is subject to change at any time. The courts and the legislatures of all fifty states are constantly revising the laws. It is possible that while you are reading this book, some aspect of the law is being changed.

In most cases, the change will be of minimal significance. A form will be redesigned, additional information will be required, or a waiting period will be extended. As a result, you might need to revise a form, file an extra form, or wait out a longer time period. These types of changes will not usually affect the outcome of your case. On the other hand, sometimes a major part of the law is changed, the entire law in a particular area is rewritten, or a case that was the basis of a central legal point is overruled. In such instances, your entire ability to pursue your case may be impaired.

# Introduction

If you are like most Americans, you are probably struggling to make payments on a mortgage, car loans, medical bills, various credit cards, student loans, home improvement loans, or other kinds of debt. Perhaps you have been laid off at work due to local or nationwide economic conditions, or due to problems with your company or industry. Maybe you or a member of your family had a serious illness or injury, and many of the medical bills were not covered by insurance.

This book is designed specifically for you. It will help you analyze your situation, decide whether you should file for bankruptcy, and guide you through the steps to either avoid bankruptcy or get through the bankruptcy procedure. This is not a law school course, but a practical guide to get you through the system as easily as possible.

This book presents fairly simplified procedures for use by non-attorneys. It does not contain all the possible loopholes or tricks of the trade that an experienced bankruptcy lawyer might use to gain a little extra advantage. On the other hand, for many people, these legal details either do not apply or their advantage will be offset by having to pay the fee of an experienced bankruptcy attorney.

If you are at a high income level, or have extensive and complicated investments and debts, you will need a lawyer. However, this book will still help you understand the system and work with your lawyer more effectively.

**NOTE:** *This book is not designed for corporate, partnership, or business-related bankruptcies.*

Bankruptcy law is covered in various chapters of the federal Bankruptcy Code. This book covers bankruptcy under Chapter 7 and Chapter 13 of the Bankruptcy Code. In order to avoid confusion between chapters of the Bankruptcy Code and what would normally be called chapters of this book, the word "section" is used instead of the word "chapter" when referring to this book. The word "chapter" is only used when referring to the Bankruptcy Code.

Sections 1 through 5 of this book explain the legal system, help you decide if bankruptcy is for you, and assist your preparation for filing for bankruptcy. Section 6 explains the details of pursuing a case under Chapter 7 of the Bankruptcy Code, and Section 7 explains the details of filing under Chapter 13 of the Bankruptcy Code. Section 8 deals with special circumstances that may arise, and Section 9 gives you some advice for the future—after you have completed your bankruptcy case in court.

Appendix A contains the federal and state lists of property that you may keep even if you file for bankruptcy. Appendix B provides some checklists for filing bankruptcy and worksheets that will help you fill in the forms in Appendix C.

Be sure to read this entire book, especially the parts of Section 6 or Section 7 on "Understanding Legal Forms," before you begin preparing any of the forms in this book. You may want to make several copies of the forms in this book and save the originals, so you can make more copies if you need them.

# Bankruptcy and the Legal System

This section gives you a basic overview of bankruptcy law and the legal system. It includes vital information about legal terminology, bankruptcy court procedures, the types of bankruptcy relief available, and the recent changes in the bankruptcy law. Do not skip this section, as it provides you with basic information you need in order to fully understand the later sections.

## HISTORY AND GENERAL INFORMATION

Simply stated, *bankruptcy* is a legal procedure that allows you to get out of oppressive debt and get a fresh start financially. The concept of bankruptcy goes back at least to the time of the Old Testament, which states:

> *At the end of every seven years you shall grant a release and this is the manner of the release: every creditor shall release what he has lent to his neighbor....*
> —(Deuteronomy 15:1-2)

In the United States, the importance of bankruptcy was recognized at the time of our nation's birth and was made a part of the U.S.

Constitution. Article I, Section 8 of the U.S. Constitution gives Congress the power to establish "uniform laws on the subject of bankruptcies throughout the United States." In 1800, Congress enacted the first bankruptcy laws.

Today, there exists a comprehensive set of federal laws that govern bankruptcy. There are so many bankruptcies filed each year that there is a special division of the federal court system devoted exclusively to bankruptcy. In recent years, personal bankruptcy filings have reached over one million annually. If you need to file for bankruptcy, you can be sure you will not be alone.

The average person filing for bankruptcy has an annual income of about $22,000, and has probably undergone a substantial period of unemployment. Many are single mothers. One study indicates that about half of all bankruptcies are the result of large, uninsured medical expenses.

## Recent Changes in Bankruptcy Law

In spite of this, creditors (mostly credit card companies) have convinced Congress that far too many people filing for bankruptcy are simply irresponsible consumers out to run up large debts that they avoid paying through bankruptcy. This resulted in Congress passing the *Bankruptcy Abuse Prevention and Consumer Protection Act of 2005* (commonly abbreviated BAPCPA). This new law consists of over 500 pages, which can be summed up by saying that it is now more difficult for people to wipe out debts through bankruptcy. The changes to the law are incorporated in the information and forms contained in this book.

## Purpose and Procedure

The bankruptcy procedure serves two purposes. First, it allows you to change your financial situation. Second, it holds your creditors at bay while you make this change.

Depending upon your financial situation, you will choose one of two bankruptcy procedures. The first is traditional bankruptcy, in which your debts are forgiven altogether. The other procedure is commonly referred to by a few different names, such as *reorganization*, a *wage-earner plan*, or a *repayment plan*. In this procedure, you arrange to pay off some or all of your debts according to a payment plan that you can handle on your income. Although this is technically not bankruptcy, it is a part of the bankruptcy law and will be referred to in this book as a bankruptcy. Due to the 2005 changes in the bankruptcy law, more people will be required to use the payment plan procedure than in the past.

**Chapters of Bankruptcy**

Traditional bankruptcy is covered in Chapter 7 of the federal Bankruptcy Code, and is often referred to as a *Chapter 7*. The payment plan procedure is covered in Chapter 13 of the Bankruptcy Code, and is referred to as a *Chapter 13*. These procedures will be discussed in greater detail in later sections of this book.

There are other chapters to the Bankruptcy Code. *Chapter 12* is specially designed for farmers, so if you are a farmer, you should consult a bankruptcy lawyer. *Chapter 11* is generally designed for corporations and partnerships. Chapter 11 is also available to individuals, although it is not used unless the person has secured debts in excess of $750,000, unsecured debts in excess of $250,000, and sufficient income to pay off a portion of these debts over several years. If you are in this situation, you should consult a lawyer.

## THE LEGAL SYSTEM

This section gives you a general introduction to the legal system of the bankruptcy court. Most people have an idea of the way the legal system should be, which usually does not match reality. If you do not learn to accept reality, you will experience much stress and frustration. Although bankruptcy can get as complicated as any other area of law, for most cases it is a bit more cut and dry, making it more predictable than many other areas of the law.

**Rules**

Our legal system is a system of rules. There are basically three types of rules.

1.  *Rules of Law*: These provide the basic substance of the law, such as defining a debt and describing what property can be kept after bankruptcy.

2.  *Rules of Procedure*: These outline how matters are to be handled in the courts, such as requiring court papers to be in a certain form or filed within a certain time.

3.  *Rules of Evidence*: These set forth the manner in which facts are to be proven.

In bankruptcy, it is not usually necessary to be concerned with rules of evidence. Most bankruptcy cases are presented to the court in the way of standard forms. It is unnecessary to call witnesses and introduce evidence as would be done in a trial of another type of case. In addition, the rules of law and procedure are so well-defined that, in most cases, they are not nearly as complicated and subject to interpretation as in many other areas. For most middle-class Americans, bankruptcy entails filling out certain forms, filing them with the court, and attending a couple of meetings. As long as you provide the court with accurate and complete information about your finances, you should not have any difficulties.

A basic rule stressed in this book is *do not panic*. If, as you read, you find yourself thinking, *I will never be able to do this myself,* keep reading. By the end of this book, you will see that it is a fairly simple task.

This advice also applies to dealing with the court. The United States is divided into numerous districts, and each district has its own bankruptcy court. Each court has a court clerk and may have some local rules. It is possible that the clerk in your district will tell you that one of your papers is not exactly correct in its form or content. This happens to lawyers with many years of experience, so there is no need to feel bad if it happens to you. If it does, you should relax, find out exactly what the clerk wants, and do it the clerk's way. Similar to the old saying about the army, there is the right way, the wrong way, and the clerk's way. Only the clerk's way will get you what you want. Fortunately, the forms are standardized all over the country, so this should not be a problem.

**The System**     Although bankruptcy is relatively simple and straightforward, there are a few realities of our nation's legal system that can apply to all areas of the law to some degree. A brief mention of these realities will help prepare you in the event you come across any of them.

***The system is not perfect.*** The rules are designed to apply to all persons in all situations. This can sometimes lead to an unfair result if one person's situation is slightly different.

It is also possible for a judge to make a bad decision, or for someone to cheat and not get caught (such as by not telling the truth, even under oath). As a well-known and respected judge once said to a young attorney, "This is a court of law, young man, not a court of justice!"

***Judges do not always follow the rules.*** Many decisions are made simply on the judge's personal view of what seems fair under the circumstances (even if the judge does not take the time to fully understand the circumstances or has a strange idea of fairness). The judge will then find some way to try to justify his or her decision, even if it means distorting or ignoring the existing law.

***The system is slow.*** Even lawyers get frustrated by how long it can take to get a case completed. Things generally take longer than you would expect. Patience is required to get through the system with a minimum amount of stress. Do not get angry or let your frustration show.

***No two cases are alike.*** If your friends or coworkers learn that you have filed for bankruptcy, you can be sure you will be getting a great deal of "legal" advice from them. *Do not listen to them!* Everyone has their own experience to relate, or a story to tell about a friend or relative who has gone through bankruptcy. *Do not listen to them!* If your friend used an attorney, remember that many attorneys are not always clear when explaining the law and procedure to their clients.

Your case is not exactly the same as the one your friend will want to tell you about, so you cannot expect your experience to be the same. After reading this book, you will know more about bankruptcy than many of your friends, and what you learn here will serve as a much better guide than a friend's advice.

**The Players**   Law and the legal system are often compared to games, and just like games, it is important to understand who the players are.

***The judge.*** The judge has the power to determine whether your debts can be discharged (or whether your payment plan can be accepted). In bankruptcy court, the judge is a U.S. District Court Judge, who is appointed to his or her position for life by the president. Bankruptcy judges have large caseloads, and like it best when your case can be conducted quickly and without hassles. This means that you should be sure that your papers are done correctly, with complete and accurate information. Most likely, you will only see the judge at your final hearing, which will only take a few minutes.

The most important thing is to show respect for the judge. This means you answer the judge's questions as simply and to the point as possible. Under no circumstances should you argue with the judge, or with a creditor while you are before the judge. Always follow the judge's instructions without argument or complaint.

***The court clerk.*** The job of the clerk is to file papers, schedule hearings, and maintain the court's files. Be sure you are friendly and cooperative toward people in the clerk's office. If you make a clerk your enemy, there is no end to the trouble he or she can cause you.

Generally, the clerk has no interest in the outcome of your case, but is only interested that all of the paperwork is in order. The clerk has the power to accept or reject your papers. If the clerk wants something changed in your papers, just find out what he or she wants and do it.

If you happen to come across a particularly unfriendly clerk, try to understand that clerks frequently deal with frustrated, angry, and rude people. You will get much better treatment by showing the clerk that you are happy to cooperate and are patient with the slowness of the system, rather than being just another rude person causing him or her stress.

***The trustee.*** After you file your first papers, your case will be assigned to a trustee. The trustee's job is to make sure that your papers are complete and accurate, ensure that all of your creditors are notified about your bankruptcy, handle the disposition of your assets, and generally assure that your case continues properly and is ready for final hearing with the judge. The trustee works for the court, and is a middle-person between you, your creditors, and the court.

The trustee's office is a division of the United States Department of Justice. There is a lot of valuable and essential information on its website at **www.usdoj.gov/ust**. Some of the information you need to complete your bankruptcy forms can be accessed through this website.

***The creditors.*** These are the people and companies to whom you owe money. These people will not be happy about your bankruptcy, because it means they will probably not get fully paid. Some of them may be allowed to take back the property they sold you and some of them will get nothing. Some of them may be very hostile and some of them will just accept your bankruptcy as part of the risk of doing business. (After all, they encouraged you to buy on credit.)

In general, once you file your bankruptcy petition, your creditors can no longer bother you for payment. You may stop making payments once you file, except on items you do not want to lose (such as your home and car). All your creditor can do is either object to the court that you do not qualify for bankruptcy or object to your plan for how their debt is to be handled. It will then be up to the judge to decide. Filing for bankruptcy will also stop any lawsuits that may have been brought by creditors or others. However, proceedings for eviction, driver's license suspension, divorce, or child support may continue.

***Lawyers.*** This either refers to your lawyer (discussed in Section 2 of this book) or to your creditor's lawyer. Generally, in bankruptcy proceedings, there is little difference between dealing with your creditor or its attorney.

Many lawyers are dignified and polite in their dealings with the other side in a case. These lawyers will try to get the best deal for their client, and will do it in a polite and honest, but firm and businesslike, manner.

Other lawyers are truly nasty people, who are impolite and cannot deal with their opponents in a civilized manner. They will not hesitate to make threats and lie in an attempt to intimidate you. These lawyers simply cannot be reasoned with, and you should not try. If you encounter one of these lawyers, simply do not speak to him or her. Just address all of your statements to the trustee or the judge. If you are uncertain of the law as stated by such an attorney, you may wish to consult an attorney yourself.

# BANKRUPTCY LAW AND PROCEDURE

The next few pages give you a summary of the law and the procedure of bankruptcy. The details and how-to file are discussed later, but it is important to get a more general overview of the process first.

**In General**    The idea of the bankruptcy law is to give you a fresh start, free from your previous debts, with enough assets to live on and help you start over. The law sets up different classes of debts and property, which determine what property you can and cannot keep, whether or not your creditors get paid, and how much your creditors get paid.

**Limitations**    There are some limits as to how often you can use bankruptcy. You may not file under Chapter 7 if:

- ✪    you obtained a discharge under a Chapter 7, 11, 12, or 13 petition filed within the past eight years;

- ✪    you had a Chapter 7 case dismissed within the past 180 days because you violated a court order; or,

- ✪    you had a Chapter 7 case dismissed within the past 180 days because you asked for dismissal after a creditor asked for the automatic stay to be lifted.

However, these limits do not apply to Chapter 13 cases, which may be filed at any time. If your secured debts exceed $750,000 or your unsecured debts exceed $250,000, you may not use Chapter 13. If you are in this situation, you should consult a lawyer about the possibility of filing under Chapter 11 of the Bankruptcy Code.

**Exempt and Nonexempt Property**    Each piece of property you own will be classified as either *exempt* (which means you may be able to keep it) or *nonexempt* (which means you will have to turn it over to the trustee). Although the Bankruptcy Code is a federal law, the available exemptions are different in each state. Appendix A of this book will tell you how to determine the property that is exempt in your state. This is also discussed in more detail later.

Most states allow you to keep a certain dollar value of:

- ✪ real estate;

- ✪ vehicles;

- ✪ tools used in your profession;

- ✪ insurance policies;

- ✪ clothing;

- ✪ household furnishings;

- ✪ retirement benefits;

- ✪ public benefits (such as workers' compensation and unemployment); and,

- ✪ other personal items.

These are examples of exempt property. However, exempt property may still be lost if you borrowed money to buy it and do not keep up your payments.

**Secured and Unsecured Debts**

Debts are classified as either *secured* or *unsecured*. A *secured debt* is one that is covered by a certain piece of property. The most common examples are home mortgages and car loans. The papers you signed when you borrowed the money specifically state that if you do not pay, the lender may take the property. You may not keep such property unless you pay for it, even if it would otherwise be exempt property in your state. If you do not want to lose your home or car, you will have to arrange a payment plan acceptable to your lender or keep your payments current.

An *unsecured debt* is not covered by any property. Examples of unsecured debts are credit cards, department store credit cards, and medical bills. In these cases, the lender does not get paid and does not get any property either. Even if you bought your dining room furniture with your credit card, it is still an unsecured debt (unless you also signed some additional paper that states that the property secured the loan).

**Mortgage Foreclosures**

Since a mortgage is a secured debt, filing for bankruptcy will not allow you to keep your home without paying for it. The best bankruptcy can do is buy you time to make arrangements to catch up on your payments, or allow you to arrange some kind of adjustment in the terms of your loan so that you can keep your home.

When you file for bankruptcy, the law imposes what is called an *automatic stay*. This prevents any creditor from taking any legal action against you unless it first gets the permission of the bankruptcy court. Therefore, if your lender has already begun a *foreclosure action*, filing bankruptcy will temporarily stop the foreclosure—probably for a few weeks at most. If your lender has not yet filed for foreclosure, it may not do so until the bankruptcy court lifts the automatic stay.

If you file under Chapter 7 of the Bankruptcy Code, you will either need to bring your payments current or work out some arrangement with your lender by the time the automatic stay is lifted. If you file for bankruptcy under Chapter 13 of the Bankruptcy Code, you may be able to get the bankruptcy court to require the lender to accept new terms for repayment (such as an extension of the time of the loan). The best thing to do is talk to your lender as soon as you find you are having trouble making payments. The longer you wait, the less likely you will be able to work something out.

When you talk to your lender, explain your financial situation and have a plan to present (such as extending the term of the loan). Just be sure you can follow through with the plan you propose. Many lenders would rather work with you than foreclose. For a lender, foreclosure is time-consuming and expensive. They really would rather not have to hassle with taking the home back and trying to resell it for enough to recoup the costs.

**Nondischargeable Debts**

One other significant part of the law is that there are a few types of debts that cannot be discharged in bankruptcy. The four most common types of nondischargeable debts are:

✪    taxes (with certain exceptions);

✪    government-guaranteed student loans;

✪    child support; and,

✪    alimony.

You still have to pay these debts even if you go through a bankruptcy.

**Bankruptcy Procedure**    The bankruptcy procedure can be viewed as a simple four-step process.

1.    You prepare and file your **VOLUNTARY PETITION** and various supporting documents. (see form 1, p.215.) This provides information about your income, expenses, property, and debts. It also requests that the court discharge your debts (or approve your payment plan) according to the law.

2.    The trustee sends notices to all of your creditors to advise them that you have filed for bankruptcy. This gives your creditors an opportunity to be sure you have given correct information in your petition, and to raise any questions or objections.

3.    You have a meeting with the trustee and your creditors. This is when any questions or objections are discussed and settled.

4.    You attend a hearing, at which time the judge will discharge your debts (or approve your payment plan). This may even be a mass discharge of many cases at one time, in which you and many others obtain a discharge at the same time.

**Other Considerations**    You should also consider the following things before you decide to file for bankruptcy.

✪    If a friend or relative co-signed a loan for you, that friend or relative will still be liable for the debt.

✪    You may have your case dismissed if the judge determines that you have enough income to pay your debts, if you defrauded your creditors, or if you charged a lot for entertainment, vacations, or luxury items just before filing.

✪    You may not need to file for bankruptcy if your only goal is to get bill collectors off your back, or to avoid having your property or wages attached. Other state and federal laws may be able to accomplish these goals without filing for bankruptcy.

**Chapter 7 Bankruptcy (Discharge of Debts)**    As mentioned earlier, there are two types of bankruptcy for individuals—the discharge of debts and the payment plan. Chapter 7 of the Bankruptcy Code is for the discharge of debts, which is the traditional bankruptcy. Under Chapter 7, you either pay for or give up your property for secured debts. You surrender any nonexempt property in order to pay off as much of your other debt as possible. You keep all of your other exempt property and are forever released from any obligation to repay the remaining debt.

One important requirement for a Chapter 7 bankruptcy is that you do not have sufficient income to allow you to pay at least a portion of your debts. Making this determination is largely a mathematical calculation, and there is a form for making the calculation. If you have enough income, you will need to file under Chapter 13 instead of under Chapter 7. This is discussed further in later sections of this book.

**Chapter 13 Bankruptcy (Payment Plan)**    In a Chapter 13 bankruptcy, you are not seeking to get rid of all of your debt entirely, but only to do one or a combination of the following:

✪    restructure your payments so they are more manageable, considering your income or

✪    get rid of part of your debt so that you can manage payments.

This can be done by spreading your payments over a longer period of time or by paying only a part of the loan. Either way, your monthly or weekly payment will be reduced. This type of payment plan can last up to five years. This means your finances will be under the watchful eye of the trustee during this time.

The two main things the trustee and the judge will consider in deciding whether to accept your plan are:

1. whether the creditors are being treated fairly and

2. whether each creditor will receive at least as much as if you had gone with the traditional Chapter 7 bankruptcy.

For a Chapter 13 bankruptcy, you will fill out some different forms than for a Chapter 7. The main difference is that you will need to fill out a form in which you offer a payment plan that you create. In a Chapter 13 case, the creditors' meeting is usually concerned with trying to reach a plan that will be acceptable to the creditors. You may spend some time negotiating with the creditors as they try to get you to change your plan so they get more money or get it faster.

It is not necessary that the creditors agree with your plan, but if they do agree, it will be easily accepted by the trustee and the judge. Even if the creditors object to your plan, it will still be approved as long as it is fair (in the judge's opinion, which usually relates to all creditors of the same type being treated equally) and as long as each creditor gets at least as much as if you had filed under Chapter 7.

**Converting to Another Chapter**

In some circumstances, it is possible to convert a Chapter 13 bankruptcy to a Chapter 7 bankruptcy. It is also possible to convert a Chapter 7 case to a Chapter 13 case. Prior to changes to the bankruptcy law in 2005, such conversions were more common because the old law was not very specific about when a person should file under either chapter of the Bankruptcy Code. A large part of the changes made it more clear as to when a Chapter 7 bankruptcy will be allowed. The qualifications for a Chapter 7 case will be explained in detail in Section 6 of this book and more about converting a case is discussed in Section 8.

# Lawyers

This section helps you decide if you want to hire a lawyer, and if so, how to go about hiring one. It also gives you advice about how to effectively work with an attorney.

You are not required to have a lawyer in order to file for bankruptcy. Most people should be able to handle their own bankruptcy. However, you will probably need an attorney if:

- ✪ you are involved in a business, either alone or in a partnership;

- ✪ you own stock in a privately held corporation;

- ✪ you are married and your spouse is not filing for bankruptcy with you;

- ✪ you are a farmer (there are special bankruptcy laws covering farm bankruptcy); or,

- ✪ you encounter a creditor, trustee, or judge who is particularly difficult.

## NEEDING A LAWYER

One of your first questions about bankruptcy probably is *How much will an attorney cost?* Attorneys come in all price ranges, although the exact range is uncertain. Due to the 2005 changes in the bankruptcy law, it is expected that attorneys will drastically increase their fees for bankruptcies. Prior to the 2005 changes, you could typically find lawyers charging between $500 and $2,500, depending upon where you live and the complexity of your case. You could also find ads in the newspapers for $150 to $200 bankruptcies, but these were usually only available in very simple cases, and were *no-frills services*. If you used one of these lawyers, it was important to be sure you knew exactly what would be provided for the fee.

Now that the new law requires more forms and places new obligations on attorneys, some experts are speculating that attorneys' fees will double. In any event, looking in the newspaper classified ads or making a few phone calls to attorneys' offices should give you a good idea of the going rate in your community. Most lawyers will want to be paid in advance. Most new (and therefore, less expensive) attorneys are quite capable of handling a simple bankruptcy, but by the time you have read this book, you will probably know as much about bankruptcy as many of them.

**Advantages to Having a Lawyer**

The following are some reasons why you may want to consider hiring a lawyer.

✪ You may be able to save more of your property. A lawyer may be able to find more loopholes in the bankruptcy law, or give you other suggestions that will preserve more assets or discharge more debt. However, these savings may be offset by the attorney's fee you will pay. Generally, the more loopholes you want, the more experienced (and expensive) of an attorney you will need.

✪ Judges and other attorneys may take you more seriously. People who represent themselves often waste time by being unfamiliar with the procedures. However, this should not be a problem with anyone who has read this book.

✪    A lawyer can serve as a buffer between you and your creditors.

✪    In the event your case becomes complicated, it is an advantage to have an attorney who is familiar with your case. It can be comforting to have a lawyer for advice and reassurance. Again, the more advice and reassurance, the higher the attorney's fee.

**Advantages to Representing Yourself**

Here are some reasons why you may want to do the work yourself.

✪    You save the cost of a lawyer.

✪    Sometimes judges and trustees feel more sympathetic toward a person who is not represented by a lawyer. They will often actually help you.

✪    The procedure may be faster. One of the most frequent complaints about lawyers involves delay in completing the case, usually due to heavy caseloads. If you are handling your own case, you will be able to keep it moving through the system.

✪    Selecting a good attorney is not easy.

**Middle Ground**

You may want to look for an attorney who will be willing to accept an hourly fee to answer your questions and give you help on an as-needed basis. Expect to pay at least $75 per hour for such consultation. Attorneys offering *free initial consultation* or a consultation *for just $20* will often not provide you with any usable advice, and will not explain how you should do something.

## SELECTING A LAWYER

If you decide that you want a lawyer to represent you in filing for bankruptcy or in dealing with your creditors to try to avoid bankruptcy, you will need to seek one out. The attorney you select should be experienced in bankruptcy, should instill confidence in you, and should be someone you feel comfortable talking to about your situation. The following pages will provide you with the things to consider when locating such a lawyer.

**Finding Lawyers**

Finding a lawyer is a two-step process. First, you need to decide which attorney (or attorneys) to make an appointment with. Second, you need to decide if you want to hire the attorney you meet.

***Ask a friend.*** A common, and frequently the best, way to find a lawyer is to ask someone you know to recommend one.

***Lawyer referral service.*** You can find a referral service by looking in the Yellow Pages of your phone directory under the heading "Attorney Referral Services" or "Attorneys." The referral service is free, but it does not guarantee the quality of the attorney's work or the level of experience or ability.

***Yellow Pages.*** Check under the heading for "Attorneys." Look for ads for firms or lawyers that indicate they handle bankruptcy or credit matters.

***Newspaper.*** In the classified ads, you should find a section for "Legal Services" that often includes the least expensive attorneys—but expect minimal services. You may even be given a set of forms to complete yourself.

***Ask another lawyer.*** If you have used an attorney in the past (such as for a will, real estate closing, or traffic ticket), call him or her and ask for a referral to a bankruptcy attorney.

**Evaluating a Lawyer**

You should select three to five lawyers worthy of further consideration. Call each attorney's office and ask the following questions.

- ✪ Does the attorney (or firm) handle bankruptcies?

- ✪ How much can I expect it to cost?

- ✪ How soon can I get an appointment?

- ✪ What is the cost for an initial consultation?

If you like the answers you get, ask if you can speak to the attorney. Once you get in contact with the attorney (either by phone or at an appointment), ask the following questions.

✪  How much will it cost?

✪  How will the fee be paid? (Usually it is paid in advance, in full.)

✪  What percentage of the attorney's cases involve bankruptcies? (Do not expect an exact answer, but you should get a rough estimate of at least 10%.)

✪  How long will it take? (Do not expect an exact answer, but the attorney should be able to give you an average range and discuss the variables.)

If you get acceptable answers to these questions, it is time to ask yourself these questions.

✪  Do I feel comfortable talking to this lawyer?

✪  Does this lawyer seem confident and knowledgeable?

✪  Is this lawyer willing and able to explain things so I can understand?

If you get satisfactory answers to all of these questions, you probably have a lawyer you will be able to work with. Remember, *you* are interviewing the lawyer to see if you want to hire him or her.

## WORKING WITH A LAWYER

You will most likely work best with your attorney if you keep an open, honest, and friendly attitude. You should also consider the following suggestions.

**Ask Questions**    If you want to know something, or if you do not understand something, ask your attorney. If you do not understand the answer, ask him or her to explain it again. There are many points of law that even lawyers do not fully understand, so you should not be embarrassed about asking questions. If your lawyer will not take the time to explain what he or she is doing, it may be time to look for a new lawyer.

**Give Complete Information**

Anything you tell your lawyer is confidential, and your lawyer cannot help you if he or she does not have all of the information. The more information you give your lawyer, the more he or she can do for you.

**Accept Reality**

Accept what your lawyer tells you about the law and the system. It is pointless to argue because the law or the system does not work the way you think it should. Remember, it is not your lawyer's fault that the system is not perfect or that the law does not say what you would like it to say.

**Be Patient**

Be patient with the system and with your attorney. Do not expect your attorney to return your phone call within an hour. Your attorney may not even be able to return it the same day. Most lawyers are very busy. It is rare that an attorney can maintain a full caseload and still make each client feel like his or her only client.

**Talk to the Secretary**

Your lawyer's secretary can be a valuable source of information. Be friendly and get to know him or her. The secretary will often be able to answer your questions, and you will not get a bill for the time you talk. Even if the secretary cannot answer your question, he or she can probably get the answer from the attorney and call you back faster than if you insist on waiting to speak directly to the lawyer.

**Be On Time**

Be on time to appointments with your lawyer and to court hearings.

**Keep Your Case Moving**

Many lawyers operate on the old principal of *the squeaking wheel gets the oil*. Work on a case tends to get put off until a deadline is near, an emergency develops, or the client calls. There is a reason for this. Many lawyers take more cases than can be effectively handled in order to increase their income. Your task is to become a squeaking wheel that does not squeak to the point of being aggravating to your lawyer and his or her office staff. Whenever you talk to your lawyer, ask the following questions.

✪  What is the next step?

✪  When do you expect it to be done?

✪  When should I talk to you next?

If you do not hear from the lawyer when you expect, call him or her the following day. Do not remind your lawyer that you did not receive a call—just ask how your case is going.

**Try to Save Money**  Of course, you do not want to spend unnecessary money for an attorney. Here are a few things you can do to avoid excess legal fees.

- ✪ Do not make unnecessary phone calls to your lawyer.

- ✪ Give information to the secretary whenever possible.

- ✪ Direct questions to the secretary first.

- ✪ Plan phone calls so you get to the point. Write down an outline if necessary.

- ✪ Do some of the legwork yourself—pick up and deliver papers, for example. Ask what you can do to assist your lawyer.

- ✪ Be prepared for appointments. Have all related papers with you, and plan your visit to get to the point. Make an outline of what you want to discuss and ask.

## FIRING YOUR LAWYER

If you find that you can no longer work with your lawyer or do not trust your lawyer, it is time to either go it alone or get a new attorney. You will need to send your lawyer a letter stating that you no longer desire his or her services and are discharging him or her from your case. Also, state that you will be coming by his or her office the following day to pick up your file.

The attorney does not have to give you his or her own notes or other work in progress, but your lawyer must give you the essential contents of your file (such as copies of papers already prepared and billed for, and any documents you provided). If your attorney refuses to give you the file for any reason, contact your state's bar association about filing a complaint or *grievance* against the lawyer. Of course, you will need to settle any remaining fees owed.

# Avoiding Bankruptcy

Before resigning yourself to the idea that bankruptcy is the only option for you, there are things you may want to consider. Perhaps there is a way for you to work with your creditors and avoid bankruptcy altogether. The first part of this section demonstrates that there are some good reasons to avoid bankruptcy. However, there are also good reasons to file for bankruptcy, in the right circumstances. The second part of this section helps you determine if the circumstances are right.

## THE EFFECTS OF BANKRUPTCY

Bankruptcy should be regarded as a last resort. Before you jump into a bankruptcy, it is a good idea to evaluate your financial situation and consider the effects of a bankruptcy. Before you make a final decision, be sure to look at Section 8 of this book to see if any of the special circumstances discussed apply to you.

**Financial Effects**    A bankruptcy is a mixed blessing. It will have both positive and negative financial effects. These can be divided into immediate and long-term effects.

*Immediate effects.* An immediate positive effect is that your creditors get off your back. However, this may only last a short time for certain kinds of debts. Such things as utility cut-offs, mortgage foreclosures, or evictions may only be delayed for a few days or weeks. Once you file for bankruptcy, your financial dealings come under the scrutiny of the bankruptcy trustee, and you will need his or her permission to sell any assets or pay any debts.

*Long-term effects.* These are the effects after your bankruptcy is completed. The fact that you now have a bankruptcy in your credit history will make it more difficult for you to obtain credit. There are stories of people who cannot get a car loan, even with a 50% down payment, ten years after filing bankruptcy. However, a study by the Purdue University Credit Research Center once revealed that 16% of people who filed for bankruptcy were able to get some credit after one year, and 53% were able to get credit after five years.

It may also make it difficult for you to get a promotion or be given a position of trust at work, or to get hired by a new employer who does a credit check. You will probably also be starting over with fewer possessions than you had before your bankruptcy. Some of your property will probably get repossessed, and some of it may have to be sold. If a relative or friend co-signed a loan for you, that relative or friend will still be liable to repay the loan.

A bankruptcy may also cause you to lose your retirement benefits. Be sure to read Section 8 of this book for more information on pension plans and how they are affected by bankruptcy.

You will have to be very careful not to get into debt problems again. You can only file for bankruptcy once every eight years.

**Emotional Effects**

In addition to the financial effects, most people experience some emotional effects when they file for bankruptcy.

*Yourself.* You may experience a feeling of failure or dishonesty. The feeling of failure may occur because you could not manage your affairs better or were not smart enough to handle your money, while the feeling of dishonesty may arise because you feel you are cheating your creditors. Although there are many logical arguments for not feeling this way, many people still cannot overcome the feeling on an emotional level. Regardless of how others really feel about your situation, you will see and interpret their reaction in terms of how you feel about yourself.

***Your family and friends.*** If you are married, your spouse and possibly your children will have to know about the bankruptcy. You will need to prepare for how you will discuss it with them. You may also have to be prepared to deal with their feelings of failure, disappointment, and guilt. Additionally, there may be extended family members involved, such as parents, siblings, aunts, uncles, and friends. These people may or may not understand and sympathize with your situation.

***Your employer.*** It is possible that you can keep your bankruptcy out of your workplace, but it is not likely. Although your employer probably will not admit it, a bankruptcy may affect your ability to obtain promotions or to be entrusted with certain responsibilities (such as handling money or accounts). Of course, the same thing may happen if you do not file and a creditor files a wage garnishment.

For some, or all, of these reasons, you should first explore whether you might avoid bankruptcy.

## INCOME AND EXPENSES WORKSHEET

In order to be considering bankruptcy, you must be in a situation in which your income is not sufficient to cover your monthly expenses. To find out just how bad your situation is, you need to examine your current budget. Complete the **INCOME AND EXPENSES WORKSHEET** in Appendix B, using the following guidelines. (see worksheet 1, p.208.)

- ✪ Be sure to use *monthly* amounts in completing this form.

- ✪ To convert a weekly amount, multiply by 4.3.

- ✪ To convert a biweekly amount, divide by 2, then multiply the answer by 4.3.

The following relates to the "INCOME" portion of worksheet 1.

- ◈ *Take-Home Pay*. This refers to your total pay after you deduct for taxes and Social Security. If you have other payroll deductions, such as for a medical or dental plan, uniforms, or a savings plan, they should be listed under the "EXPENSES" section of this form. You should add these deductions back to the take-home pay shown on your paycheck. If your pay changes from paycheck to paycheck, obtain an average by dividing your yearly income by 12, or by some other appropriate method.

- ◈ *Self-Employment Income*. Calculate an average monthly income if you are self-employed (either as your main job or as a second job). Consult a book that covers business bankruptcies or see a lawyer if you are self-employed and are incorporated, have employees, or have a financially complex business operation.

- ◈ *Interest and Dividends*. This includes things such as interest on bank accounts, certificates of deposit (CDs), stocks, bonds, mutual funds, and so on.

- ◈ *Income from Real Estate*. Income from any rental you own.

- ◈ *Retirement Income*. This includes pensions and other retirement payments from your prior employment.

- ◈ *Alimony or Support Payments*. This includes money you receive as alimony, maintenance, child support, and so on. Only count these payments if you receive them on a fairly regular and dependable basis.

- ◈ *Other*. This might include things such as Social Security, unemployment compensation, disability benefits, welfare benefits, or income from loans you made to other people.

- ◈ Add all of your monthly income and write the total in the space for "TOTAL MONTHLY INCOME."

The following relates to the "EXPENSES" section of worksheet 1.

◈ *Homeowners or Renters Insurance*. If homeowners insurance is included in your mortgage payment, it should not be listed here again. If you rent and have renters insurance on your possessions, you will be paying it separately from your rent payment, so list it here.

◈ *Real Estate Taxes*. If these are included in your mortgage payment, they should not be listed here again.

◈ *Other Installment Loan Payments*. This relates to all loans except your mortgage and auto loan payments. This will include such things as credit cards, home equity loans, boat loans, vacation loans, home improvement loans, and swimming pool loans.

The remaining items of the form are self-explanatory. Just make sure everything is converted to a *monthly* amount.

◈ Next, add all of your monthly expenses and write the total in the space for "TOTAL MONTHLY EXPENSES."

◈ Finally, subtract the "TOTAL MONTHLY EXPENSES" from the "TOTAL MONTHLY INCOME," and write that amount in the space for "DEFICIT." This should give you a negative number, which will tell you how much money you are falling short each month. If you get a positive number (that is, your monthly income is more than your monthly expenses), then you have either forgotten to list some of your expenses, or you are making enough money to meet your monthly expenses and should not be thinking about bankruptcy.

## PROPERTY WORKSHEET

The two things you will consider in trying to avoid bankruptcy are whether you can cut your expenses and whether you can sell any assets to pay off some of your debts. The best way to start this process is by completing the **PROPERTY WORKSHEET**. (see worksheet 2, page 209.)

To put it simply, *property* is something you own (such as money, a house, a car, or furniture) and a *debt* is money you owe. Property may also be referred to as an *asset*. To understand the **PROPERTY WORKSHEET**, first it is necessary to explain the types of property and debts involved in a bankruptcy.

Property is divided into *exempt* and *nonexempt* categories. Remember, the purpose of bankruptcy is to help you start over financially. It would not be helpful to leave you without any property, so the bankruptcy laws allow you to keep a certain amount of your property. The types and amounts of property you are allowed to keep are *exempt property*. The type and amount of property that is exempt is a matter of state law (and alternative federal law, in some states).

Although the Bankruptcy Code is a federal law, the question of exempt property is generally determined by your state government. Most states exempt the following types of property, at least up to a certain value or amount:

- motor vehicles;

- clothing and personal effects;

- household furnishings;

- tools used in your trade or profession;

- equity in a home;

- life insurance;

- public employee pensions; or,

- Social Security, welfare, unemployment, workers' compensation, or other public benefits accumulated in a bank account.

Typical examples of nonexempt property are:

- the previously mentioned exempt items over a certain amount;

- a second car;

- ✪   a boat or recreational vehicle;

- ✪   a vacation home;

- ✪   cash, bank accounts, certificates of deposit; or,

- ✪   other investments, such as stocks, bonds, coin collections, etc.

The **PROPERTY WORKSHEET** in Appendix B will divide your property into exempt and nonexempt categories. (see worksheet 2, p.209.) If you live in Arkansas, Connecticut, the District of Columbia, Hawaii, Massachusetts, Michigan, Minnesota, New Jersey, New Mexico, Pennsylvania, Rhode Island, South Carolina, Texas, Vermont, Washington, or Wisconsin, you have the following choices in determining what property is exempt.

- ✪   Use the exemptions listed for your state *and* the Federal Nonbankruptcy Exemptions, both of which are listed in Appendix A of this book. (If you use your state exemptions, you may not use any of the Federal Bankruptcy Exemptions.)

- ✪   Use the Federal Bankruptcy Exemptions *and* the Federal Nonbankruptcy Exemptions, both of which are listed in Appendix A of this book. (If you use the Federal Bankruptcy Exemptions, you may not use any of your state exemptions.)

If you live in any other state, you may only use your state exemptions and the Federal Nonbankruptcy Exemptions.

---

### – Warning –

Even if the property is exempt, you may still lose the property if it is tied to a secured debt. For example, your home is exempt property under your state's laws. If you borrowed money from a bank to buy the house, and the bank holds a mortgage on the house, the bank can still foreclose and take your house if you do not pay.

---

The **Property Worksheet** is divided into six columns, each of which have both a number and a title. The following instructions refer to each column by number. (see worksheet 2, p.209.)

⬦ In Column (1), list all of your property. Do not list anything in more than one category. For each category of property in worksheet 2, check if any such items are exempt on your state's list in Appendix A of this book. If so, be sure to list those items separately.

---

### Example:
If your state exempts wedding rings, be sure to list your wedding rings as a separate item in the Jewelry category in worksheet 2.

---

If you live in Arkansas, Connecticut, the District of Columbia, Hawaii, Massachusetts, Michigan, Minnesota, New Jersey, New Mexico, Pennsylvania, Rhode Island, South Carolina, Texas, Vermont, Washington, or Wisconsin, you should also compare your state's exemptions with the Federal Bankruptcy Exemptions at the beginning of Appendix A.

Column (1) is divided into several categories of property, as follows.

✪ *Real Estate*. List any real estate you own by each property's address or other brief description.

✪ *Autos*. Include cars, trucks, motorcycles, etc.

✪ *Boats*. Include boats, engines, boating equipment, and any other recreational vehicles.

✪ *Cash on Hand*. This is cash in your pocket, wallet, purse, mattress, and so on. It does not include money in a bank.

✪ *Bank Accounts*. List all of your bank accounts by your bank name and account number.

✪ *Clothing.* You can just give an estimate of the total value of your clothing. Only list specific items if they have great value (such as a mink coat or original designer items).

✪ *Jewelry.* Costume jewelry need not be listed by item, but gold, diamonds, and other precious metals and gems should be listed by each item.

✪ *Household Goods.* This includes all of your furniture, pots and pans, dishes, and personal items. A general estimate can be given for most things. Any items of great value should be listed separately, but first check to see if they fit in one of the other categories on this form.

✪ *Collections.* This is for such things as coins, stamps, paintings, books, and other valuable collectibles.

✪ *Sports Equipment.* Include firearms, pool tables, golf clubs, and so on.

✪ *Business Goods or Trade Tools.* This includes any items you need in order to conduct your business or engage in your occupation.

✪ *Investments.* This includes any stocks, bonds, patents, copyrights, licenses, etc.

✪ *Insurance.* This includes any cash value in life insurance policies, annuities, etc.

✪ *Other Property.* This is where you list anything that does not fit into one of the other categories. Again, be sure to check your state's listing in Appendix A.

◈ Column (2) is titled "Value." Fill in the approximate value of each of the items of property you listed under Column (1). For some items you will know the exact value, but for others you will have to make a good estimate. For such things as automobiles and boats, you may be able to find a *blue book* (which may be any color) at your local library or at a local dealer that will give approximate values. For other items, such as clothing, personal belongings, and furniture, just estimate what you think you could sell these items for at a garage sale. Estimate low, but do not get ridiculous.

◈    Column (3) is used to fill in how much money, if any, you still owe on any of the items listed under Column (1). For the purposes of this form, you only *owe* something if the item can be foreclosed on or repossessed if you fail to pay.

---

### Example:

If you bought your dining set with your Visa card, it cannot be repossessed. Therefore, you do not owe anything on the dining set.

---

◈    Next, subtract the amount owed in Column (3) from the value in Column (2), and write in the difference in Column (4). This will give you the *equity* in each piece of property. *Equity* is the amount of cash you would have if you sold the property and paid off the amount you owe.

◈    For Column (5), refer to your state's listing in Appendix A, where you will find a list of the items and amounts that are exempt. Also, look at the beginning of Appendix A to see if you are in a state that permits use of the Federal Bankruptcy Exemptions. If so, compare the state and Federal Bankruptcy Exemptions to see which would make more of your property exempt.

The state exemptions will usually give you a better result, but not always. If you will get more exempt property under the Federal Bankruptcy Exemptions, use them instead of the state exemptions. For each item of property, you may find that item completely exempt, or only exempt to a certain value. The following examples will help illustrate this point.

### Example 1:

If you live in Florida, the home you live in (your *homestead*) is completely exempt, no matter what its value. If you have a home worth $100,000, it is fully exempt. This means you do not have to sell your house to pay off your creditors. (However, if you have a mortgage, you have to make your payments.)

### Example 2:

If you live in Illinois, only $7,500 of the value of your home is exempt. If your home is worth $100,000, you may only claim an exemption of $7,500. You would have to sell your home, or take out a new mortgage for $92,500 so that your equity is only $7,500. Of course, you would have to make your mortgage payments if you could get a loan with your financial problems. Illinois does not allow the Federal Bankruptcy Exemptions, so you can only exempt the $7,500 allowed by Illinois.

### Example 3:

If you live in New Jersey, your home is not exempt at all. Whether your equity is $100,000 or $1, you would lose it in a bankruptcy if you use the New Jersey exemptions. However, New Jersey allows you to use the alternative Federal Bankruptcy Exemptions, which would allow you to keep up to $15,000 in a home.

Look at your available exemptions in Appendix A and determine what property is exempt. Fill in the amount of the exemption in Column (5).

◆ In Column (6), place a check mark beside each item of property for which the debt is secured. (If necessary, reread the part of this section on secured and unsecured debts.) If the debt for that property is secured, you will need to keep up your payment, or at least work out something with the creditor, in order to keep the property (even if the property is exempt in your state).

◆ Write the totals of each column at the bottom.

# DEBT ASSESSMENT

The next step is to assess how much money you owe and the kinds of debts you have.

**Dischargeable and Nondischargeable Debts**

In a bankruptcy, debts are first divided into two types—*dischargeable* and *nondischargeable*. A dischargeable debt is one that the bankruptcy laws allow you to *discharge*, or cancel. The best examples of dischargeable debts are the money you owe on credit cards—such as a Visa, MasterCard, or department store cards—and medical bills. Most consumer debts are dischargeable in bankruptcy, and these are the types of debts that lead most people into a situation that requires them to file for bankruptcy. If you have several credit cards and you charge them all up to the limit, it is easy to get in over your head.

A nondischargeable debt is one that you will still owe after the bankruptcy is completed. Examples of nondischargeable debts are:

- ✪ student loans;

- ✪ child support;

- ✪ alimony obligations;

- ✪ delinquent taxes;

- ✪ some court-ordered judgments; and,

- ✪ debts arising from fraud (such as providing false credit application information or obtaining credit with the intention of filing for bankruptcy to avoid payment).

**Secured and Unsecured Debts**

Debts are also divided into two other categories—*secured* and *unsecured*. A secured debt is one that can be viewed as *attached* to a particular piece of property. The property that secures the debt can be taken by the creditor to pay the debt. The prime example of a secured debt is a mortgage. The mortgage means that if you do not pay the money you borrowed to buy your house, the lender can take your house. Most car loans also include a *financing statement*, which is essentially the same as a mortgage. If you do not pay, the lender gets your car.

An *unsecured* debt is not tied to any particular piece of property. Most credit card loans are unsecured. If you do not pay, the bank cannot seize any particular piece of property (at least, not without suing you and trying to attach your property later to satisfy the debt).

**Debt Worksheet**

Now, complete the **DEBT WORKSHEET** in Appendix B according to the following guidelines. (see worksheet 3, p.210.) This form is divided into six columns, each of which are numbered and titled. The following instructions refer to each column by number.

⬧ In Column (1), list all of your debts.

⬧ In Column (2), list the lender's name and account number for each debt.

⬧ In Column (3), list what the loan was for, such as home, car, boat, vacation, etc. For your credit cards, you do not need to list each little purchase you made. The only purpose of this column is to help you remember what the loan is for and to determine whether the loan is secured by any property.

⬧ In Column (4), write down the balance due on each loan. You do not need to have each one exact to the penny, but be as accurate as possible.

⬧ In Column (5), write in the same amount as Column (4) for each loan that is secured by a piece of property.

⬧ In Column (6), write in the same amount as Column (4) for each loan that is a dischargeable loan. For worksheet 3, a secured loan is not considered dischargeable, unless you are willing to give up that item of property.

⬧ Write the totals of each column at the bottom.

## GENERAL GUIDELINES

In order to determine whether you should file for bankruptcy, you need to evaluate your situation according to the following four factors.

1.    Can you reduce your total monthly payments so that you can manage things on your income?

2.    How much of your debt is dischargeable?

3.    How much of your debt is secured by your property?

4.    How much of your property is exempt?

Once you have done this, you will have a good idea of whether you can avoid bankruptcy and where things would stand after a bankruptcy. You will be able to estimate how much property you would be able to keep and how much money you would still owe to creditors.

Look at your monthly budget first. (Refer to your completed **INCOME AND EXPENSES WORKSHEET** (worksheet 1).) Examine each of your monthly expenses.

✪    Are there any that you can reduce or eliminate?

✪    Can you sell some of your property to pay off some of your debts?

✪    Can you move to a cheaper apartment, or sell your home and find an apartment that will reduce your monthly housing costs?

✪    Can you sell your late model car and buy a less expensive one?

This is no time to think about maintaining your lifestyle. After all, it may be your lifestyle that got you into financial trouble in the first place. If you can make such adjustments to your expenses, you may be able to avoid bankruptcy. If such adjustments still will not help your situation, look at the types of debts and property you have.

A general rule of thumb is that if you can discharge more than 50% of your debts, a Chapter 7 bankruptcy would probably improve your financial situation. To determine if your situation fits this guideline, refer to worksheet 3. On worksheet 3, take the total of Column (4) and divide it by 2. If the answer is equal to or less than the total of Column (6), you can probably benefit from a Chapter 7 bankruptcy. If the answer is greater than the total of Column (6), you may benefit from a Chapter 13 bankruptcy or may even avoid bankruptcy.

Be sure to read the rest of this section on alternatives to bankruptcy. Following the instructions on planning a budget will help you to better understand your situation, even if you already know that you need to file for bankruptcy.

## ALTERNATIVES TO BANKRUPTCY

If, after filling out worksheets 1, 2, and 3 from Appendix B of this book, it looks as if you may be able to avoid bankruptcy, read the next few pages for some ideas on how you can get your debt problems under control. Of course, the first step is to *stop charging*.

**Credit Counseling**

One alternative to bankruptcy is to seek credit counseling. Even if you decide to file for bankruptcy, you will first need to see a credit counselor. The 2005 revisions to the Bankruptcy Code prohibit you from filing a bankruptcy petition until you have gone through credit counseling. A credit counselor will contact your creditors to try to establish a new payment plan, and will help you set up a budget you can handle.

---

### – Warning –

Beware of private *debt counselors* or offers for *debt consolidation loans*. Such "help" often only results in one large payment instead of many smaller payments, and you will still have trouble making that monthly payment. Furthermore, such operations charge counseling fees that only take away needed cash. Soon you may be facing bankruptcy again. Also, avoid the now-famous *home equity loan*. This can end up converting your unsecured debts into secured debts, which means that you may not be able to file for bankruptcy without losing your home.

---

You will want to use one of the numerous credit counseling agencies that have been approved by the U.S. Trustee's Office. You can obtain information about the approved credit counselors in your area from the local trustee's office, or through its website. To access the information on the Web, go to **www.usdoj.gov/ust**. Click on "Bankruptcy Abuse Prevention and Consumer Protection Act of 2005," then "Credit Counseling and Debt or Education Information." Click on "Approved Credit Counseling Agencies," then select your state. You can then scroll down and look for the agencies in or near your town. If there are any fees for credit counseling, you will be responsible for paying them.

A consumer credit counseling plan is similar to a Chapter 13 bankruptcy, but on a less formal basis. It is also cheaper than court filing fees and other costs associated with bankruptcy. Your credit report will look better with a record of credit counseling assistance than it will with a record of having filed for bankruptcy. A credit counseling plan will require you to pay your debts in full, whereas a Chapter 13 plan may only require the payment of a portion of your debts.

**Be Your Own Credit Counselor**

In theory, there is nothing a credit counselor can do that you cannot do. On a practical level, creditors are more inclined to listen to a credit counselor. Your creditors do not want you to file for bankruptcy, because it means they will not get paid in full. Therefore, they should have a strong incentive to be reasonable. Your main goal is to get the creditor to allow you to make smaller payments. This is typically accomplished by reducing the interest rate, extending the length of the loan, or both.

---

### Example:

George has a $1,500 balance on a credit card from a local department store. His payments are $74.89 a month, and the balance will take two years to pay off. If the department store will agree to accept payments over an additional year, George's monthly payment will be lowered to $54.23 a month. This lowers his monthly payment by $20.66. If he has ten loans like this, he could save over $200 per month, which may be enough to enable him to keep up his payments based on his income.

---

*Planning a budget.* The place to begin is by reviewing the **INCOME AND EXPENSES WORKSHEET** (worksheet 1) that you completed earlier. You will need this worksheet and a calculator to plan your budget.

The copy of worksheet 1 you completed shows your budget as it is right now. Use a blank copy to start your new budget.

Your total income will remain the same, so write it in under "TOTAL MONTHLY INCOME." Enter this amount in your calculator. Now go through all of your expenses, and subtract each one from the "TOTAL MONTHLY INCOME" figure.

First, identify the most important item, which is probably your rent or mortgage payment (unless you are prepared to go live with friends and relatives). Write this amount in the appropriate place on the worksheet, and subtract it from your total income.

Second, identify your next most important expense, and so on. For each item, ask yourself if there is any way to reduce the amount you spend each month. If you can reduce the amount, then use the reduced amount and subtract it from the total. Your essential payments are for housing (including utilities), food, and transportation (probably your car).

There are also a few things to consider as a means of paying off some of your debts. These include making a real effort to stop buying nonessential items, borrowing from a retirement plan or life insurance policy, and taking money from a college tuition or other savings account.

In order to survive and earn a living, you need a place to live, food, and a way to get to and from work. If you are unable to find a way to make these essential payments with your income, you may want to apply for some type of public assistance (welfare) in addition to filing for bankruptcy.

Once you have subtracted the essential living expenses, you will be left with the total remaining income available to pay your creditors and other expenses. (Absolutely last on your list should be the expenses for recreation, travel, or entertainment.) Now, start subtracting your payments for loans that are secured loans. These are any loans in which your property can be repossessed if you do not pay. Most credit card debts are not secured by any particular property. The most common secured loans are for homes (including home equity loans), automobiles, boats, and occasionally, furniture. If the only paper you signed was the typical charge card receipt for Visa, MasterCard, Sears, or other department store charges, the loan is not secured.

By now, you are probably left with a small amount of income (if any at all) with which you can make payments on the rest of your loans. Add up the remaining loan payments, and subtract them from your remaining income. If your answer is -0- or more, whatever adjustments you made to your expenses were enough to eliminate your debt problem. Now your only problem is to try to live according to your new budget.

However, if your answer is less than -0-, it represents how much you need to reduce your monthly payments in order to avoid having to file for bankruptcy. Your next step is to try to persuade your creditors to adjust your payments to fit your remaining income.

***Dealing with creditors.*** Your next task is to create a new payment plan to present to your unsecured creditors. You need to come up with a plan that is fair to all of your creditors. For your unsecured creditors, you will want to reduce each payment by a proportional amount. First, take the total monthly payments of your remaining debts, and divide it by the monthly shortage. This will give you the percentage you need to reduce each debt by in order to match your remaining income.

---

### Example:

Sue has subtracted all of her essential expenses and secured loan payments from her income, and is left with $245. She has five monthly credit card payments as follows.

| | |
|---|---|
| Visa | $150.00 |
| Mastercard | 65.00 |
| Sears | 50.00 |
| Discover | 23.00 |
| Local Department Store | 75.00 |
| TOTAL | $363.00 |

Sue's income is $118 short ($363 - $245 = $118). If she divides the amount she is short ($118) by the total payments ($363), she gets a figure of .325, which she will round up to .33 (or just about ⅓). If she reduces each payment by .33, she will have enough income to meet the new payments. To find the amount to reduce each payment by, Sue will multiply each payment amount by .33, round off each answer, and then subtract this amount from each payment.

| Creditor | Old Payment | Subtract | New Payment |
|---|---|---|---|
| Visa | $150.00 | $50.00 | $100.00 |
| Mastercard | 65.00 | 21.50 | 43.50 |
| Sears | 50.00 | 16.50 | 33.50 |
| Discover | 23.00 | 7.50 | 15.50 |
| Local Department Store | 75.00 | 25.00 | 50.00 |
| TOTAL | $363.00 | $120.50 | $242.50 |

As you can see, Sue has lowered her payments to fit her income, and has treated each creditor the same. If she can persuade these creditors to accept the lower payments, she has her new budget (and she has an extra $2.50 left over). Of course, this will increase the number of payments needed to pay off the loans.

---

Once you have worked out your new proposed payment amounts, it is time to contact your creditors with your plan. There is an example of such a letter on page 42.

Fill in the date, the name of each creditor, and the creditor's address at the top. You will need to make a copy of this letter for each creditor. Just fill in the blanks according to your new payment plan, fill in your name and address (so it can be read), sign your name, and mail a copy to each creditor. Be sure to type in your name, address, and account number below your signature.

CERTIFIED MAIL
RETURN RECEIPT REQUESTED
No. _____

Dear Sir or Madam:

My current financial situation may require me to file for bankruptcy protection. In order to avoid this, I am requesting that my payments on your account be restructured. This will allow me to pay you the full amount you are owed.

My net monthly income is $_____. After paying essential expenses, such as housing, utilities, food, clothing, transportation for work, and medical expenses, I am left with a monthly disposable income of $_____. Out of this balance I am able to pay my creditors as follows.

| CREDITOR | OLD AMOUNT | REVISED AMOUNT |
| --- | --- | --- |

This schedule represents an equal pro rata reduction for each unsecured creditor. Please let me know if this new arrangement is acceptable. Unless I hear from you before the next payment is due, I will assume this proposal is acceptable, and will make my next payment according to the revised amount.

Thank you for your attention to this matter.

**NOTE:** *It is a good idea to send these letters by certified, return-receipt mail. This will cost you a couple of dollars per letter, but you will be able to prove the creditor received it, if needed.*

Now, sit back and wait for your creditors to answer. You will note that the form letter states that your next payment will be according to the new schedule, unless you hear from the creditor beforehand.

You may be asking, *Why should the creditors accept reduced payments?* If the creditors really believe you are serious about bankruptcy and see that you have a workable budget, they have every reason to accept your plan. The alternative is to let you declare bankruptcy, in which case they will receive less than the full amount owed (and possibly nothing at all).

You should try to get your unsecured creditors to lower their payment requirements in order to fit your budget. Only after this fails should you contact your secured creditors about a new payment schedule. You may wonder why secured creditors would agree to lower payments, when all they have to do is repossess or foreclose. Even a secured creditor would usually rather get paid than take back the property. It takes a lot of time and money to repossess and resell property. If you do file for bankruptcy, it will take even more time and expense. A bankruptcy will not stop foreclosure or repossession, but it will delay it. Therefore, most lenders will work with you to try to avoid foreclosure, repossession, or bankruptcy.

The key to success is showing the creditor a fair and reasonable payment plan that is clearly within your ability to maintain. If this does not work, you can still go to a credit counselor, and can ultimately proceed with a bankruptcy if necessary.

# Preparing for Bankruptcy

This section discusses some things you must do, or may wish to do, prior to filing for bankruptcy. It explains some techniques that may be used to help improve your situation, and discusses some serious problems that can be encountered by certain attempts to gain an advantage.

## BASIC LEGAL REQUIREMENTS

Under the 2005 changes to the Bankruptcy Code, there are certain basic requirements that must be met in order to file for bankruptcy. Some of these apply to Chapter 7 cases, some apply to Chapter 13 cases, and some apply to both.

**Means Testing**
In general, you will not be able to file under Chapter 7 of the Bankruptcy Code unless you meet certain financial requirements. If, under the guidelines established by Congress, your financial means (ability to pay) are too great, you will not be permitted to discharge your debts under Chapter 7. Instead, you will need to work out a debt payment plan under Chapter 13.

First, your family income over the past six months will be examined, and if it falls below the median income for your state, you will be able to use Chapter 7. If it is above the median income, the court will then look at your ability to pay your debts. The judge takes your income, subtracts certain allowable expenses, and determines whether you have enough money left over to pay at least $100 per month to your creditors, and whether you will be able to pay at least $10,000 or 25% of your unsecured debts over a five-year period. If you do have such sufficient leftover money, you will need to file under Chapter 13.

**Credit Counseling**

Before you can file for bankruptcy under either Chapter 7 or Chapter 13, you will need to see a credit counselor who is approved by the U.S. Trustees Program. This must be done within the six-month period before filing. To find approved credit counseling agencies near you, contact your local bankruptcy court clerk, your local trustee's office, or go online to **www.usdoj.gov/ust**.

**Financial Management Course**

Before your case can be concluded under either Chapter 7 or Chapter 13, you will need to complete a course on financial management given by an agency approved by the U.S. Trustees Program. This does not need to be done before you file, but must be done before the court will discharge any of your debts. To find approved financial management education agencies near you, contact your local bankruptcy court clerk or your local trustee's office, or go online to **www.usdoj.gov/ust**.

## ARRANGING YOUR FINANCES

There are some things you might do before you file that will improve your situation after your bankruptcy is complete.

---

### – Warning –

*Use this section with extreme caution.* Before you file for bankruptcy, you may want to review your financial situation to see if there is anything you can rearrange to your advantage. You need to be aware that you may be walking a fine line between acceptable practices and what the court might consider to be cheating your creditors. At a very minimum, you should not file for bankruptcy for at least ninety days after you make any of the changes discussed in this section. If any changes involve a relative, you should not file for at least one year. However, each bankruptcy judge has his or her own ideas and attitudes, and some have determined that there was an intent to defraud where transfers were made more than a year before filing.

**Incurring New Debts**

If you will need to borrow more money to pay for necessities (such as for medical treatment, buying clothing for your family, or getting your car repaired so you can get to work), you may want to wait to file for bankruptcy until you have incurred these debts. This way, these debts can be included in your bankruptcy. A bankruptcy only affects those debts that you incur *before* you file. Any debts you incur *after* you file are not included in the bankruptcy. Just make sure you are incurring these new debts for necessary things and not for luxuries (such as a vacation, a new stereo, or a night on the town).

**Converting Nonexempt Property to Exempt Property**

It is permissible to convert nonexempt property to exempt property, provided this is not done with the specific intent to defraud creditors. Whether there is intent to defraud creditors is decided on a case-by-case basis, and is based on the individual circumstances. The big risk here is that if the court determines there was an intent to defraud creditors, it can deny your request for a discharge of your debts.

The most obvious thing you could do is sell nonexempt property and use the money to buy exempt property.

### Example:
If you live in New York, exempt property includes furniture, a radio, a television, a refrigerator, and clothing. However, boats and second cars are not exempt. Therefore, you may want to sell your boat or second car and use the money you get to buy some furniture, a radio, a television, a refrigerator, or some clothing.

Another possibility is to take money (either from an existing nonexempt financial account or from selling nonexempt property) and place it in some type of exempt investment.

---

### Example:

If you live in Florida, there are only minimal exemptions for cash in bank accounts or personal property items. However, *Individual Retirement Accounts* (IRAs) are exempt. Therefore, you could put money into an IRA account. There is a court opinion that approved of such a transfer (in the amount of $5,000), even though the money was deposited in the IRA about three months before filing for bankruptcy, the debtors were unemployed, and "their future prospects looked rather gloomy." (*In re Horvath*, 116 B.R. 835 (M.D. Fla. 1990).)

---

To consider this concept more fully, you will need to carefully read the list of exemptions for your state in Appendix A of this book.

**Using Nonexempt Property to Pay Certain Debts**

It is also permissible to use nonexempt cash, or money from the sale of nonexempt property, to pay off a nondischargeable debt (such as a student loan or overdue taxes) or to pay on a secured debt on exempt property (such as catching up with an overdue mortgage payment).

---

### Example 1:

You have a nonexempt boat. You sell it and use the money to pay off a student loan. In the bankruptcy you would lose the boat anyway, so you may as well use it to reduce or eliminate the number of payments you will need to make after bankruptcy on your nondischargeable student loan.

### Example 2:

You have a nonexempt second car. You sell it and use the money to pay off the balance of the loan for your primary car, which is exempt in your state. You get to keep your primary car after bankruptcy, and you will have one less payment to make (provided your primary car is not worth more than the allowable exemption).

---

---

**– Warning –**

Be sure you do not pay off a loan on a nonexempt piece of property, because you will lose the property in bankruptcy anyway.

---

**Example:**

You sell your second car and use the money to pay off your secured boat loan. The boat, being nonexempt property, is then taken by the trustee, to be sold and used to pay off other unsecured creditors. You have gained nothing.

---

You may also want to sell nonexempt property to pay off an unsecured loan. Paying an unsecured loan will only be of advantage under one or both of the following circumstances.

- ✪ A friend or relative has co-signed the loan and you do not want to stick that friend or relative with having to pay the loan for you.

- ✪ You want to maintain good relations with that particular creditor (such as your doctor or car repairman), and possibly be able to keep your ability to buy there on credit.

**Bankruptcy Abuse and Defrauding Creditors**

Under the 2005 changes to the Bankruptcy Act, if certain facts become apparent from the papers you file, it can trigger a presumption of fraud. One of the forms you will complete and file with the court will analyze whether there is such a presumption of fraud. This will be discussed more in later sections of this book. Even if there is a presumption of fraud, it does not mean there is fraud. However, your case will become subject to greater scrutiny by the trustee, your creditors, and the court.

Rearranging your asset and debt situation can get you into trouble. If it appears to the court that you have made changes in order to cheat your creditors, the judge can let the trustee take and sell the new property you bought. He or she can even dismiss your case and not let you have a discharge of any debts. This will leave you in a much worse situation than when you began. These problems most often occur when it appears that the debtor has incurred significant debts with the idea of declaring bankruptcy in order to avoid paying (such as if you and your spouse charge an expensive Alaskan cruise on your credit card, and then file for bankruptcy shortly after returning home).

In order to minimize the chances of problems, keep the following points in mind.

- ✪ Do not make so many sales that you would have enough money to pay off most or all of your debts (unless this is your goal in order to avoid bankruptcy). If you sell enough property to be able to pay off your debts, and then do not pay them off, it will be considered fraud.

- ✪ Sell and buy property at market value prices. If you sell something for less than reasonable or market price, or buy something for more than it is worth, your creditors may object.

- ✪ Avoid sales to, or purchases from, relatives. If you decide this is absolutely necessary, be sure you make the exchange at market value.

- ✪ Do not sell something expensive and buy something cheap, planning to secretly pocket the cash. The judge or trustee can make you account for all of the cash you get from a sale, and then either you come up with the extra cash or get your case dismissed.

- ✪ If the trustee, judge, or creditor asks you about your transactions before you filed, tell the truth. One of the main things the court will consider in deciding if your action was fraudulent is your intention. Furthermore, if you are asked about a particular transaction, you can be sure that the person asking the questions already knows about it. Judges do not like people who lie or are sneaky, so do not try to hide things. You are bound to get caught.

- ✪ Do not buy more nonexempt property on credit, then sell the items to buy exempt property. This is fraud.

- ✪ Do not go overboard and sell all of your nonexempt property. Leave something for the unsecured creditors so they do not feel cheated and challenge the transactions.

If all of this leaves you confused and you want to take advantage of the things discussed in this section, you should consider consulting a lawyer.

# Gathering Information

Before you start preparing any forms, you will need to gather information about your finances. You should already have most, if not all, of the information you need. Your petition for bankruptcy consists mostly of describing your financial situation at a certain point in time. You need to gather all of your papers regarding your income, monthly expenses, assets, and debts.

This information is necessary for you to adequately fill out the forms to file for bankruptcy, and is also useful in the event a judge, creditor, or trustee asks you how you came up with the figures on your forms. The following comments regarding the type of information you need should answer any questions you have.

There are also certain papers you will be required to file along with your bankruptcy petition. These are your federal income tax return for the last year, and either a recent paystub or some other proof of income. If you did not file a tax return for the last year, you will need to do so before you can file your petition. These requirements are discussed more in the following sections of this book.

## INCOME

For most people, income information will come from three primary sources: paystubs, tax returns, and W-2 statements. Your paystub should give the most current information. Look for a space that shows your *year-to-date* (YTD) income. This will give your total earnings since the beginning of the current year. You can then count the number of weeks that have passed since January 1st and divide your year-to-date earnings by the number of weeks that have passed to get an average weekly amount. If your paystub does not show a year-to-date figure, you can always add up the totals of all paystubs since the beginning of the year.

Another good source of income information is your previous year's income tax return, or W-2 statement. This information will be useable as long as you did not get a raise, change jobs, or have any other change in income.

If you have additional income from things such as bank account interest, stock dividends, or alimony, get out any statements or other records that show this income.

If you have income from self-employment, you should gather your accounting records and tax returns.

## EXPENSES

Get out any papers or records showing the amount of your monthly expenses. These should include housing, utilities, food, loans, and other debts. Under the 2005 changes to the Bankruptcy Act, expenses are limited by certain IRS guidelines, which are discussed in more detail in the following sections of this book. In spite of these IRS limits, you should still know your actual expenses. This should include at least the following categories.

**Housing**  If you have a mortgage, you probably have a payment book that shows your monthly payment. If not, look for cancelled checks to the mortgage holder, a copy of the note and mortgage showing the payment, an escrow statement showing the amount withheld each month for taxes and insurance, or some similar record. If you rent, you should have a copy of a lease that shows the monthly rent, or at least cancelled checks or receipts. If you cannot find any of these, ask your mortgage company or landlord to send you a statement to verify the amount of your payment.

**Utilities**  Get out your monthly statements for your electric, gas, telephone, trash pick-up, and any other utility bill. Hopefully, you have kept at least the last couple of bills. If not, be sure to keep the next one that comes. You could also write to the utility company and ask for a month-by-month statement for the past year. This information may be on some of your bills.

**Food**  Since most people do not keep their sales receipts for food, this documentation will not be as easy to find. However, if you normally write a check for your food shopping, you can get an average from your checkbook information. If you cannot find any such information, you probably still have a good idea of how much you spend on food for a week or month.

**Loan Payments**  Loan information should be easy to find in the form of a monthly statement or payment book. For credit cards, you should get a monthly billing statement, which will give the balance owed and the minimum monthly payment. For other debts, such as auto loans, you will probably have a payment book.

**Other Debts**  Other debts include such things as insurance premiums, gas and maintenance expenses for your car, child day care, and any other expenses. Some of these items will have some sort of documentation and some you will simply have to estimate. This information should already be on the **INCOME AND EXPENSES WORKSHEET** you prepared earlier. (see worksheet 1, p.208.)

## PROPERTY

Next, you need to make a list of everything you own. At this point, do not be concerned with how much you owe or what it is worth. Your list will include items such as real estate, vehicles, bank accounts, financial assets, jewelry, and other personal belongings.

**Real Estate**    A deed or mortgage will sufficiently describe the property, by way of a legal description. You will probably only need the street address, but it is a good idea to have the legal description on hand.

**Vehicles**    You will need the year, make, and model of each vehicle you own. You probably already know this information, but it is a good idea to have some paperwork on hand, such as the title, bill of sale, registration, or loan papers.

**Bank Accounts, CDs, etc.**    You will need copies of your most current statements, or some other records, showing the current balance in all checking and savings accounts, certificates of deposit (CDs), IRA accounts, etc.

**Other Financial Assets**    Other financial assets include such things as stocks and bonds, mutual funds, annuities, life insurance policies with a cash value, and any kind of retirement account or fund. All of these things should have some kind of statement or other paperwork to show current values.

**Jewelry and Other Collectibles**    These items will probably not have any papers to document their value, unless you had the item appraised or insured for a certain amount, or have borrowed money to buy the item. (Unless you still happen to have the receipt for an item that has not gone up in value much since its purchase.) When there is no documentation, make a list of the items and estimate what you could sell it for.

**Other Personal Belongings**    This category includes all of your furniture, clothing, pots and pans, dishes, and other everyday personal possessions. Of course, if any of these items are especially valuable, you need to treat them the same as jewelry and collectibles. Otherwise, just make a note in each category with an amount you think it would cost to replace the entire category. It is not necessary for you to list each piece of clothing or each pan separately.

## DEBTS

The most common debts are a mortgage, auto loan, and credit cards. A *debt* will have an outstanding balance, and almost certainly an interest rate. This distinguishes debts from other monthly obligations, such as rent and utility payments. There will also be either a monthly statement or payment book, and probably some other paperwork you completed or received when you first obtained the credit. Mainly, you will need to know the name and address of the person or company the money is owed to, the account number, and the amount owed.

## LEGAL RESEARCH

As the law is subject to change at any time, it is strongly suggested that you do some checking before you file. If you have Internet access, this can be done online. Otherwise, the best places to get current information are at the bankruptcy clerk's office, the bankruptcy trustee's office, or a local law library. The best place to find a law library is at your local courthouse. Law schools also have good law libraries.

There are two things you primarily need to check. First, since the 2005 changes to the Bankruptcy Act are so new, it is very likely that the bankruptcy court will change some of the official forms and rules. At the time this book goes to print, the courts have indicated that some of the forms are "under revision." There will probably be legal challenges to various aspects of the law, and it cannot be known how the courts will rule. Court rulings may force the bankruptcy courts to change both forms and rules. Second, you should review your state's exemption laws, which are summarized in Appendix A. Exemption laws do not change often, but occasionally a state will increase the amount of an exemption.

The following information helps you find your state's exemption laws and gives you more information about doing further legal research if you desire.

**State Laws**    State laws are most often referred to as *statutes* or *codes*, and contain the exact law as passed by your state legislature. The laws are identified by numbers called *articles*, *titles, chapters*, or *sections*, depending upon your state's system. A few states (namely Maryland, New York, and Texas) break the laws down by subject first, then break each subject down into sections. Once you find the particular law relating to your exemption, read the exact language to be sure there are not any special qualifications required for the exemption.

***Supplement.*** In addition to the main volume, there is another place you should look. All of the states periodically update their statutes. Some states do this by a paperback supplement that slides into a pocket in the back of the hardcover volume. Other states publish a separate hardcover or paperback volume, which you can find as the last book of the series of laws. A few states have their statutes in loose-leaf binders, with separate supplement sections. Be sure to check the supplement.

***Annotation.*** Many states also have sets of laws that are *annotated*. This means that, after each law is stated, there is more information to help you understand what the law means. This includes brief summaries of court decisions interpreting that law. The supplements will also be annotated, which is where you will find the most recent information.

**Bankruptcy Reporter**

The *Bankruptcy Reporter* is a multi-volume set of books containing court decisions in bankruptcy cases. In most cases, you will only be concerned with the more recent, paperback volumes. The index in the front of each volume contains a summary of the court decisions. Look for decisions from your state, which are abbreviated at the beginning of each summary.

**Practice Manuals**

If you really want to study the details of bankruptcy law, look for a practice manual on bankruptcy. A practice manual is a book, or set of books, that gives detailed information on a specific area of law. A leading practice manual in the field of bankruptcy law is *Collier Bankruptcy Manual*, published by Matthew Bender, along with its companion *Collier Forms Manual*. Your law library will probably have a section devoted to such bankruptcy books. These books will contain additional forms, as well as detailed information on all aspects of bankruptcy law.

If you have any difficulty, ask the librarian for assistance. However, do not expect the librarian to give you any legal advice.

**Online Research**

There are several sources of bankruptcy information and forms on the Internet.

- ✪ The basic website for the Federal Bankruptcy Courts, which includes special information for bankruptcy courts in certain states, is **www.uscourts.gov/bankruptcycourts.html**.

- ✪ The basic Federal Bankruptcy Court site for forms is **www.uscourts.gov/bkforms**.

- ✪ New and revised forms pursuant to the 2005 changes in the law can be found at **www.uscourts.gov/rules**.

- ✪ Valuable information can also be found at the U.S. Trustees Office website, at **www.usdoj.gov/ust**.

- ✪ Findlaw (**www.findlaw.com**) offers information on legal topics and includes links to the text of federal and state laws. Go directly to bankruptcy information and forms at **http://forms.lp.findlaw.com/federal/fjnbf_1.html**.

- ✪ The text of the Bankruptcy Code can also be found at **www.law.cornell.edu**. Under "Law about..." click on "Federal statutes by topic," then click on "Title 11—Bankruptcy."

Some other sites of interest include:

- ✪ InterNet Bankruptcy Library at **http://bankrupt.com**;

- ✪ American Bankruptcy Institute at **www.abiworld.org**; and,

- ✪ Bankruptcy Alternatives at **www.berkshire.net/~mkb**.

# Chapter 7 Bankruptcy

This section takes you through the forms and procedures for a Chapter 7 bankruptcy case.

## QUALIFYING FOR CHAPTER 7 BANKRUPTCY

There are certain financial requirements that must be met in order to be allowed to file for bankruptcy under Chapter 7 of the Bankruptcy Code. If your situation does not meet these requirements, you will need to file under Chapter 13 instead. This is commonly referred to as a *means test*.

Basically, you will *not* be allowed to file under Chapter 7 if:

✪   your income is above the median income for people in your state and

✪   you have sufficient income to pay at least 25% of your unsecured debts over a period of three to five years, at the rate of at least $100 per month.

Whether you meet this criteria is determined by a form you prepare and file with the court. If you have any doubt that your income is low enough to qualify, you may want to first prepare the **STATEMENT OF CURRENT MONTHLY INCOME AND MEANS TEST CALCULATION** (form 18), as instructed later in this section. If you find that you do not satisfy the means test to qualify for Chapter 7 bankruptcy, you can follow the instructions in Section 7 of this book for a Chapter 13 bankruptcy.

**Filing Fee**    The filing fee for a Chapter 7 bankruptcy is $274. This is paid at the time you file your case. If you do not have the money to pay the fee at that time, you can ask the court to allow you to pay the fee in four installments. This is done by preparing and filing an **APPLICATION TO PAY FILING FEE IN INSTALLMENTS** (see form 2, p.219), which is explained later in this section. If you are unable to pay the fee at all, you can ask the court to waive the fee entirely. This is done by preparing and filing an **APPLICATION FOR WAIVER OF THE CHAPTER 7 FILING FEE** (see form 3, p.221), which is also explained later in this section.

## UNDERSTANDING LEGAL FORMS

Legal forms are simply means of communicating necessary information to the court. Forms serve two main functions. First, they ask the court to do something (such as give you a discharge of your debts). Second, they provide the court with the information it needs to decide whether to give you what you ask for.

Most of this section explains how to fill in each specific form. You will notice that some of the forms begin as follows.

UNITED STATES BANKRUPTCY COURT

_____ DISTRICT OF _____

This is to show which court you are filing your papers with. Anyone who looks at your papers later will be able to know which court to go to in order to find more details about your bankruptcy case. Your creditors may need this information during the bankruptcy case. Also, as you are applying for a mortgage or car loan after your case is completed, your prospective lender may need this information.

Each state has both state and federal courts. The first line tells you that this case is in the federal district bankruptcy court. Each state has at least one federal district bankruptcy court, and most have two or more. States that are divided into two districts will be divided one of the two following ways:

1.  Eastern District and Western District or

2.  Northern District and Southern District.

States that are divided into three districts will also be divided one of the two ways listed above, but will also have a Middle District. To find out which district you live in (and will file your case in), look in your phone directory for the number of the U.S. District Court or U.S. Bankruptcy Court. This should be listed in the government section of your phone directory. Call the court and ask which district covers your area.

The district designation will need to be typed in the first space on each form you use. If you live in a state with only one district, leave this space blank. The name of your state needs to be typed in the second space. For example, if you live in Florida and you are in the Southern District, your forms will look like this when completed:

---

**UNITED STATES BANKRUPTCY COURT**

_____Southern_____ DISTRICT OF _____Florida_____

---

You may want to make a trip to your bankruptcy court clerk's office and ask to see a Chapter 7 case that someone else has filed. This may help you in completing your forms. The court records are open to the public; however, you will not be allowed to take the case file out of the clerk's office. There will probably be an area at the clerk's office where you can sit down and review a file.

The forms in this book follow those approved by the bankruptcy courts throughout the country. The bankruptcy rules require all of the bankruptcy courts to accept these forms. It may also be possible to access court files online. See pages 55–57 on "Legal Research" in Section 5 of this book for information about how to access online information for the bankruptcy courts.

It is not absolutely necessary that you use a typewriter to fill in the forms, although typing is preferred by the court and gives a much more professional appearance than handwriting. If typing is not possible, then print the information and be sure that your writing can be easily read. The remainder of each form will be discussed in detail in the following pages of this section. Just remember to complete the top part of each form.

Many of these forms are new as a result of the 2005 changes to the Bankruptcy Code. The law requires certain procedures be followed for establishing new court rules and forms. In enacting the changes, Congress did not allow sufficient time for these procedures to be followed. As a result, temporary (or *interim*) rules and forms were set up. It is anticipated that proposed permanent forms and rules will be announced by late 2006. Then, time frames will be established for the public to comment on these proposed forms and rules. Meanwhile, the courts may change the interim forms. Therefore, you should check to be sure you are using the current versions of the forms. This can be done best by checking the Bankruptcy Court website at:

www.uscourts.gov/rules/new_and_revised_official_forms.html

The bankruptcy rules require all papers filed with the court clerk to be two-hole punched so the clerk can insert them at the top of a file folder. Get a paper punch and punch out two circles at the top of each form.

The following material gives you detailed instructions for filling out the forms necessary for a Chapter 7 bankruptcy and for taking your case through the court system. The forms may be found in Appendix C. In Appendix B, you will find a checklist for Chapter 7 bankruptcy to help you keep track of your case, and help ensure that you have all of the necessary forms and information. The instructions that follow relate to the form's number, which is located in the upper, outside corner of the first page of the form. Some of the forms are more than one page, and several have continuation pages for use if there is not enough room on the first page.

## VOLUNTARY PETITION

The following directions explain how to complete the **VOLUNTARY PETITION**. (see form 1, p.215.)

- ❖ Fill in the designation of the bankruptcy court in which you will be filing your case, according to the instructions on page 60 under "Understanding Legal Forms."

- ❖ Fill in the names, last four digits of Social Security numbers, and addresses in the appropriate boxes as indicated.

- ❖ Under the heading "Type of Debtor," check the box for "Individual (includes Joint Debtors)."

- ❖ Ignore the boxes under "Nature of Business."

- ❖ Under "Chapter of Bankruptcy Code Under Which the Petition is Filed," check the box for "Chapter 7."

- ❖ Under "Nature of Debts," check the box for "Consumer/ Non-Business."

- ❖ Under "Filing Fee," check whichever box applies to your situation. If you are financially unable to pay the full fee, but will be able to pay it in several installments, you will need to complete the **APPLICATION TO PAY FILING FEE IN INSTALLMENTS** (form 2), which is explained on page 219. If your financial situation is so bad that you cannot even make installment payments, you will need to complete the **APPLICATION FOR WAIVER OF THE CHAPTER 7 FILING FEE** (form 3), which is explained on page 221. Reviewing, or even completing, either or both of these forms now will help you determine if you qualify.

- ❖ Ignore the boxes under "Chapter 11 Debtors."

◈ Under "Statistical/Administrative Information," check whichever boxes apply to your situation. Whether funds will be available for unsecured creditors, the number of creditors, the estimated assets, and the estimated debts can be determined from the information you completed on worksheets 1, 2, and 3.

◈ At the top of the second page of the **VOLUNTARY PETITION**, type in your name (and your spouse's name, if you are filing a joint petition). If you have filed for bankruptcy within the past eight years, or if your spouse has filed a bankruptcy case that is currently pending, you will need to fill in the information where indicated.

◈ Ignore the sections marked "Exhibit A" and "Exhibit B."

◈ The section marked "Exhibit C" is primarily designed for use by businesses that may have chemicals or other hazardous materials, to alert trustees to potential dangers. Unless you have such materials, check the box marked "No."

◈ In the section marked "Certification Concerning Debt Counseling by Individual/Joint Debtor(s)," you will most likely check the first box. You must complete debt counseling before filing your petition. If you have not done so, see Section 4 for more information about debt counseling. The second box is to request a waiver of this requirement, but you need to be able to show some type of emergency situation that would justify not completing the debt counseling requirement.

◈ The information under the heading "Information Regarding the Debtor" is to show that you are in the proper bankruptcy court. You will need to be able to check one box, which will probably be the first box. The second box is for businesses. If you have an affiliate, general partner, or partnership, you should consult a lawyer or a business bankruptcy book.

◈ If you are renting the place where you live and your landlord has sued you for eviction due to nonpayment of rent, you will need to review the heading "Statement by a Debtor Who Resides as a Tenant of Residential Property." If your landlord has already obtained a court judgment against you to recover possession of the property, you will need to check the first box and fill in the name and address of the landlord. If this is the case, the automatic bankruptcy stay would not apply and your landlord will be able to proceed with having you evicted. However, there is a situation in which you may be able to stop or delay the eviction. This is possible if your state law allows you to stop the eviction by paying the entire amount you owe the landlord, and you deposit with the court the rent that would be due over the thirty-day period after filing your bankruptcy petition. If this applies to you, check the second and third boxes. If you rent, but your landlord has not filed for eviction, or has filed but has not already obtained a judgment, you can leave this section of the form blank.

◈  At the top of the third page of the **VOLUNTARY PETITION**, type in your name (and the name of your spouse, if you are filing a joint petition).

◈  In the section marked "Signature(s) of Debtor(s) (Individual/Joint)," sign your name, and fill in your telephone number and the date on the lines where indicated. If you and your spouse are filing a joint petition, your spouse must also sign. Ignore the other sections on this page.

## APPLICATION TO PAY FILING FEE IN INSTALLMENTS

Use the **APPLICATION TO PAY FILING FEE IN INSTALLMENTS** (see form 2, p.219) if you are unable to pay the full filing fee at the time you file your **VOLUNTARY PETITION**. (If your situation is so bad that you cannot pay the filing fee in installments, you may ask the judge to waive the filing fee altogether. To do this, you will need to complete form 3 instead of form 2, which is explained on page 221.) If you *are* able to pay the full filing fee when you file your **VOLUNTARY PETITION**, you can ignore form 2.

Call the court clerk's office to confirm the amount of the filing fee for a Chapter 7 case. You can expect it to cost about $274. You may pay the filing fee in installments, provided that there are no more·than four installments and that the last payment is made no later than 120 days after the **VOLUNTARY PETITION** is filed. Exact fees can be found on various bankruptcy court websites and at 28 U.S.C. §1930.

◈   Complete the top portion of the form according to the instructions in "Understanding Legal Forms" at the beginning of this section. On the line marked "Chapter," fill in the number "7." You will need to leave the "Case No." blank, as you will not have a case number until the clerk assigns one at the time you take your papers in for filing.

◈   Fill in the amount of the filing fee on the line in paragraph 1.

◈   In paragraph 4, fill in the installment payment terms on the lines provided.

◈   Sign your name on the line marked "Signature of Debtor" and fill in the date. If you and your spouse are filing a joint petition, your spouse will need to sign on the line marked "Signature of Joint Debtor" and fill in the date. Ignore the other items on the first page of this form.

◈   The second page of this form is the order the judge will sign to give you permission to pay in installments. All you need to do here is fill in the designation of the court at the top of the page.

◈   Fill in your name on the line marked "Debtor" (and your spouse's name, if filing jointly).

◈   On the line marked "Chapter," fill in the number "7."

The court clerk will fill in the case number and the judge will complete the remainder of the page.

## APPLICATION FOR WAIVER
## OF THE CHAPTER 7 FILING FEE

If your financial situation is so bad that you cannot come up with the filing fee ($274) and cannot even pay it in four installments over a period of 120 days, you can ask the court to waive the filing fee entirely. This is done by filing an **APPLICATION FOR WAIVER OF THE CHAPTER 7 FILING FEE**. (see form 3, p.221.) However, a waiver can only be approved by the judge if your income is less than 150% of the official poverty line for the size of your family. The poverty guidelines may be obtained from the bankruptcy clerk's office, or online at **www.uscourts.gov**. By completing the various forms required to go along with the waiver request, you will find out if you meet this requirement. In order to fill in the information that will be required in form 3, you should first complete Schedules A, B, I, and J, which are explained in detail later in this section of the book. Complete form 3 as follows.

♦ Complete the top portion of the form by filling in your name (and your spouse's name, if filing jointly). You will need to leave the "Case No." blank, as you will not have a case number until the clerk assigns one at the time you take your papers in for filing.

♦ Fill in the required information for items 1 through 17. These items are self-explanatory, and the information will mostly come from the various schedules you will need to prepare as instructed throughout this section.

♦ The last page of this form, with the heading "Order on Debtor's Application for Waiver of the Chapter 7 Filing Fee," will be completed by the judge. You will note that the judge has three options: (1) to grant your request for a waiver; (2) to deny your request and order you to pay the filing fee in installments; and, (3) to schedule a hearing on your waiver request. A copy of this order will be mailed to you after the judge completes it.

---

## – Warning –

The **SUMMARY OF SCHEDULES** appears at this point in Appendix C. (see form 4, p.225.) Skip this form for now. It will be completed after you complete Schedules A through J.

---

## SCHEDULE A—REAL PROPERTY

**SCHEDULE A—REAL PROPERTY** is the form on which you will list all real estate you own or have an interest in. (see form 5, p.227.) First of all, be sure to carefully read the instructions contained at the top of the form itself. In general, *real property* means land and things permanently attached to it (like a house).

◈ If you do not have an interest in any real property, simply write "None" in the first column that is headed "DESCRIPTION AND LOCATION OF PROPERTY." If you do have an interest in real property, you will need to complete the rest of this form.

◈ In the first column, describe the property and tell where it is located. This does not have to be the formal legal description, but you should state the type of property (such as home, unimproved lot, or condominium) and the address (including the city, county, and state). If you are renting the property, it should not be listed on this form, but should be listed on **SCHEDULE G—EXECUTORY CONTRACTS AND UNEXPIRED LEASES** instead. (see form 11, p.243.)

◈ In the second column, designated "NATURE OF DEBTOR'S INTEREST IN PROPERTY," state the type of interest you have in the property. For most people who own a home, the ownership interest in the property is known as *fee simple*. The most common interests in real property are as follows.

○ *Fee Simple*. This is where you own the property, with no obligation other than to pay the mortgage and taxes. You may own the property with someone else or by yourself.

✪ *Life Estate.* This is where you have the right to live on the property during your lifetime, but you cannot sell or give it away during your lifetime, or leave it to anyone upon your death. This is commonly set up when a spouse dies, and is usually done for tax purposes. One spouse gives the other a life estate so that he or she can live on the property until death, but then the property goes to their children.

✪ *Future Interest.* The most common example of this kind of interest is what the children have after a life estate for their widowed parent. A person with a future interest will get the property someday, but only after some event occurs (such as the death of the person with the life estate).

One of these types of interests should be listed in the second column. If you own the property with another person who is not your husband or wife, you should also indicate the portion of the interest you own (such as one-half fee simple, or one-third future interest).

◈ If you are not married, you may ignore the third column. If you are married, you need to indicate whether each piece of property is owned by the husband (H), the wife (W), both of you jointly (J), or both of you as *community property* (C).

   **NOTE:** *Community property only applies if you live in Arizona, California, Idaho, Louisiana, Nevada, New Mexico, Texas, Washington, or Wisconsin. Generally, this means that all the property either spouse obtains during the marriage is owned by both of them, and can be taken by the trustee even if they do not file for bankruptcy jointly. If you live in one of these states and are considering filing separately from your spouse, you should consult a bankruptcy lawyer.*

◈ In the fourth column, indicate the value of the property. This will typically be the current market value. Do not take into account any money you owe on a mortgage. Be sure to total these amounts at the bottom of this column.

⟡ In the fifth column, indicate the amount of money you owe on the mortgage or any liens on the property. If you do not owe any money on the property, write "None" in the fifth column.

## SCHEDULE B—PERSONAL PROPERTY

On **SCHEDULE B—PERSONAL PROPERTY**, you will list all of your property that is *not* real estate. (see form 6, p.229.) Be sure to carefully read the instructions on the form itself. Note that this form is several pages long. *Personal property* is all of your property that is *not* land or permanently attached to the land. This will be everything you listed in the **PROPERTY WORKSHEET**, except for the real estate items. (see worksheet 2, p.209.)

---

### – Warning –

Be sure to list all of your property, even if you think it has no value. Otherwise, it may appear that you are trying to hide property from creditors, which could result in the dismissal of your case.

---

⟡ At the top of each page, fill in your name (or your name and your spouse's name, if filing jointly) and the case number, once it is issued by the clerk.

⟡ The types of personal property are listed in the first column of this form. Simply read each item and write down what you own in that category.

⟡ If you do not own anything in a particular category, simply check the second column marked "NONE."

⟡ In the third column, marked "DESCRIPTION AND LOCATION OF PROPERTY," describe each item in the category, and indicate where it is located by street address, city, county, and state. If most of the property is at your home, you may write "Unless otherwise indicated, all property is located at the debtor's residence." If you do this, be sure to indicate any property that is located somewhere else.

Refer to Appendix A of this book for the list of the exemptions for your state and for the alternate Federal Bankruptcy Exemptions. Any item for which you may claim an exemption should be listed separately in this form.

---

### Example:
Item 12 relates to pension plans. If your state offers an exemption for a certain type of plan, be sure to indicate that your plan is of that type. (See Section 8, pages 137–138 of this book regarding pension plans.)

---

◈    If you are not married, you may ignore the fourth column. If you are married, you will need to indicate whether the property is owned by the husband (H), the wife (W), both of you jointly (J), or both of you as community property (C).

◈    In the last column, indicate the current value of the property.

◈    Total the amounts in this column at the bottom of the third page of the form.

## SCHEDULE C—PROPERTY CLAIMED AS EXEMPT
The property you are claiming as exempt from your creditors must be listed in **SCHEDULE C—PROPERTY CLAIMED AS EXEMPT**. (see form 7, p.233.)

◈    At the top of each page, fill in your name (or your name and your spouse's name, if filing jointly) and the case number, once it is issued by the clerk.

◈    You will need to check one of the two boxes at the top, left-hand side of the form. Check the first box if you are using the Federal Bankruptcy Exemptions, and check the second box if you are using the exemptions for your state. The Federal Bankruptcy Exemptions and the Federal Nonbankruptcy Exemptions, as well as your state's exemptions, are found in Appendix A.

The Federal Bankruptcy Exemptions are only available in the following states: Arkansas, Connecticut, District of Columbia, Hawaii, Massachusetts, Michigan, Minnesota, New Jersey, New Mexico, Pennsylvania, Rhode Island, South Carolina, Texas, Vermont, Washington, and Wisconsin. If you will not be filing in one of these states, check the second box.

**NOTE:** *If the Federal Bankruptcy Exemptions are available in your state, you need to compare them with those of your state to see which set will allow you to keep more of your property. If you select the state exemptions, you may also use the Federal Nonbankruptcy Exemptions.*

⟐ If you are claiming a homestead exemption that is more than $125,000, you will need to check the box at the top, right-hand of the page. This can only apply if you will be filing in one of the following states, and only if you have lived there for at least forty months: Arkansas, California, District of Columbia, Florida, Iowa, Kansas, Louisiana, Massachusetts, Minnesota, Nevada, Oklahoma, Rhode Island, South Dakota, and Texas. If you will be filing in one of these states, but you have not lived there for at least forty months, your homestead exemption is limited to $125,000. If you have lived in one of these states for at least forty months before filing your petition, you can use the state's homestead exemption in excess of $125,000.

⟐ To complete the rest of **SCHEDULE C—PROPERTY CLAIMED AS EXEMPT**, refer to Column (5) of the **PROPERTY WORKSHEET**, where you have already identified the items you are claiming as exempt. (see worksheet 2, p.209.) You may want to refer once again to the information in Appendix A of this book to be sure you are claiming everything to which you may be entitled.

If you are not sure whether you can claim an item, but it seems to fit one of the exemptions, then claim it. Let the trustee or a creditor question it. (Of course, do not claim something you know is not exempt, but if you genuinely are not sure, give yourself the benefit of the exemption.)

◈ In the first column, write in a description of the property. Try to use the same categories as those for your state in Appendix A.

> **NOTE:** *All of the property listed in this form should also be listed in either* **SCHEDULE A—REAL PROPERTY** *(form 5) or in* **SCHEDULE B—PERSONAL PROPERTY** *(form 6).*

◈ In the second column, indicate the statute or law that gives you the exemption you are claiming. Again, refer to Appendix A of this book for the statute or law number. Examples of how to refer to these laws appear at the beginning of each state's listing in Appendix A.

◈ In the third column, marked "VALUE OF CLAIMED EXEMPTION," state the amount of the exemption you are claiming. Be sure you are not exceeding the maximum amount of the exemption allowed as indicated in Appendix A.

---

### Example:
If your state only allows up to a $2,000 exemption for a car, do not show a $30,000 exemption for your Mercedes.

---

◈ In the last column, indicate the full market value of the property.

## SCHEDULE D—CREDITORS HOLDING SECURED CLAIMS

Any secured creditors need to be listed on **SCHEDULE D—CREDITORS HOLDING SECURED CLAIMS**. (see form 8, p.235.) Be sure to carefully read the instructions at the beginning of the form itself. To complete this form, refer to the **DEBT WORKSHEET**, Column (5), which will show the creditors holding a security interest in your property. (see worksheet 3, p.210.) These will most likely be the mortgage holders on your home and any other real property, as well as the lenders on auto, boat, or home improvement loans. (They are not likely to be credit card companies.)

A creditor holding security is one who loaned you money to buy something and has the right to take some of your property if you do not pay. This also includes anyone having a lien on your property, such as for work done on your home.

◈ At the top of each page, fill in your name (or your name and your spouse's name, if filing jointly) and the case number, once it is issued by the clerk.

◈ In the first column, fill in the last four digits of the account number, and the creditor's name and address. (To protect against theft, do not list the entire account number.)

◈ Place an "X" in the second column, marked "CODEBTOR," if another person is also liable for the repayment of the debt. However, do not check this column if the other person is your spouse *and* you have filed a joint bankruptcy with your spouse.

◈ If you are not married, ignore the third column. If you are married, then indicate here whether the debt is owed by the husband (H), the wife (W), both of you jointly (J), or both of you as a community property debt (C).

◈ In the fourth column, first indicate the date the debt was created. Next, indicate the nature of the lien on the property. Refer to the first paragraph of instructions on the form itself for examples of the types of liens. If you are not sure of the type of lien, simply write "nature uncertain" and ask the trustee later, or call the person or company you owe the money to and ask. Next, give a description of the property that is subject to the lien, and indicate the full value of the property in the space labeled "VALUE $."

◈ In the fifth, sixth, and seventh columns, indicate (by an "X") if the debt is *contingent, unliquidated*, or *disputed*. These concepts are very confusing, so do not hesitate to ask the trustee if you are not sure.

A *contingent debt* is one that will only be owed if some future event occurs (such as if a tax audit shows that a debt claimed by the IRS is really owed).

An *unliquidated debt* is one in which the exact amount has not been determined (such as where you know you owe a tax, but will not know the exact amount until you know the full amount of your income or expenses).

A *disputed debt* is one you are contesting (someone is claiming you owe the debt, but you do not think you do or do not think you owe as much as he or she is claiming).

If none of these apply, leave these columns blank.

◈ In the eighth column, marked "AMOUNT OF CLAIM WITH-OUT DEDUCTING VALUE OF COLLATERAL," indicate the amount of the debt you owe.

◈ In the last column, indicate if any of the debt is *unsecured* (not attached to any piece of property).

---

### Example:
If you owe $8,000 on your car, but the car is only worth $6,000, then $2,000 of the debt is unsecured.

---

◈ Total the eighth column, and indicate at the bottom left if there are any continuation sheets attached.

> **NOTE:** *The second page of this form is a continuation sheet. Indicate at the bottom left whether there are any continuation sheets attached.*

◈ If you only use the first page, total the eighth column and type in the amount in the box marked "Total."

◈ If you use one or more continuation pages, total the eighth column for each page and type the amount in the box marked "Subtotal." Then, add all of the subtotals and type the amount in the box marked "Total" on the last page.

## SCHEDULE E—CREDITORS HOLDING UNSECURED PRIORITY CLAIMS

Certain types of creditors have *priority*, which means that they will be paid from your nonexempt and nonsecured property before other creditors. Most creditors with priority relate to the operation of a business, so they will not apply to most people filing for personal bankruptcy under Chapter 7 or 13. The priority claims are listed on **SCHEDULE E—CREDITORS HOLDING UNSECURED PRIORITY CLAIMS** as follows. (see form 9, p.237.)

- ✪ *Domestic Support Obligations.* This applies if you owe court-ordered alimony, maintenance, or support to a former spouse or a child.

- ✪ *Extensions of credit in an involuntary case.* Since you are filing a voluntary petition, this does not apply to you.

- ✪ *Wages, salaries, and commissions.* This relates to money that you would owe to your employee. If you have employees, you should either consult an attorney or a book that deals with business bankruptcy.

- ✪ *Contributions to employee benefit plans.* Again, if you have employees, you should consult a lawyer or a book dealing with business bankruptcy.

- ✪ *Certain farmers and fishermen.* This only applies to operators of grain or fish storage facilities.

- ✪ *Deposits by individuals.* This would apply to you only if you owe someone money for a deposit they gave you to purchase or rent real estate, goods, or services that you have not provided.

- ✪ *Taxes and certain other debts owed to the government.* If you owe taxes to the federal, state, or local government, you will need to check this box and list the debt.

- ✪ *Commitments to maintain the capital of an insured depository institution.* This only applies to banks or other similar depository institutions.

✪    *Claims for Death or Personal Injury While Debtor was Intoxicated.* This applies if you are paying on a claim that resulted from you driving a car while intoxicated and causing damages to another.

Be sure to carefully read the instructions at the beginning of form 9.

◈    At the top of each page, fill in your name (or your name and your spouse's name, if filing jointly) and the case number, once it is issued by the clerk.

◈    If you do not have any of these types of debts, check the first box on the first page that states: "Check this box if the debtor has no creditors holding unsecured priority claims to report on this Schedule E."

◈    If you do have any of these types of debts, check the appropriate box or boxes on the first page, and list the debt on the continuation sheet. Complete a separate continuation sheet for each type of debt listed.

   **NOTE:** *There is a space at the top of the continuation sheet for indicating the type of priority debt.*

◈    To complete the remainder of the continuation sheet, follow the same directions for the **Schedule D—Creditors Holding Secured Claims** given on page 235. Be sure to total the amounts in the eighth column, and indicate at the bottom left how many continuation sheets are provided for **Schedule E**. Remember to only fill in the last four digits of your account number.

## SCHEDULE F—CREDITORS HOLDING UNSECURED NONPRIORITY CLAIMS

All of the creditors not listed on any of the previous forms will be listed on **Schedule F—Creditors Holding Unsecured Nonpriority Claims**. (see form 10, p.241.) In most cases, this will be primarily credit cards and other personal debts, such as unpaid bills. Be sure to carefully read the instructions at the beginning of the form itself. This form also has a continuation sheet.

**NOTE:** *There is a box to check if you have no creditors to report on this form. If you have no creditors to report here, you need to go back to Section 3 of this book and take another look at whether you can, or should, avoid bankruptcy.*

The main benefit of bankruptcy is getting rid of these unsecured nonpriority claims. If you have none to get rid of, you probably should not file for bankruptcy and may want to consult a lawyer or credit counselor.

◈    At the top of each page, fill in your name (or your name and your spouse's name, if filing jointly) and the case number, once it is issued by the clerk.

◈    Complete the first, second, and third columns according to the instructions for **Schedule D—Creditors Holding Secured Claims**, as indicated on page 74. Remember to only fill in the last four digits of your account number.

◈    In the fourth column, indicate the date the claim was incurred, the consideration for the claim, and any setoff you are claiming. (A *setoff* is a debt the creditor owes to you.)

   For the *consideration*, simply state what the debt was for, such as student loan, vacation loan, dental bill, car repair, Visa, or Sears.

   In some cases, a store may have required you to pledge some property as collateral in order to obtain the credit card. You should know if this is the case because you probably had to sign some additional papers instead of a simple credit card application.

   If this is the case with one of your credit cards, you should list it on **Schedule D** instead of here. (see form 8, p.235.)

---

### Example:

If you owe your landlord $800 in back rent, but he owes you $50 for plumbing repairs that you paid for, you have a setoff of $50.

---

◈ Complete the remaining columns according to the instructions for the same columns in **Schedule D**, as indicated on pages 73–75.

◈ This form also has a continuation sheet, so be sure to indicate at the bottom the number of continuation sheets attached.

◈ Total the amounts in the last column.

## SCHEDULE G—EXECUTORY CONTRACTS AND UNEXPIRED LEASES

Any contracts or leases to which you are a party must be listed and described on **Schedule G—Executory Contracts and Unexpired Leases**. (see form 11, p.243.)

◈ At the top of each page, fill in your name (or your name and your spouse's name, if filing jointly) and the case number, once it is issued by the clerk.

◈ If you are not a party to any contracts or leases, simply check the box near the top of the form before the sentence "Check this box if debtor has no executory contracts or unexpired leases." Be sure to carefully read the instructions at the beginning of the form itself.

◈ In the first column, indicate the name and address of the other parties to the contract or lease. This includes anyone who is obligated the same as you, such as your apartment roommate if his or her name is also on the lease. It also includes the person to whom you are obligated, such as your landlord.

◈ In the second column, describe the contract or lease. Examples of such descriptions are "apartment lease," "auto lease," or "lawn maintenance contract." In this column, you must also list the nature of your interest, such as lessee, seller, or purchaser. (If you are a landlord, you will state this as "lessor.") If you have a lease for nonresidential property, you need to indicate this. If you are a party to a government contract, the contract number must be stated.

## SCHEDULE H—CODEBTORS

Anyone who is also obligated to pay all or part of any of your debts must be listed on **SCHEDULE H—CODEBTORS**. (see form 12, p.245.) You do not need to include your spouse if you are filing a joint bankruptcy petition. Be sure to carefully read the instructions at the beginning of the form itself. At the top of each page, fill in your name (or your name and your spouse's name, if filing jointly) and the case number, once it is issued by the clerk.

There is a box to check if you have no codebtors. If you do have codebtors, then indicate their names and addresses in the first column, and the creditors' names and addresses in the second column.

## SCHEDULE I—CURRENT INCOME OF INDIVIDUAL DEBTOR(S)

**SCHEDULE I—CURRENT INCOME OF INDIVIDUAL DEBTOR(S)** is where you list your income, as well as your spouse's income if you are married and are filing a joint petition for bankruptcy. (see form 13, p.247.)

The top portion of this form asks for information about your family status and employment, and is self-explanatory. The lower part asks for a breakdown of your income and payroll deductions (and that of your spouse, if you are married and filing a joint petition). All amounts should be converted to a monthly amount. The last sentence in the form asks you to describe any increase or decrease of more than 10% in any of the listed categories that you expect to occur within the year after filing the petition. Examples would be the termination of unemployment benefits, an anticipated layoff or wage reduction, or the loss of rental income from the imminent sale of the property.

## SCHEDULE J—CURRENT EXPENDITURES OF INDIVIDUAL DEBTOR(S)

The previous schedule listed your income. **SCHEDULE J—CURRENT EXPENDITURES OF INDIVIDUAL DEBTOR(S)** is used to list your monthly expenses. (see form 14, p.249.) Convert all amounts to monthly figures. If you and your spouse are filing a joint petition, but do not live together, you will need to check the box near the top of the form, and your spouse will also need to complete a separate **SCHEDULE J**. (In this case, you will need to make another copy of this form for your spouse to complete.)

◈ At the top of each page, fill in your name (or your name and your spouse's name, if filing jointly) and the case number, once it is issued by the clerk.

◈ In items 1–17, list monthly expenses for the categories listed. Item 17 is for other recurring monthly expenses.

◈ In item 18, add up your totals and list your "TOTAL MONTHLY EXPENSES."

◈ Item 19 provides space to describe any anticipated increase or decrease in the numbers listed above.

◈ In item 20a, use the total income figure from form 13.

◈ In item 20b, use the "TOTAL MONTHLY EXPENSES" from item 18 of this form.

◈ Item 20c will give the total amount you have available to pay your creditors.

## SUMMARY OF SCHEDULES

On the **SUMMARY OF SCHEDULES** you will give the totals from each of the schedules you have completed. (see form 4, p.225.) At the top of each page, fill in the court information, your name (or your name and your spouse's name, if filing jointly), and the case number, once it is issued by the clerk. Also fill in "7" on the line marked "Chapter." You will be attaching all of the schedules to your **VOLUNTARY PETITION**, so fill in "Yes" in the column marked "Attached (Yes/No)."

On the second page of the form, fill in the top portion as you did in the previous forms, then fill in the amount of each of the indicated liabilities from the appropriate schedule.

NOTE: *For each schedule you are to indicate the number of sheets used. You will need to count the number of continuation sheets for each schedule. Do not forget to count your spouse's separate* SCHEDULE J—CURRENT EXPENDITURES OF INDIVIDUAL DEBTOR(S) *if appropriate.*

Be sure to add the totals of the columns where indicated. Do not leave any spaces blank. If there is no entry for an item, type "0" in the space for that item. Although you are completing this form after the other schedules, this form will come before the other schedules when you file your petition.

## DECLARATION CONCERNING DEBTOR'S SCHEDULES

By completing and signing the DECLARATION CONCERNING DEBTOR'S SCHEDULES, you swear that your schedules are accurate to the best of your knowledge. (see form 15, p.251.) To complete this form, follow these steps.

◈ At the top of each page, fill in your name (or your name and your spouse's name, if filing jointly) and the case number, once it is issued by the clerk.

◈ Type in the total number of sheets as indicated on the form.

◈ Type in the date.

◈ Sign your name where indicated (your spouse must do the same if you are filing jointly).

NOTE: *There are fine and jail penalties listed on the form for giving false information.*

◈ Ignore the sections titled "DECLARATION AND SIGNATURE OF NON-ATTORNEY BANKRUPTCY PETITION PREPARER" and "DECLARATION UNDER PENALTY OF PERJURY ON BEHALF OF A CORPORATION OR PARTNERSHIP."

# STATEMENT OF FINANCIAL AFFAIRS

The **STATEMENT OF FINANCIAL AFFAIRS** is a lengthy form, but one that is not difficult to complete, because the instructions on the form itself are rather clear. (see form 16, p.253.) At the top of each page, fill in your name (or your name and your spouse's name, if filing jointly) and the case number, once it is issued by the clerk. All you need to do is read each item and provide the information it asks for. For each item there is a box marked "None" to check if that item does not apply to you. Be sure you mark the "None" box instead of leaving an item unanswered.

Some of the questions may require you to go back through your records for the past few years. Just answer the questions as best you can with the information you can recall or locate. Use additional sheets of paper if necessary, and be sure to indicate the number of the item being continued on the additional sheet.

Item 14 asks about property you have that belongs to someone else. This is to protect that person's property from your creditors. Of course, an easier way to deal with this situation is for you to return that property to the other person.

Read the instructions immediately before Item 14 carefully. You will not need to complete any more of the numbered items in this form (and can skip to the last page for your signature) unless you have been in one of the following positions within the past six years:

- ✪   an officer, director, or managing executive of a corporation;

- ✪   an owner of more than 5% of the voting stock of a corporation;

- ✪   a general partner in a partnership; or,

- ✪   a sole proprietor of a business or otherwise self-employed.

Once you have completed all of the items you are required to complete, type in the date and sign your name where indicated on the last page of the **STATEMENT OF FINANCIAL AFFAIRS**. Your spouse must also date and sign this form if you are filing a joint petition. Also, indicate the number of continuation sheets attached (type in "0" if there are none).

**NOTE:** *There are fine and jail penalties listed at the end of the form for giving false information.*

## CHAPTER 7 INDIVIDUAL DEBTOR'S STATEMENT OF INTENTION

The purpose of the **CHAPTER 7 DEBTOR'S STATEMENT OF INTENTION** is to indicate what secured property you intend to give up to your creditors and what property you intend to keep. (see form 17, p.265.) This form only applies to the following two types of property.

1. *Secured property*, which would be property listed on **SCHEDULE D—CREDITORS HOLDING SECURED CLAIMS** (form 8).

2. *Personal property subject to an unexpired lease*, which would be listed on **SCHEDULE G—EXECUTORY CONTRACTS AND UNEXPIRED LEASES** (form 11).

To complete form 17 do the following.

⟐ Complete the caption according to the instructions on page 61.

⟐ Note the three statements preceded by boxes at the top of the form. If you do not have any secured property or personal property subject to an unexpired lease, leave these blank. Check the first box if you have completed **SCHEDULE D** listing secured debts. Check the second box if you have completed **SCHEDULE G** listing personal property subject to an unexpired lease. If you checked either of the first two boxes (or both), check the third box.

⟐ You will note there are two charts on the form. The first chart on the form relates to secured property, and should be completed as follows.

⟐ In the first column, list the secured property from **SCHEDULE D**. This should be a sufficiently clear description of the property to avoid any confusion with other property.

(For example, if you have two cars, it would not be sufficient to simply state "automobile." Instead, you should list
the year, make, and model.)

◈   In the second column, fill in the name of the creditor. The
remaining columns are to indicate what you intend to do
with each item of property.

◈   Check the third column if the item is to be surrendered to
pay creditors.

◈   Check the fourth column if you are claiming the item as
exempt property. If so, it should also be listed on
**SCHEDULE C—PROPERTY CLAIMED AS EXEMPT** (form 7).

◈   Check the fifth column if the property is to be redeemed.
There can be many complications to redeeming property.
Be sure to read more about this subject in Section 8 of this
book. It is suggested that you see a lawyer if you think you
want to redeem property.

◈   Check the sixth column if you will be reaffirming the debt.
There can be many complications to reaffirming a debt. It
is the common practice of many creditors to attempt to
talk the debtor into reaffirming the debt, often to the
debtor's detriment. Be sure to read more about this subject
in Section 8 of this book. If you think you want to reaffirm
a debt, it is suggested that you see a lawyer.

◈  The second chart on this form relates to leased property, and
should be completed as follows.

◈   In the first column, list the leased property.

◈   In the second column, fill in the lessor's name.

◈   Check the third column if the lease is to be assumed.
*Assuming a lease* means that you intend to keep the
property and continue paying what is owed under the
lease. If you do so, you will also need to cure any default
under the lease.

◈ Date and sign the form on the lines indicated. Ignore the section of the form titled "Declaration of Non-Attorney Bankruptcy Petition Preparer."

Although this form is very poorly designed, it is the official form approved by the bankruptcy courts. There can be many complications to redeeming property or reaffirming a debt. Be sure to read more about these subjects in Section 8 of this book. It is the common practice of many creditors to attempt to talk the debtor into reaffirming the debt, often to the debtor's detriment. If you run into a situation where you are not certain that your creditor will not foreclose or repossess, and will allow you to continue payments, you should see a lawyer.

## STATEMENT OF CURRENT MONTHLY INCOME AND MEANS TEST CALCULATION

The **STATEMENT OF CURRENT MONTHLY INCOME AND MEANS TEST CALCULATION** is used to determine whether you meet the requirements to be allowed to file for bankruptcy under Chapter 7 of the Bankruptcy Code. (see form 18, p.267.) Part of this form uses expenses allowed by the Internal Revenue Service (IRS).

Most of this form is self-explanatory. From reading each item, you can easily determine what information is being requested. The following information may help clarify a few points.

◈ At the top of the first page, fill in your name (or your name and your spouse's name, if filing jointly) and the case number, once it is issued by the clerk. For now, ignore the box at the top right of the first page (with boxes marked "Presumption arises" and "Presumption does not arise"), as it will be addressed later.

◈ Part I of this form only applies if you are a disabled veteran. If you are a disabled veteran, check the box in Part I and check the box at the top right of the first page marked "Presumption does not arise." You can then skip to Part VIII of this form.

◈ Part II of this form is to fill in all of your sources of income. Line 12 will be your total monthly income.

◈ Part III of this form will determine if you meet one of the basic qualifications for filing under Chapter 7 of the Bankruptcy Code—that your income is no more than the median family income for your state and family size. For Line 13, take your total monthly income from Line 12 and multiply it by 12 to get your total annual income.

Line 14 asks for the "Applicable median family income." This is determined by information from the U.S. Census Bureau, which takes into account the number of people in the family. This amount varies from state to state. The values for your state can be obtained from your local bankruptcy court clerk, or online at **www.usdoj.gov/ust**.

If the amount on Line 13 is less than, or equal to, the amount on Line 14, you automatically meet the requirement for Chapter 7 bankruptcy. Check the first box in Line 15, then go back to the top of the first page and check the box marked "Presumption does not arise." You can then skip down to Part VIII of this form. On the other hand, if the amount on Line 13 is more than the amount on Line 14, you will need to continue on to Part IV of this form. You may still be able to use Chapter 7, but more calculations are needed to be sure.

◈ Part IV of this form reverts back to monthly income.

◈ Part V, Subpart A of this form is to determine your allowed expenses. The amount for Line 19 comes from national standards set forth in tables created by the IRS. There is one table for Alaska, one table for Hawaii, and one table for all other states and the District of Columbia. The amounts for Line 20 through Line 23 come from local standards, which also come from IRS tables. Both the national and local standards are available from the bankruptcy court clerk or online at **www.usdoj.gov/ust**. The amounts for Line 25 through Line 32 will come from your records. Enter the total of the allowed expenses on Line 33.

◈ Part V, Subpart B of this form lists various additional expenses. Read each item and determine if it applies to you. If so, fill in the appropriate amount. Note that documentation to prove some of these items is required. Add the figures in Lines 34 through 40, and enter the total on Line 41.

◈    Part V, Subpart C of this form is to list various debts you will continue to pay. Much of this information will come from the various schedules you filed with your **Voluntary Petition**.

◈    Part VI of this form is used to determine if you qualify for filing under Chapter 7 of the Bankruptcy Code. Follow the instructions for Lines 48 through 51. The amount on Line 51 represents the amount of money you have available to make debt payments over the next five years.

   ◈    If the amount on Line 51 is less than $6,000, you automatically qualify for a Chapter 7 bankruptcy. You will check the first box in Line 52; then go back to the top of the first page and check the box marked "Presumption does not arise." You can skip down to Part VIII of this form.

   ◈    If the amount on Line 51 is more than $10,000, a legal presumption arises that you are attempting to defraud your creditors by filing for Chapter 7. If this is the case, you should consider filing under Chapter 13 of the Bankruptcy Code, or you should see a bankruptcy attorney. If you intend to continue with Chapter 7, you will need to check the second box in Line 52; then, go back to the top of the first page and check the box marked "Presumption arises."

   ◈    If the amount on Line 51 is at least $6,000, but less than $10,000, continue on to Lines 53 through 55.

◈    If the amount on Line 51 is less than the amount on Line 54, check the first box in Line 55; then go back to the top of the first page and check the box marked "Presumption does not arise." If Line 51 is more than, or equal to, Line 54, the legal presumption of fraud is again triggered. If this is the case, you should consider filing under Chapter 13 of the Bankruptcy Code or you should see a bankruptcy attorney. If you intend to continue with Chapter 7, you will need to check the second box in Line 55; then, go back to the top of the first page and check the box marked "Presumption arises." Your other option is to complete Part VII, if you think you can make a good case that you have other expenses that are "required for the health and welfare of you and your family."

## DEBTOR'S CERTIFICATION OF COMPLETION OF INSTRUCTIONAL COURSE CONCERNING PERSONAL FINANCIAL MANAGEMENT

As mentioned earlier, one requirement for filing for bankruptcy is that you complete a course on personal financial management. The only time you do *not* need to do this is if one of the following situations applies:

✪ you are disabled or incapacitated;

✪ you are on active military duty in a military combat zone; or,

✪ you live in a federal bankruptcy court district where the trustee's office has determined that the approved instructional courses are not adequate at this time to serve the additional individuals who would otherwise be required to complete such courses (whatever that means). You will need to check with the court clerk or trustee's office to find out if you live in one of these districts.

To prove to the court that you have completed the required course, you will need to file the **DEBTOR'S CERTIFICATION OF COMPLETION OF INSTRUCTIONAL COURSE CONCERNING PERSONAL FINANCIAL MANAGEMENT**. (see form 21, p.281.) Prepare form 21 as follows.

◈ At the top of the page, fill in the court information, your name (or your name and your spouse's name, if filing jointly), and the case number, once it is issued by the clerk. On the line marked "Chapter," type in "7."

◈ If you do not fall within any of the exceptions and have completed the course, you will need to check the first box and fill in your name(s), the date you completed the course, and the name of the agency that conducted the course. You should also have received some type of paper verifying the course completion, and you need to staple a copy to this form.

◈    If you fall within any of the exceptions listed on page 89, you will need to check the second box, fill in your name(s), and check one of the three exception boxes to indicate which exception applies to you.

◈    You will then sign your name on the line marked "Signature of Debtor" and fill in the date. If you and your spouse are filing jointly, your spouse will need to sign on the line marked "Signature of Joint Debtor" and fill in the date.

**Hurricane Katrina Victims**    Although not covered in form 21, the U.S. Trustee's Office has decided to grant waivers of the financial management course requirement to victims of Hurricane Katrina. If you are a victim of Hurricane Katrina, you need to mention this to the court clerk and ask how to go about getting the waiver.

## MASTER ADDRESS LISTS AND MAILING MATRIX

All bankruptcy courts require the debtor to provide information on creditors so that the court clerk can mail the required notices to the creditors. You need to check with the bankruptcy court clerk where you file your case to determine the requirements you need to meet. Some courts have their requirements set forth online. To find out if your court has online information, go to **www.uscourts.gov**. You can then click on "Court Links" and do a search on the U.S. map that appears to see if your state is listed.

All courts previously required the debtor to prepare a list of the creditors' names and addresses in rows and columns that corresponded to sheets of mailing labels. To properly align the rows and columns of addresses, it was necessary to take a blank sheet of paper and insert it in a typewriter with a **MAILING MATRIX** behind it. (see form 22, p.283.) A sheet of addresses prepared in this manner allowed the clerk to photocopy the list onto a mailing label sheet. If your court still uses a **MAILING**

**MATRIX**, you can use form 22 to prepare it. However, be sure to check with the court clerk to be sure you know how to properly prepare it.

The bankruptcy courts in many states have entered the computer age. These courts take a more simply prepared list of creditors' names and addresses, scan them into a computer, then have the computer generate the addressed envelopes. These courts typically have detailed instructions about how the list is to be prepared and submitted by the debtor. To get these instructions, check with the court clerk or online at **www.uscourts.gov**.

## FILING WITH THE COURT CLERK AND NOTIFYING CREDITORS

Once all of your papers have been prepared, you are ready to file them with the court clerk. This is not difficult; however, things will go smoother if you are organized and know what you can expect.

**Finding the Clerk's Office**

By now you should have found out where the bankruptcy court is located. If not, the first place to check is the government listings in your local telephone directory. Look in the U.S. Government section for "Bankruptcy Court," "District Court," or "Clerk of the District Court." If this fails, there is probably a general U.S. government information listing that you can call to get the location and mailing address of the bankruptcy court clerk's office.

Only a few cities in each state have a federal court, so you may need to do some digging to find the one closest to you. If you are having trouble, try calling the law library at the county courthouse in your county, or try your local public library.

**What to Bring**

There is a checklist in Appendix B to indicate what you should bring with you to the court clerk's office when you go to file your papers.

**Filing**

Although it is possible to file by mail, it is strongly advised that you go to the clerk's office and file in person. It is easier to establish a friendly relationship in person, and the more time you spend at the bankruptcy court, the more comfortable you will feel with the entire process.

As you enter the clerk's office, look around for any signs that may help you figure out exactly where to go. There may be several windows, which may be marked for different purposes, such as filing, cashier,  or file checkout. Go to the appropriate window, or to any window if you are uncertain, and tell the clerk that you would like to file a Chapter 7.

The clerk will take your papers and examine them. If everything looks in order, the clerk will then tell you how to go about paying the filing fee. Either that clerk will handle the payment or you will be directed to the cashier's window.

You will pay the filing fee and receive a receipt. The clerk will also assign a case number and will stamp or write the number on your papers. The case number should also be on your receipt. Your papers are now filed.

If the clerk determines that something is not correct with your papers, you will be told what is wrong. *Do not argue with the clerk.* The clerk controls your access to the bankruptcy system and you do not want to make an enemy of the clerk. Clerks cannot give you legal advice, but they will usually tell you what is wrong with your papers and give you some idea of how you can fix the problem.

The kind of problem the clerk will identify is one of form, such as you forgot to sign something, forgot to fill in a space, need another type of form, or need to submit an extra copy. All you can do is find out what the clerk wants, then do it. You may be able to correct the problem at the clerk's office.

If you try to satisfy the clerk, but are still getting your papers rejected or do not understand what is required, you may want to consult a lawyer. You can also politely tell the clerk that you are not under-standing the problem, and ask him or her to explain it again, or have another clerk try to explain it to you.

Although most clerks are pleasant, helpful people, you sometimes run into a simply nasty clerk. You must still be polite, and try to win over the clerk. If this does not work, there is nothing wrong with asking for the clerk's supervisor. Just do not get angry under any circumstances. Remain calm and polite.

**Stopping Payments**

If you have not already stopped making payments, you should stop once your petition is filed (except for payments on any secured debts if you want to keep the property). From this point on, all payments for anything must be approved by the trustee. It is acceptable to buy food, and gas for your car so you can get to work, and to pay for any necessary medical expenses, but that is about all.

It will take awhile to have a trustee appointed, but once you receive a notice in the mail with the name of the trustee, contact the trustee as soon as possible. Tell the trustee that you just wanted to make an initial contact, and ask him or her if you may pay any bills you feel you need to pay. Also, ask the trustee any other questions you have. If you are continuing to make payments on secured property (such as your mortgage or car payment), mention this to the trustee.

**Automatic Stay**    Filing your petition operates as an *automatic stay*. This prohibits your creditors from taking any collection action or from cutting off any services to you. Once your petition is filed, you may want to be sure to get your creditors off your back by sending them a letter notifying them that you have filed. The following is an example of such a letter.

---

Dear Sir or Madam:

YOU ARE HEREBY ADVISED that on _____
_____, I filed a voluntary petition with the U.S. Bankruptcy Code. You may not:

✪    take any action to evict me from my residence;

✪    discontinue any service or benefit being provided to me; or,

✪    take any action against me or my property, or repossess any of my property.

Any violation of these prohibitions may constitute contempt of court and be punished accordingly.

---

Space is left at the top for the date and the creditor's address. Sign your name at the bottom, and below your signature, type in your name, address, and account number. If you have a particularly bothersome creditor, you may want to send the letter by certified, return-receipt mail. Let the trustee know if any creditors continue to bother you.

# CREDITORS' MEETING

After you have filed your case, the clerk will do several things. Using the master address list you provided and the information in your supporting documents, the clerk will send a notice to all of your creditors, indicating that you have filed for bankruptcy. A trustee will also be appointed to your case, who will then schedule a meeting of creditors. Copies of any documents issued by the clerk or the trustee will be sent to you. Read them carefully, and call the clerk's office if you do not understand them. Most of these papers will not require you to do anything, but some may require some type of response.

You may also receive copies of any papers your creditors may file with the clerk. Again, these do not require you to do anything, but keep the copies anyway.

You will receive a notice of the date, time, and place of the meeting of creditors, which you must attend. In a large number of cases, no creditors come to the meeting. The trustee will review your papers and ask you some questions. The questions are usually to verify what is in your papers, or to fill in information that you may have left out.

A few days before the meeting, call the trustee and ask him or her to tell you what information you should bring to the creditors' meeting. In all cases, be sure to bring copies of all the papers you filed and all the papers you have received regarding your case. You should also bring tax returns and other documents that support the information in the papers you filed. Each court may have its own particular requirements, which is why it is a good idea to ask the trustee.

If creditors do attend the meeting, they also have the right to ask you questions. A creditor's usual concern is whether you have identified all of your nonexempt property, and whether such property has been turned over to the trustee for sale. Answer all of the questions honestly, as you will be under oath.

If the trustee decides that your any nonexempt property is not worth enough to justify trying to sell it, he or she may *abandon* the property. This means that you will get to keep it, even though it is not exempt.

# COURT HEARING AND APPROVAL OF PLAN

If the trustee determines that everything is in order, you should receive a discharge. Depending upon the procedures in your particular bankruptcy court, you may or may not have to appear before the judge. If you do have to appear, the judge will probably only:

✪ talk to you about the effects of the bankruptcy discharge;

✪ caution you to avoid getting in debt again;

✪ possibly ask a few questions to assure the court that everything has been done properly; and,

✪ make sure that you understand the meaning of the discharge.

Your particular bankruptcy court may even have mass discharge hearings, in which many debtors are discharged at the same time and no questions are asked. All the judge does is give everyone a brief lecture about how your debts are now discharged, and how you should avoid getting into financial trouble again.

Once you have done all that is required to settle the case (turned over your nonexempt assets to the trustee, paid the filing fee and any other costs required, etc.), an order will be entered discharging all of your dischargeable debts. As has already been discussed, you will not be discharged from:

✪ taxes, fines, or penalties owed to the government;

✪ alimony or child support;

✪ certain types of student loans;

✪ obligations as a result of criminal or fraudulent actions; or,

✪ any debts that were not declared in your bankruptcy or that involve creditors who were not notified in a timely manner.

# Chapter 13 Bankruptcy

This section takes you through the forms and procedures for a Chapter 13 bankruptcy case.

## QUALIFYING FOR CHAPTER 13 BANKRUPTCY

Before filing for bankruptcy under Chapter 13 of the Bankruptcy Code, you should be certain that you do not qualify for a Chapter 7 bankruptcy. Under Chapter 7 you are able to wipe out more of your debts, and do not have to go through a three- to five-year payment plan as you do under Chapter 13.

There are certain financial requirements that must be met in order to be allowed to file for bankruptcy under Chapter 7. If your situation does not meet these requirements, you will need to file under Chapter 13 instead. This is commonly referred to as a *means test*. Basically, you will *not* be allowed to file under Chapter 7 if:

✪   your income is above the median income for people in your state and

✪   you have sufficient income to pay at least 25% of your unsecured debts over a period of three to five years, at the rate of at least $100 per month.

If you have any doubt that your income is high enough to require filing under Chapter 13, you may want to first fill out the **Statement of Current Monthly Income and Means Test Calculation** (form 18), as instructed in Section 6 of this book. (This form is not one of the forms used in a Chapter 13, but can be used to determine whether you would qualify for Chapter 7 instead.) If you find that you do not satisfy the means test to qualify for Chapter 7 bankruptcy, you can continue with the instructions in this section for a Chapter 13 bankruptcy.

**Filing Fee**  The filing fee for a Chapter 13 bankruptcy is $189. This is to be paid at the time you file your case. If you do not have the money to pay the fee at that time, you can ask the court to allow you to pay the fee in four installments. This is done by preparing and filing an **Application to Pay Filing Fee in Installments** (see form 2, p.219), which is explained later in this section.

## UNDERSTANDING LEGAL FORMS
Legal forms are simply means of communicating necessary information to the court. Forms serve two main functions. First, they ask the court to do something (such as give you a discharge of your debts). Second, they provide the court with the information it needs to decide whether to give you what you ask for.

Most of this section explains how to fill in each specific form. You will notice that some of the forms begin as follows.

---

UNITED STATES BANKRUPTCY COURT

_____ DISTRICT OF _____

---

This is to show which court you are filing your papers with. Anyone who looks at your papers later will be able to know which court to go to in order to find more details about your bankruptcy case. Your creditors may need this information during the bankruptcy case. Also, as you are applying for a mortgage or car loan after your case is completed, your prospective lender may need this information.

Each state has both state and federal courts. The first line tells you that this case is in the federal district bankruptcy court. Each state has at least one federal district bankruptcy court, and most have two or more. States that are divided into two districts will be divided one of the two following ways:

1.    Eastern District and Western District or

2.    Northern District and Southern District.

States that are divided into three districts will also be divided one of the two ways listed above, but will also have a Middle District. To find out which district you live in (and will file your case in), look in your phone directory for the number of the U.S. District Court or U.S. Bankruptcy Court. This should be listed in the government section of your phone directory. Call the court and ask which district covers your area.

The district designation will need to be typed in the first space on each form you use. If you live in a state with only one district, leave this space blank. The name of your state needs to be typed in the second space. For example, if you live in Florida and you are in the Southern District, your forms will look like this when completed:

---

### UNITED STATES BANKRUPTCY COURT

_____Southern_____ DISTRICT OF _____Florida_____

---

You may want to make a trip to your bankruptcy court clerk's office and ask to see a Chapter 13 case that someone else has filed. This may help you in completing your forms. The court records are open to the public; however you will not be allowed to take the case file out of the clerk's office. There will probably be an area at the clerk's office where you can sit down and review a file. It may also be possible to access court files online. See pages 55–57 on "Legal Research" in Section 5 of this book for information about how to access online information for the bankruptcy courts.

The forms in this book follow those approved by the bankruptcy courts throughout the country. The bankruptcy rules require all of the bankruptcy courts to accept these forms. However, many of these forms are new as a result of the 2005 changes to the Bankruptcy Code. The law requires certain procedures be followed for establishing new court rules and forms. In enacting the changes, Congress did not allow sufficient time for these procedures to be followed. As a result, temporary (or *interim*) rules and forms were set up. It is anticipated that proposed permanent forms and rules will be announced by late 2006. Then, time frames will be established for the public to comment on these proposed forms and rules. Meanwhile, the courts may change the interim forms. Therefore, you should check to be sure you are using the current versions of the forms. This can be done best by checking the Bankruptcy Court website at:

www.uscourts.gov/rules/new_and_revised_official_forms.html

It is not absolutely necessary that you use a typewriter to fill in the forms, although typing is preferred by the court and gives a much more professional appearance than handwriting. If typing is not possible, then print the information and be sure that your writing can be easily read. The remainder of each form will be discussed in detail in the following pages of this section. Just remember to complete the top part of each form.

The bankruptcy rules require all papers filed with the court clerk to be two-hole punched so the clerk can insert them at the top of a file folder. Get a paper punch and punch out two circles at the top of each form.

The following sections give you detailed instructions for filling out the forms necessary for a Chapter 13 bankruptcy and for taking your case through the court system. The forms are found in Appendix C. In Appendix B you will find a checklist for Chapter 13 bankruptcy, which will help you keep track of your case and help ensure that you have all of the necessary forms and information. The instructions in this section relate to the form's number, which is located in the upper, outside corner of the first page of the form. Some of the forms are more than one page, and several have continuation pages for use if there is not enough room on the first page.

# VOLUNTARY PETITION

The following directions explain how to complete the **VOLUNTARY PETITION**. (see form 1, p.215.)

◈ Fill in the designation of the bankruptcy court in which you will be filing your case.

◈ Fill in the names, last four digits of Social Security numbers, and addresses in the appropriate boxes as indicated.

◈ Under the heading "Type of Debtor," check the box for "Individual (includes Joint Debtors)."

◈ Ignore the boxes under "Nature of Business."

◈ Under "Chapter of Bankruptcy Code Under Which the Petition is Filed," check the box for "Chapter 13."

◈ Under "Nature of Debts," check the box for "Consumer/ Non-Business."

◈ Under "Filing Fee," check whichever box applies to your situation. If you are financially unable to pay the full fee of $189, but will be able to pay it in several installments, you will need to complete the **APPLICATION TO PAY FILING FEE IN INSTALLMENTS** (form 2), which is explained on page 219. Reviewing, or even completing, form 2 now will help you determine if you qualify.

◈ Ignore the boxes under "Chapter 11 Debtors."

◈ Under "Statistical/Administrative Information," check whichever boxes apply to your situation. Whether funds will be available for unsecured creditors, the number of creditors, the estimated assets, and the estimated debts can be determined from the information you provided on worksheets 1, 2, and 3. As a practical matter, you would probably not be filing under Chapter 13 if you did not have funds available for unsecured creditors.

◈   At the top of the second page of the **VOLUNTARY PETITION**, type in your name (and your spouse's name, if you are filing a joint petition). If you have filed for bankruptcy within the past eight years, or if your spouse has filed a bankruptcy case that is currently pending, you will need to fill in the information where indicated.

◈   Ignore the sections marked "Exhibit A" and "Exhibit B."

◈   The section marked "Exhibit C" is primarily designed for use by businesses that may have chemicals or other hazardous materials, to alert trustees to potential dangers. Unless you have such materials, check the box marked "No."

◈   In the section marked "Certification Concerning Debt Counseling by Individual/Joint Debtor(s)," you will most likely check the first box. You must complete debt counseling before filing your petition. If you have not done so, see Section 4 for more information about debt counseling. The second box is to request a waiver of this requirement, but you need to be able to show some type of emergency situation that would justify not completing the debt counseling requirement.

◈   The information under the heading "Information Regarding the Debtor" is to show that you are in the proper bankruptcy court. You will need to be able to check one box, which will probably be the first box. The second box is for businesses. If you have an affiliate, general partner, or partnership, you should consult a lawyer or a business bankruptcy book.

◈   If you are renting the place where you live and your landlord has sued you for eviction due to nonpayment of rent, you will need to review the heading "Statement by a Debtor Who Resides as a Tenant of Residential Property." If your landlord has already obtained a court judgment against you to recover possession of the property, you will need to check the first box and fill in the name and address of the landlord. If this is the case, the automatic bankruptcy stay would not apply and your landlord will be able to proceed with having you evicted. However, there is a situation in which you may be able to stop or delay the eviction.

This is possible if your state law allows you to stop the eviction by paying the entire amount you owe the landlord, and you deposit with the court the rent that would be due over the thirty-day period after filing your bankruptcy petition. If this applies to you, check the second and third boxes. If you rent, but your landlord has not filed for eviction, or has filed but has not already obtained a judgment, you can leave this section of the form blank.

◈ At the top of the third page of the **VOLUNTARY PETITION**, type in your name (and the name of your spouse, if you are filing a joint petition).

◈ In the section marked "Signature(s) of Debtor(s) (Individual/Joint)," sign your name, and fill in your telephone number and the date on the lines where indicated. If you and your spouse are filing a joint petition, your spouse must also sign. Ignore the other sections on this page.

## APPLICATION TO PAY FILING FEE IN INSTALLMENTS

Use the **APPLICATION TO PAY FILING FEE IN INSTALLMENTS** (see form 2, p.219) if you are unable to pay the full filing fees at the time you file your **VOLUNTARY PETITION**. If you *are* able to pay the full filing fee when you file your **VOLUNTARY PETITION**, you can ignore form 2.

Call the court clerk's office to confirm the amount of the filing fee for a Chapter 13 case. You can expect it to cost about $189. You may pay the filing fee in installments, provided that there are no more than four installments and that the last payment is made no later than 120 days after the **VOLUNTARY PETITION** is filed. Exact fees can be found on various bankruptcy court websites and at 28 U.S.C. §1930.

◈ Complete the top portion of the form according to the instructions in "Understanding Legal Forms" at the beginning of this section. On the line marked "Chapter," fill in the number "13." You will need to leave the "Case No." blank, as you will not have a case number until the clerk assigns one at the time you take your papers in for filing.

❖ Fill in the amount of the filing fee on the line in paragraph 1.

❖ In paragraph 4, fill in the installment payment terms on the lines provided.

❖ Sign your name on the line marked "Signature of Debtor" and fill in the date. If you and your spouse are filing a joint petition, your spouse will need to sign on the line marked "Signature of Joint Debtor" and fill in the date. Ignore the other items on the first page of this form.

❖ The second page of this form is the order the judge will sign to give you permission to pay in installments. All you need to do here is fill in the designation of the court at the top of the page.

❖ Fill in your name, on the line marked "Debtor" (and your spouse's name, if filing jointly).

❖ On the line marked "Chapter," fill in the number "13."

The court clerk will fill in the case number and the judge will complete the remainder of the page.

---

## – Warning –

In Appendix C there is the **SUMMARY OF SCHEDULES**. (see form 4, p.225.) Skip this form for now. It will be completed after you complete Schedules A through J.

---

# SCHEDULE A—REAL PROPERTY

**SCHEDULE A—REAL PROPERTY** is the form on which you will list all real estate you own or have an interest in. (see form 5, p.227.) First of all, be sure to carefully read the instructions contained at the top of the form itself. In general, *real property* means land and things permanently attached to it (like a house).

◈ If you do not have an interest in any real property, simply write "None" in the first column that is headed "DESCRIPTION AND LOCATION OF PROPERTY." If you do have an interest in real property, you will need to complete the rest of this form.

◈ In the first column, describe the property and tell where it is located. This does not have to be the formal legal description, but you should state the type of property (such as home, unimproved lot, or condominium) and the address (including the city, county, and state). If you are renting the property, it should not be listed on this form, but should be listed on **Schedule G—Executory Contracts and Unexpired Leases** instead. (see form 11, p.243.)

◈ In the second column, designated "NATURE OF DEBTOR'S INTEREST IN PROPERTY," state the type of interest you have in the property. For most people who own a home, the ownership interest in the property is known as *fee simple*. The most common interests in real property are as follows.

 ✪ *Fee Simple.* This is where you own the property, with no obligation other than to pay the mortgage and taxes. You may own the property with someone else or by yourself.

 ✪ *Life Estate.* This is where you have the right to live on the property during your lifetime, but you cannot sell or give it away during your lifetime, or leave it to anyone upon your death. This is commonly set up when a spouse dies, and is usually done for tax purposes. One spouse gives the other a life estate so that he or she can live on the property until death, but then the property goes to their children.

 ✪ *Future Interest.* The most common example of this kind of interest is what the children have after a life estate for their widowed parent. A person with a future interest will get the property someday, but only after some event occurs (such as the death of the person with the life estate).

One of these types of interests should be listed in the second column. If you own the property with another person who is not your husband or wife, you should also indicate the portion of the interest you own (such as one-half fee simple, or one-third future interest).

◈ If you are not married, you may ignore the third column. If you are married, you need to indicate whether each piece of property is owned by the husband (H), the wife (W), both of you jointly (J), or both of you as *community property* (C).

> **NOTE:** *Community property only applies if you live in Arizona, California, Idaho, Louisiana, Nevada, New Mexico, Texas, Washington, or Wisconsin. Generally, this means that all the property either spouse obtains during the marriage is owned by both of them, and can be taken by the trustee even if they do not file for bankruptcy jointly. If you live in one of these states and are considering filing separately from your spouse, you should consult a bankruptcy lawyer.*

◈ In the fourth column, indicate the value of the property. This will be the current market value of the property. Do not take into account any money you owe on a mortgage. Be sure to total these amounts at the bottom of this column.

◈ In the fifth column, indicate the amount of money you owe on the mortgage or any liens on the property. If you do not owe any money on the property, write "None" in the fifth column.

# SCHEDULE B—PERSONAL PROPERTY

On **SCHEDULE B—PERSONAL PROPERTY**, you will list all of your property that is *not* real estate. (see form 6, p.229.) Be sure to carefully read the instructions on the form itself. Note that this form is several pages long. *Personal property* is all of your property that is *not* land or permanently attached to the land. This will be everything you listed in the **PROPERTY WORKSHEET**, except for the real estate items. (see worksheet 2, p.209.)

## – Warning –

Be sure to list all of your property, even if you think it has no value. Otherwise, it may appear that you are trying to hide property from creditors, which could result in the dismissal of your case.

◈  At the top of each page, fill in your name (or your name and your spouse's name, if filing jointly) and the case number, once it is issued by the clerk.

◈  The types of personal property are listed in the first column of this form. Simply read each item and write down what you own in that category.

◈  If you do not own anything in a particular category, simply check the second column marked "NONE."

◈  In the third column, marked "DESCRIPTION AND LOCATION OF PROPERTY," describe each item in the category and indicate where it is located by street address, city, county, and state. If most of the property is at your home, you may write "Unless otherwise indicated, all property is located at the debtor's residence." If you do this, be sure to indicate any property that is located somewhere else.

Refer to Appendix A of this book for the list of the exemptions for your state and for the alternate Federal Bankruptcy Exemptions. Any item for which you may claim an exemption should be listed separately in this form.

### Example:

Item 12 relates to pension plans. If your state offers an exemption for a certain type of plan, be sure to indicate that your plan is of that type. (See Section 8, pages 137–138 of this book regarding pension plans.)

◈ If you are not married, you may ignore the fourth column. If you are married, you will need to indicate whether the property is owned by the husband (H), the wife (W), both of you jointly (J), or both of you as community property (C).

◈ In the last column, indicate the current value of the property.

◈ Total the amounts in this column at the bottom of the third page of the form.

## SCHEDULE C—PROPERTY CLAIMED AS EXEMPT

The property you are claiming as exempt from your creditors must be listed in **Schedule C—Property Claimed as Exempt**. (see form 7, p.233.)

◈ At the top of each page, fill in your name (or your name and your spouse's name, if filing jointly) and the case number, once it is issued by the clerk.

◈ First, you need to check one of the boxes at the top, indicating whether you are using the Federal Bankruptcy Exemptions (the first box) or the exemptions for your state (the second box). Both types of federal exemptions and your state's exemptions are found in Appendix A of this book. The Federal Bankruptcy Exemptions are only available in certain states, which are listed under the federal exemptions in Appendix A.

  **NOTE:** *If the Federal Bankruptcy Exemptions are available in your state, you need to compare them with those of your state to see which set will allow you to keep more of your property. If you select the state exemptions, you may also use the Federal Nonbankruptcy Exemptions.*

◈ If you are claiming a homestead exemption that is more than $125,000, you will need to check the box at the top, right-hand of the page. This can only apply if you will be filing in one of the following states, and only if you have lived there for at least forty months: Arkansas, California, District of Columbia,

Florida, Iowa, Kansas, Louisiana, Massachusetts, Minnesota, Nevada, Oklahoma, Rhode Island, South Dakota, and Texas. If you will be filing in one of these states, but you have not lived there for at least forty months, your homestead exemption is limited to $125,000. If you have lived in one of these states for at least forty months before filing your petition, you can use the state's homestead exemption in excess of $125,000.

◈    To complete the rest of **Schedule C—Property Claimed as Exempt**, refer to Column (5) of the **Property Worksheet**, where you have already identified the items you are claiming as exempt. (see worksheet 2, p.209.) You may want to refer once again to the information in Appendix A of this book to be sure you are claiming everything to which you may be entitled.

If you are not sure whether you can claim an item, but it seems to fit one of the exemptions, then claim it. Let the trustee or a creditor question it. (Of course, do not claim something you know is not exempt, but if you genuinely are not sure, give yourself the benefit of the exemption.)

◈    In the first column, write in a description of the property. Try to use the same categories as those for your state in Appendix A.

**NOTE:** *All of the property listed in this form should also be listed in either* **Schedule A—Real Property** *(form 5) or in* **Schedule B—Personal Property** *(form 6).*

◈    In the second column, indicate the statute or law that gives you the exemption you are claiming. Again, refer to Appendix A of this book for the statute or law number. Examples of how to refer to these laws appear at the beginning of each state's listing in Appendix A.

◈    In the third column, marked "VALUE OF CLAIMED EXEMPTION," state the amount of the exemption you are claiming. Be sure you are not exceeding the maximum amount of the exemption allowed as indicated in Appendix A.

**Example:**

If your state only allows up to a $2,000 exemption for a car, do not show a $30,000 exemption for your Mercedes.

---

◈  In the last column, indicate the property's full market value.

## SCHEDULE D—CREDITORS HOLDING SECURED CLAIMS

Any secured creditors need to be listed on **SCHEDULE D—CREDITORS HOLDING SECURED CLAIMS**. (see form 8, p.235.) Be sure to carefully read the instructions at the beginning of the form itself. To complete this form, refer to the **DEBT WORKSHEET**, Column (5), which will show the creditors holding a security interest in your property. (see worksheet 3, p.210.) These will most likely be the mortgage holders on your home and any other real property, as well as the lenders on auto, boat, or home improvement loans. (They are not likely to be credit card companies.)

A creditor holding security is one who loaned you money to buy something and has the right to take some of your property if you do not pay. This also includes anyone having a lien on your property, such as for work done on your home.

◈  At the top of each page, fill in your name (or your name and your spouse's name, if filing jointly) and the case number, once it is issued by the clerk.

◈  In the first column, fill in the last four digits of the account number, and the creditor's name and address. (To protect against theft, do not list the entire account number.)

◈  Place an "X" in the second column, marked "CODEBTOR," if another person is also liable for the repayment of the debt. However, do not check this column if the other person is your spouse *and* you have filed a joint bankruptcy petition with your spouse.

❖   If you are not married, ignore the third column. If you are married, then indicate here whether the debt is owed by the husband (H), the wife (W), both of you jointly (J), or both of you as a community property debt (C).

❖   In the fourth column, first indicate the date the debt was created. Next, indicate the nature of the lien on the property. Refer to the first paragraph of instructions on the form itself for examples of the types of liens. If you are not sure of the type of lien, simply write "nature uncertain" and ask the trustee later, or call the person or company you owe the money to and ask. Next, give a description of the property that is subject to the lien, and indicate the full value of the property in the space labeled "VALUE $."

❖   In the fifth, sixth, and seventh columns, indicate (by an "X") if the debt is *contingent, unliquidated,* or *disputed.* These concepts are very confusing, so do not hesitate to ask the trustee if you are not sure.

A *contingent debt* is one that will only be owed if some future event occurs (such as if a tax audit shows that a debt claimed by the IRS is really owed).

An *unliquidated debt* is one in which the exact amount has not been determined (such as where you know you owe a tax, but will not know the exact amount until you know the full amount of your income or expenses).

A *disputed debt* is one you are contesting (someone is claiming you owe the debt, but you do not think you do or do not think you owe as much as he or she is claiming).

If none of these apply, leave these columns blank.

❖   In the eighth column, marked "AMOUNT OF CLAIM WITHOUT DEDUCTING VALUE OF COLLATERAL," indicate the amount of the debt you owe.

❖ In the last column, indicate if any of the debt is *unsecured* (not attached to any piece of property).

---

### Example:

If you owe $8,000 on your car, but the car is only worth $6,000, then $2,000 of the debt is unsecured.

---

❖ Total the eighth column, and indicate at the bottom left if there are any continuation sheets attached.

> **NOTE:** *The second page of this form is a continuation sheet. Indicate at the bottom left whether there are any continuation sheets attached.*

❖ If you only use the first page, total the eighth column and type in the amount in the box marked "Total."

❖ If you use one or more continuation pages, total the eighth column for each page and type the amount in the box marked "Subtotal." Then, add all of the subtotals and type the amount in the box marked "Total" on the last page.

## SCHEDULE E—CREDITORS HOLDING UNSECURED PRIORITY CLAIMS

Certain types of creditors have *priority*, which means that they will be paid from your nonexempt and nonsecured property before other creditors. Most creditors with priority relate to the operation of a business, so they will not apply to most people filing for personal bankruptcy under Chapter 7 or 13. The priority claims are listed on **Schedule E—Creditors Holding Unsecured Priority Claims** as follows. (see form 9, p.237.)

✪ *Domestic Support Obligations*. This applies if you owe court-ordered alimony, maintenance, or support to a former spouse or a child.

✪ *Extensions of credit in an involuntary case.* Since you are filing a voluntary petition, this does not apply to you.

✪ *Wages, salaries, and commissions.* This relates to money that you would owe to your employee. If you have employees, you should either consult an attorney or a book that deals with business bankruptcy.

✪ *Contributions to employee benefit plans.* Again, if you have employees, you should consult a lawyer or a book dealing with business bankruptcy.

✪ *Certain farmers and fishermen.* This only applies to operators of grain or fish storage facilities.

✪ *Deposits by individuals.* This would apply to you only if you owe someone money for a deposit they gave you to purchase or rent real estate, goods, or services that you have not provided.

✪ *Taxes and certain other debts owed to the government.* If you owe taxes to the federal, state, or local government, you will need to check this box and list the debt.

✪ *Commitments to maintain the capital of an insured depository institution.* This only applies to banks or other similar depository institutions.

✪ *Claims for Death or Personal Injury While Debtor was Intoxicated.* This applies if you are paying on a claim that resulted from you driving a car while intoxicated and causing damages to another.

Be sure to carefully read the instructions at the beginning of form 9.

◈ At the top of each page, fill in your name (or your name and your spouse's name, if filing jointly) and the case number, once it is issued by the clerk.

◈ If you do not have any of these types of debts, check the first box on the first page that states: "Check this box if the debtor has no creditors holding unsecured priority claims to report on this Schedule E."

◈ If you do have any of these types of debts, check the appropriate box or boxes on the first page, and list the debt on the continuation sheet. Complete a separate continuation sheet for each type of debt listed.

> **NOTE:** *There is a space at the top of the continuation sheet for indicating the type of priority debt.*

◈ To complete the remainder of the continuation sheet, follow the same directions for the **SCHEDULE D—CREDITORS HOLDING SECURED CLAIMS** given on page 110. Be sure to total the amounts in the eighth column, and indicate at the bottom left how many continuation sheets are provided for **SCHEDULE E**. Remember to only fill in the last four digits of your account number.

## SCHEDULE F—CREDITORS HOLDING UNSECURED NONPRIORITY CLAIMS

All of the creditors not listed on any of the previous forms will be listed on **SCHEDULE F—CREDITORS HOLDING UNSECURED NONPRIORITY CLAIMS**. (see form 10, p.241.) In most cases, this will be primarily credit cards and other personal debts, such as unpaid bills. Be sure to carefully read the instructions at the beginning of the form itself. This form also has a continuation sheet.

> **NOTE:** *There is a box to check if you have no creditors to report on this form. If you have no creditors to report here, you need to go back to Section 3 of this book and take another look at whether you can, or should, avoid bankruptcy.*

The main benefit of bankruptcy is getting rid of these unsecured nonpriority claims. If you have none to get rid of, you probably should not file for bankruptcy and may want to consult a lawyer or credit counselor.

◈ At the top of each page, fill in your name (or your name and your spouse's name, if filing jointly) and the case number, once it is issued by the clerk.

◈ Complete the first, second, and third columns according to the instructions for **Schedule D—Creditors Holding Secured Claims**, as indicated on page 110. Remember to only fill in the last four digits of your account number.

◈ In the fourth column, indicate the date the claim was incurred, the consideration for the claim, and any setoff you are claiming. (A *setoff* is a debt the creditor owes to you.)

For the *consideration*, simply state what the debt was for, such as student loan, vacation loan, dental bill, car repair, Visa, or Sears.

In some cases, a store may have required you to pledge some property as collateral in order to obtain the credit card. You should know if this is the case because you probably had to sign some additional papers instead of a simple credit card application.

If this is the case with one of your credit cards, you should list it on **Schedule D** instead of here. (see form 8, p.235.)

---

### Example:
If you owe your landlord $800 in back rent, but he owes you $50 for plumbing repairs that you paid for, you have a setoff of $50.

---

◈ Complete the remaining columns according to the instructions for the same columns in **Schedule D**, as indicated on pages 73–75.

◈ This form also has a continuation sheet, so be sure to indicate at the bottom the number of continuation sheets attached.

◈ Total the amounts in the last column.

## SCHEDULE G—EXECUTORY CONTRACTS AND UNEXPIRED LEASES

Any contracts or leases to which you are a party must be listed and described on **SCHEDULE G—EXECUTORY CONTRACTS AND UNEXPIRED LEASES**. (see form 11, p.243.)

⬧     At the top of each page, fill in your name (or your name and your spouse's name, if filing jointly) and the case number, once it is issued by the clerk.

⬧     If you are not a party to any contracts or leases, simply check the box near the top of the form before the sentence "Check this box if debtor has no executory contracts or unexpired leases." Be sure to carefully read the instructions at the beginning of the form itself.

⬧     In the first column, indicate the name and address of the other parties to the contract or lease. This includes anyone who is obligated the same as you, such as your apartment roommate if his or her name is also on the lease. It also includes the person to whom you are obligated, such as your landlord.

⬧     In the second column, describe the contract or lease. Examples of such descriptions are "apartment lease," "auto lease," or "lawn maintenance contract." In this column, you must also list the nature of your interest, such as lessee, seller, or purchaser. (If you are a landlord, you will state this as "lessor.") If you have a lease for nonresidential property, you need to indicate this. If you are a party to a government contract, the contract number must be stated.

## SCHEDULE H—CODEBTORS

Anyone who is also obligated to pay all or part of any of your debts must be listed on **SCHEDULE H—CODEBTORS**. (see form 12, p.245.) You do not need to include your spouse if you are filing a joint bankruptcy petition. Be sure to carefully read the instructions at the beginning of the form itself. At the top of each page, fill in your name (or your name and your spouse's name, if filing jointly) and the case number, once it is issued by the clerk.

There is a box to check if you have no codebtors. If you do have codebtors, then indicate their names and addresses in the first column, and the creditors' names and addresses in the second column.

## SCHEDULE I—CURRENT INCOME OF INDIVIDUAL DEBTOR(S)

**SCHEDULE I—CURRENT INCOME OF INDIVIDUAL DEBTOR(S)** is where you list your income and your spouse's income if you are married (even if you are *not* filing a joint petition). (see form 13, p.247.) At the top of each page, fill in your name (or your name and your spouse's name, if you are married) and the case number (once it is issued by the clerk.)

The top portion of this form asks for information about your family status and employment, and is self-explanatory. The lower part asks for a breakdown of your income and payroll deductions (and that of your spouse if you are married, even if not filing a joint petition). All amounts should be converted to a monthly amount. The last sentence in the form asks you to describe any increase or decrease of more than 10% in any of the listed categories that you expect to occur within the year after filing the petition. Examples would be the termination of unemployment benefits, an anticipated layoff or wage reduction, or the loss of rental income from the imminent sale of the property.

## SCHEDULE J—CURRENT EXPENDITURES OF INDIVIDUAL DEBTOR(S)

The previous schedule listed your income. **SCHEDULE J—CURRENT EXPENDITURES OF INDIVIDUAL DEBTOR(S)** is used to list your monthly expenses. (see form 14, p.249.) Convert all amounts to monthly figures. If you and your spouse are filing a joint petition, but do not live together, you will need to check the box near the top of the form, and your spouse will also need to complete a separate **SCHEDULE J**. (In this case, you will need to make another copy of this form for your spouse to complete.)

◈ At the top of each page, fill in your name (or your name and your spouse's name, if filing jointly) and the case number, once it is issued by the clerk.

◈ In items 1–17, list monthly expenses for the categories listed. Item 17 is for other recurring monthly expenses.

◈ In item 18, add up your totals and list your "TOTAL MONTHLY EXPENSES."

◈ Item 19 provides space to describe any anticipated increase or decrease in the numbers listed above.

◈ In item 20a, use the total income figure from form 13.

◈ In item 20b, use the "TOTAL MONTHLY EXPENSES" from item 18 of this form.

◈ Item 20c will give the total amount you have available to pay your creditors.

## SUMMARY OF SCHEDULES

On the **SUMMARY OF SCHEDULES** you will give the totals from each of the schedules you have completed. (see form 4, p.225.) At the top of each page, fill in the court information, your name (or your name and your spouse's name, if filing jointly) and the case number, once it is issued by the clerk. Also fill in "13" on the line marked "Chapter." You will be attaching all of the schedules to your Voluntary Petition, so fill in "Yes" in the column marked "Attached (Yes/No)."

On the second page of the form, fill in the top portion as you did in the previous forms, then fill in the amount of each of the indicated liabilities from the appropriate schedule.

**NOTE:** *For each schedule you are to indicate the number of sheets used. You will need to count the number of continuation sheets for each schedule. Do not forget to count your spouse's separate* **SCHEDULE J—CURRENT EXPENDITURES OF INDIVIDUAL DEBTOR(S)** *if appropriate.*

Be sure to add the totals of the columns where indicated. Do not leave any spaces blank. If there is no entry for an item, type "0" in the space for that item. Although you are completing this form after the other schedules, this form will come before the other schedules when you file your petition.

## DECLARATION CONCERNING DEBTOR'S SCHEDULES

By completing and signing the **DECLARATION CONCERNING DEBTOR'S SCHEDULES**, you swear that your schedules are accurate to the best of your knowledge. (see form 15, p.251.) To complete this form, follow these steps.

⟡ At the top of each page, fill in your name (or your name and your spouse's name, if filing jointly) and the case number, once it is issued by the clerk.

⟡ Type in the total number of sheets as indicated on the form.

⟡ Type in the date.

⟡ Sign your name where indicated (your spouse must do the same if you are filing jointly).

   **NOTE:** *There are fine and jail penalties listed on the form for giving false information.*

⟡ Ignore the sections titled "DECLARATION AND SIGNATURE OF NON-ATTORNEY BANKRUPTCY PETITION PREPARER" and "DECLARATION UNDER PENALTY OF PERJURY ON BEHALF OF A CORPORATION OR PARTNERSHIP."

## STATEMENT OF FINANCIAL AFFAIRS

The **STATEMENT OF FINANCIAL AFFAIRS** is a lengthy form, but one that is not difficult to complete, because the instructions on the form itself are rather clear. (see form 16, p.253.) All you need to do is read each item and provide the information it asks for. At the top of each page, fill in your name (or your name and your spouse's name, if filing jointly) and the case number, once it is issued by the clerk. For each item there is a box marked "None" to check if that item does not apply to you. Be sure you mark the "None" box instead of leaving an item unanswered.

Some of the questions may require you to go back through your records for the past few years. Just answer the questions as best you can with the information you can recall or locate. Use additional sheets of paper if necessary, and be sure to indicate the number of the item being continued on the additional sheet.

Item 14 asks about property you have that belongs to someone else. This is to protect that person's property from your creditors. Of course, an easier way to deal with this situation is for you to return that property to the other person.

Read the instructions immediately before Item 14 carefully. You will not need to complete any more of the numbered items in this form (and can skip to the last page for your signature) unless you have been in one of the following positions within the past six years:

- ✪ an officer, director, or managing executive of a corporation;

- ✪ an owner of more than 5% of the voting stock of a corporation;

- ✪ a general partner in a partnership; or,

- ✪ a sole proprietor of a business or otherwise self-employed.

Once you have completed all of the items you are required to complete, type in the date and sign your name where indicated on the last page of the **STATEMENT OF FINANCIAL AFFAIRS**. Your spouse must also date and sign this form if you are filing a joint petition. Also, indicate the number of continuation sheets attached (type in "0" if there are none).

**NOTE:** *There are fine and jail penalties listed at the end of the form for giving false information.*

# CHAPTER 13 PLAN

The **CHAPTER 13 PLAN** is simply a statement of how you intend to pay your creditors from your disposable income. (see form 20, p.279.) At the bottom of **SCHEDULE J—CURRENT EXPENDITURES OF INDIVIDUAL DEBTOR(S)**, you will find your disposable, or *excess,* income. (see form 14, p.249.) This is the amount of money you have available to turn over to the trustee in order to pay your debts. The following instructions will help you complete your **CHAPTER 13 PLAN**.

◈ At the top of each page, fill in your name (or your name and your spouse's name, if filing jointly) and the case number, once it is issued by the clerk.

◈ In the paragraph before numbered paragraph 1, type in the amount and indicate the payment interval from the bottom of **SCHEDULE J—CURRENT EXPENDITURES OF INDIVIDUAL DEBTOR(S)**. (see form 14, p.249.) In deciding the interval to use, you may want to make it the same as your paycheck schedule.

◈ In the paragraph numbered 2, describe how you want to pay your secured debts.

> **NOTE:** *If you do not pay secured debts, the lender can repossess the property. Therefore, you will want to keep up the full payments on these debts.*

List the name of the lender, the amount of the debt, and the periodic payment to be made.

◈ In the paragraph numbered 3, describe how you want to pay your unsecured debts.

◈ Deduct the total amount of your payments on your secured debts from your disposable income. This will give you how much is left to pay your unsecured creditors. Generally, you must pay each unsecured creditor the same percentage of the debt as the other unsecured creditors. This may be done over a period of up to five years.

If you have enough income to pay all of these debts in full within five years, you will set up a schedule to accomplish this by dividing the amount owed to each creditor by 60 months. This will give you the amount to pay each creditor each month.

If you do not have enough income to pay all of your debts in full within five years, the following paragraph helps you determine how much you can pay.

⟡ To determine how much debt you can pay, use the following five steps.

1.  Take your monthly disposable income, subtract the total monthly payments to secured creditors, and multiply the answer by 60. This will give you the total amount you have available to pay over five years.

2.  Add the total amount you owe to all of your unsecured creditors.

3.  Divide the total from step 2 above by the total in step 1. This will give you the percentage of each debt you will be able to pay.

4.  For each debt, multiply the total amount owed by the answer from step 3.

5.  Take the answer from step 4 and divide it by 60. This will give you how much of your monthly disposable income should be applied to each debt. Convert this to match your pay period if necessary (such as to a weekly or semi-monthly amount).

⟡ In paragraph 3, type in the name of each creditor, the amount to be paid each month, and percentage of the amount due that will be paid (from step 3 above).

◈ Paragraph 5 contains a box to check if there is an addendum to the form. This will be used if you need additional space, or if there are any special arrangements regarding the payment of your debts.

◈ Date and sign the form. This form should be filed along with your petition, and *must* be filed no more than fifteen days after filing your petition.

## STATEMENT OF CURRENT MONTHLY INCOME AND DISPOSABLE INCOME CALCULATION

The **STATEMENT OF CURRENT MONTHLY INCOME AND DISPOSABLE INCOME CALCULATION** is used to determine how much income you have available to pay creditors, after paying your essential living expenses. (see form 19, p.273.) Part of this form uses expenses allowed by the Internal Revenue Service (IRS).

Most of this form is self-explanatory. From reading each item, you can easily determine what information is being requested. The following information may help clarify a few points.

◈ At the top of the first page, fill in your name (or your name and your spouse's name, if filing jointly) and the case number, once it is issued by the clerk. For now, ignore the box at the top right of the first page (with boxes marked "Disposable income determined under §1325(b)(3)" and "Disposable income not determined under §1325(b)(3)" inside). This box is addressed later.

◈ Part I of this form is to fill in all of your sources of income. Line 11 will be your total monthly income.

◈ Part II of this form is used to determine if you have sufficient disposable income for filing under Chapter 13 of the Bankruptcy Code. For Line 12, you will take your total monthly income from Line 11 and multiply it by 12 to get your total annual income. Line 13 asks for the "Applicable median family income." This is determined by information from the U.S. Census Bureau, which takes into account the number of people in the family. The amount varies from state to state. The values for your state can be obtained from your local bankruptcy court clerk or online at **www.usdoj.gov/ust**.

If the amount on Line 12 is less than, or equal to, the amount on Line 13, you will check the first box in Line 14. Then go back to the top of the first page and check the box marked "Disposable income not determined under §1325(b)(3)." You can then skip down to Part VI of this form. On the other hand, if the amount on Line 12 is more than the amount on Line 13, you will check the second box in Line 14. Then go back to the top of the first page and check the box marked "Disposable income determined under §1325(b)(3). In this case, you will need to continue on to Part III of this form.

◈   Part III, Subpart A of this form is used to determine your allowed expenses. The amount for Line 15 comes from national standards set forth in tables created by the IRS. There is one table for Alaska, one table for Hawaii, and one table for all other states and the District of Columbia. The amounts for Line 16 through Line 19 come from local standards, which also come from IRS tables. Both the national and local standards are available from the bankruptcy court clerk or online at **www.usdoj.gov/ust**. The amounts for Line 20 through Line 27 will come from your records. Enter the total of the allowed expenses on Line 28.

◈   Part III, Subpart B of this form lists various additional expenses. Read each item and determine if it applies to you. If so, fill in the appropriate amount. Note that documentation to prove some of these items is required. Add the figures in Lines 29 through 35, and enter the total on Line 36.

◈   Part III, Subpart C of this form is used to list various debts you will continue to pay. Much of this information will come from the various schedules you filed with your **VOLUNTARY PETITION**. Information for completing Line 40 can be obtained from the bankruptcy court clerk or online at **www.usdoj.gov/ust**.

◈  Part IV of this form is used to determine your monthly disposable income. You may also complete Part V, if you think you can make a good case that you have other expenses that are "required for the health and welfare of you and your family."

## DEBTOR'S CERTIFICATION OF COMPLETION OF INSTRUCTIONAL COURSE CONCERNING PERSONAL FINANCIAL MANAGEMENT

As mentioned earlier, one requirement for filing for bankruptcy is that you complete a course on personal financial management. The only time you do *not* need to do this is if one of the following situations applies:

✪  you are disabled or incapacitated;

✪  you are on active military duty in a military combat zone; or,

✪  you live in a federal bankruptcy court district where the trustee's office has determined that the approved instructional courses are not adequate at this time to serve the additional individuals who would otherwise be required to complete such courses (whatever that means). You will need to check with the court clerk or trustee's office to find out if you live in one of these districts.

To prove to the court that you have completed the required course, you will need to file the **DEBTOR'S CERTIFICATION OF COMPLETION OF INSTRUCTIONAL COURSE CONCERNING PERSONAL FINANCIAL MANAGEMENT**. (see form 21, p.281.) Prepare form 21 as follows.

◈  At the top of the page, fill in the court information, your name (or your name and your spouse's name, if filing jointly) and the case number, once it is issued by the clerk. On the line marked "Chapter," type in "13."

◈  If you do not fall within any of the exceptions and have completed the course, you will need to check the first box and fill in your name(s), the date you completed the course, and the name of the agency that conducted the course. You should also have received some type of paper verifying the course completion, and you need to staple a copy to this form.

❖    If you fall within any of the exceptions listed on page 125, you will need to check the second box, fill in your name(s), and check one of the three exception boxes to indicate which exception applies to you.

❖    You will then sign your name on the line marked "Signature of Debtor" and fill in the date. If you and your spouse are filing jointly, your spouse will need to sign on the line marked "Signature of Joint Debtor" and fill in the date.

**Hurricane Katrina Victims**

Although not covered in form 21, the U.S. Trustee's Office has decided to grant waivers of the financial management course requirement to victims of Hurricane Katrina. If you are a victim of Hurricane Katrina, you need to mention this to the court clerk and ask how to go about getting the waiver.

## MASTER ADDRESS LISTS AND MAILING MATRIX

All bankruptcy courts require the debtor to provide information on creditors so that the court clerk can mail the required notices to the creditors. You need to check with the bankruptcy court clerk where you file your case to determine the requirements you need to meet. Some courts have their requirements set forth online. To find out if your court has online information, go to **www.uscourts.gov**. You can then click on "Court Links" and do a search on the U.S. map that appears to see if your state is listed.

All courts previously required the debtor to prepare a list of the creditors' names and addresses in rows and columns that corresponded to sheets of mailing labels. To properly align the rows and columns of addresses, it was necessary to take a blank sheet of paper and insert it in a typewriter with a **MAILING MATRIX** behind it. (see form 22, p.283.) A sheet of addresses prepared in this manner allowed the clerk to photocopy the list onto a mailing label sheet. If your court still uses a **MAILING**

**MATRIX**, you can use form 22 to prepare it. However, be sure to check with the court clerk to be sure you know how to properly prepare it.

The bankruptcy courts in many states have entered the computer age. These courts take a more simply prepared list of creditors' names and addresses, scan them into a computer, then have the computer generate the addressed envelopes. These courts typically have detailed instructions about how the list is to be prepared and submitted by the debtor. To get these instructions, check with the court clerk or online at **www.uscourts.gov**.

# FILING WITH THE COURT CLERK AND NOTIFYING CREDITORS

Once all of your papers have been prepared, you are ready to file them with the court clerk. This is not difficult; however, things will go smoother if you are organized and know what you can expect.

**Finding the Clerk's Office**

By now you should have found out where the bankruptcy court is located. If not, the first place to check is the government listings in your local telephone directory. Look in the U.S. Government section for "Bankruptcy Court," "District Court," or "Clerk of the District Court." If this fails, there is probably a general U.S. government information listing that you can call to get the location and mailing address of the bankruptcy court clerk's office.

Only a few cities in each state have a federal court, so you may need to do some digging to find the one closest to you. If you are having trouble, try calling the law library at the county courthouse in your county, or try your local public library.

**What to Bring**

There is a checklist in Appendix B to indicate what you should bring with you to the court clerk's office when you go to file your papers.

**Filing**

Although it is possible to file by mail, it is strongly advised that you go to the clerk's office and file in person. It is easier to establish a friendly relationship in person, and the more time you spend at the bankruptcy court, the more comfortable you will feel with the entire process.

As you enter the clerk's office, look around for any signs that may help you figure out exactly where to go. There may be several windows, which may be marked for different purposes, such as filing, cashier, or file checkout. Go to the appropriate window, or to any window if you are uncertain, and tell the clerk that you would like to file a Chapter 13.

The clerk will take your papers and examine them. If everything looks in order, the clerk will then tell you how to go about paying the filing fee. Either that clerk will handle the payment or you will be directed to the cashier's window.

You will pay the filing fee and receive a receipt. The clerk will also assign a case number and will stamp or write the number on your papers. The case number should also be on your receipt. Your papers are now filed.

If the clerk determines that something is not correct with your papers, you will be told what is wrong. *Do not argue with the clerk.* The clerk controls your access to the bankruptcy system and you do not want to make an enemy of the clerk. Clerks cannot give you legal advice, but they will usually tell you what is wrong with your papers and give you some idea of how you can fix the problem.

The kind of problem the clerk will identify is one of form, such as you forgot to sign something, forgot to fill in a space, need another type of form, or need to submit an extra copy. All you can do is find out what the clerk wants, then do it. You may be able to correct the problem at the clerk's office.

If you try to satisfy the clerk, but are still getting your papers rejected or do not understand what is required, you may want to consult a lawyer. You can also politely tell the clerk that you are not understanding the problem, and ask him or her to explain it again, or have another clerk try to explain it to you.

Although most clerks are pleasant, helpful people, you sometimes run into a simply nasty clerk. You must still be polite, and try to win over the clerk. If this does not work, there is nothing wrong with asking for the clerk's supervisor. Just do not get angry under any circumstances. Remain calm and polite.

**Stopping Payments**

If you have not already stopped making payments, you should stop once your petition is filed (except for payments on any secured debts if you want to keep the property). From this point on, all payments for anything must be approved by the trustee. It is acceptable to buy food and gas for your car so you can get to work, and to pay for any necessary medical expenses, but that is about all.

It will take awhile to have a trustee appointed, but once you receive a notice in the mail with the name of the trustee, contact the trustee as soon as possible. Tell the trustee that you just wanted to make an initial contact, and ask him or her if you may pay any bills you feel you need to pay. Also, ask the trustee any other questions you have. If you are continuing to make payments on secured property (such as your mortgage or car payment), mention this to the trustee.

**Automatic Stay**

Filing your petition operates as an *automatic stay*. This prohibits your creditors from taking any collection action or from cutting off any services to you. Once your petition is filed, you may want to be sure to get your creditors off your back by sending them a letter notifying them that you have filed. The following is an example of such a letter.

---

Dear Sir or Madam:

YOU ARE HEREBY ADVISED that on _____
_____, I filed a voluntary petition with the U.S. Bankruptcy Code. You may not:

✪    take any action to evict me from my residence;

✪    discontinue any service or benefit being provided to me; or,

✪    take any action against me or my property, or repossess any of my property.

Any violation of these prohibitions may constitute contempt of court and be punished accordingly.

---

Space is left at the top for the date and the creditor's address. Sign your name at the bottom, and below your signature, type in your name, address, and account number. If you have a particularly bothersome creditor, you may want to send the letter by certified, bother you.

## CREDITORS' MEETING

After you have filed your case, the clerk will do several things. Using the master address list you provided and the information in your supporting documents, the clerk will send a notice to all of your creditors, indicating that you have filed for bankruptcy. A trustee will also be appointed to your case, who will then schedule a meeting of creditors. Copies of any documents issued by the clerk or the trustee will be sent to you. Read them carefully, and call the clerk's office if you do not understand them. Most of these papers will not require you to do anything, but some may require some type of response.

You may also receive copies of any papers your creditors may file with the clerk. Again, these do not require you to do anything, but keep the copies anyway.

You will receive a notice of the date, time, and place of the meeting of creditors, which you must attend. Creditors are more likely to attend the meeting in a Chapter 13 case than in a Chapter 7 case. They are concerned about getting the most out of your proposed payment plan. They will ask questions about the reasonableness of your payment plan and the likelihood that you will be able to carry it out. The trustee will also ask some questions. You are under oath, so answer honestly.

If the creditors and the trustee approve of your plan, it will be accepted by the court. If the plan is not approved, you may either negotiate changes in the plan to make it acceptable, stick to your plan and let the judge decide if it is acceptable, or convert your case to a Chapter 7 bankruptcy. To convert your case, see Section 8, page 134, of this book.

Once your plan is approved, the trustee will probably order that the payments be deducted directly from your paycheck by your employer. This amount will be sent to the trustee, who will make the required payments to the individual creditors.

Until the paycheck deduction goes into effect, however, you are responsible for making sure that the payments are made. Unless the court orders something different, payments must begin thirty days after you file your plan with the court. This may be before the creditors' meeting, in which case you should still begin your payments. If your plan ends up not being approved, the creditors will be required to refund any payments you have made.

## COURT HEARING AND APPROVAL OF PLAN

Depending upon the procedures in your particular bankruptcy court, you may or may not have to appear before the judge. If the trustee determines that everything is in order, you may receive a discharge without having to attend a hearing.

In a Chapter 13 case, you will be entitled to a discharge once you have completed all of the payments required by your payment plan. This is likely to require a brief court hearing with the judge.

At the hearing, the judge will probably only:

❂    talk to you about the effects of the bankruptcy discharge;

❂    caution you to avoid getting in debt again;

❂    possibly ask a few questions to assure the court that everything has been done properly; and,

❂    make sure that you understand the meaning of the discharge.

Your particular bankruptcy court may even have mass discharge hearings, in which many debtors are discharged at the same time and no questions are asked. All the judge does is give everyone a brief lecture about how your debts are now discharged, and how you should avoid getting into financial trouble again.

# Special Circumstances

This section discusses several matters that do not apply to most simple bankruptcy cases. If any of these situations apply to your case, you may want to discuss them with a lawyer. Of course, you should take a look at how much you may save in contrast to how much a lawyer may cost you. The first two items mentioned have forms in Appendix C of this book, and you can probably complete them without an attorney. However, the other items will often require an attorney's assistance.

## AMENDING YOUR PAPERWORK

If, after you file your **VOLUNTARY PETITION** (form 1) and other papers, you discover that you have made an error, you may amend whatever papers are necessary to correct the error. This will involve completing the **AMENDMENT COVER SHEET**, as well as whatever forms you need to amend. (see form 25, p.289.)

Some courts will require you to fully complete the new form, while others will allow you to simply note the item being changed. You will need to call the court clerk to find out which you need to do. At the same time, ask the clerk if there is any filing fee for the amended form.

To complete the **AMENDMENT COVER SHEET** (form 25), do the following.

◈ After the first sentence, type in the name of the form or forms you are amending. Be sure to also complete the top portion of the form, as well as the date and signature portions at the bottom.

◈ Attach the amended forms containing the new or changed information.

◈ You need to check whether the new information on one form also requires new information on other forms, and include all forms that need changing. Also, certain changes may mean that you need to re-notify creditors, especially if the creditors' meeting has already been held.

Check with the trustee or clerk to see if you need to re-notify all of your creditors. If you do, you will need to send a copy of your **AMENDMENT COVER SHEET** and the changed documents to each creditor. You will also need to complete a **PROOF OF SERVICE BY MAIL (CERTIFICATE OF MAILING)**. (see form 24, p.287.)

To complete a **PROOF OF SERVICE BY MAIL (CERTIFICATE OF MAILING)**, do the following.

◈ Fill in the title of the documents you send.

◈ Fill in the names and addresses of all the creditors or others you send copies to.

If the creditors' meeting has already been held, another meeting may need to be scheduled.

## CHANGING FROM CHAPTER 13 TO CHAPTER 7

If you filed your case under Chapter 13 of the Bankruptcy Code and have determined that you need to convert your case to Chapter 7, you need to complete a **MOTION TO CONVERT TO CHAPTER 7**. (see form 26, p.291.) This form only requires you to complete the top portion, as well as the date and signature portion. At the time you file this form, also include any other forms needed for a Chapter 7 bankruptcy as described in Section 6 of this book. Usually, only the **CHAPTER 7 INDIVIDUAL DEBTOR'S STATEMENT OF INTENTION** is needed. (see form 17, p.265.)

## LIEN AVOIDANCE

*Lien avoidance* is a procedure that allows a debtor to keep certain property that might otherwise be subject to repossession. Before reading about this any further, you should know that this is not available if you live in Kentucky, Louisiana, Maryland, Mississippi, Tennessee, and Utah. Also, it is only available in Connecticut, Texas, and Washington if you use the Federal Bankruptcy Exemptions. With the possible exception of Connecticut, it is most likely that you will find the state exemptions more advantageous in these states, especially if you own a home. Furthermore, lien avoidance only applies to exempt property, and you cannot avoid more than the exemption allows.

Next, you need to see if you have either of the two types of liens to which this can apply. The two types of liens are:

1.   those created by a court judgment and

2.   those created when you used property you already had as security for a new loan.

You may not avoid a lien if you took out the loan in order to buy the secured piece of property. Therefore, if you have no court judgments and your secured debts all relate to the items you purchased, you are not eligible for lien avoidance.

There are three other important limitations on the use of lien avoidance.

1.   You cannot avoid a lien on your vehicle, unless it is used as a part of your business (which does not include using it to get to and from work).

2.   If the lien is for more than the exemption amount for that item, the lien will only be reduced and the creditor may still repossess if the amount remaining is not paid immediately.

3. Lien avoidance can only be accomplished by filing more papers with the court, possibly leading to a court battle with the creditor and even the necessity for an appraisal of the property.

## REDEMPTION

*Redemption* is where you agree to pay the creditor a lump sum, based upon the market value of a piece of exempt property. This is generally only advisable if the property is worth less than the amount owed on the loan. Instead of paying off the full loan, you only pay the amount the property is worth. This is done because if the creditor repossesses the property, it will only be able to sell it for the market value, as the remainder of the loan is discharged in the bankruptcy.

However, there are limitations here also. Three conditions must be met.

1. The debt must be a *consumer debt*, meaning it is for personal use (as opposed to business use).

2. It must be for tangible, personal property (as opposed to items like stocks and bonds).

3. You must be claiming the property as exempt or the trustee must abandon the property (which is usually done because the property is of little value).

## REAFFIRMING A DEBT

*Reaffirming* a debt (also called *reaffirmation*) is when you and your creditor agree that the debt will still be owed after the bankruptcy and that you will continue to make payments. This requires a written agreement, signed by you and your creditor, and must contain certain provisions. A preferable alternative to this is for you to bring your payments current before filing for bankruptcy, and keep up your payments so the loan is not in default.

Reaffirmation should be a last resort, as it requires negotiating with the creditor, leaves you still liable for a debt, and requires the preparation of a written, legal agreement. Economically, reaffirmation often only makes sense if the loan is not current, you owe considerably less money than the property is worth, and the property is exempt.

## LAWSUITS

If you are involved in a lawsuit in which anyone is suing for money (such as a lawsuit for personal injuries or to collect a debt), to foreclose or repossess your property, or to evict you from your residence, you need to immediately notify the court and the creditor that you have filed for bankruptcy. This will bring the lawsuit to a dead stop, and your creditor will have to get the bankruptcy court judge's permission to continue with the lawsuit.

The formal way to do this is to file a form, called a **SUGGESTION OF BANKRUPTCY**, with the court where the lawsuit is pending. (see form 23, p.285.) *Do not* file this form in the bankruptcy court. You will need to complete the top portion of the form in exactly the same manner as your other court papers in the lawsuit read (*not* the way the bankruptcy papers read), and file it with the clerk of that court (*not* the bankruptcy clerk).

## PENSIONS AND RETIREMENT PLANS

The question here is whether you can keep your pension plan as exempt property. If you have a sizable pension plan that you are relying upon to see you through retirement, you may want to consult a bankruptcy attorney. Over the years, the issue of pension plans and bankruptcy has involved numerous court decisions and much confusion. It is not a simple area of bankruptcy law. However, the following discussion will summarize some of the basics.

You should first determine whether your pension plan is one that qualifies under the federal *Employee Retirement Income Security Act* (ERISA). You can find out if yours is an *ERISA-qualified* plan by looking at the information you have received about your plan, or by asking your employer's pension plan administrator. If it is an ERISA-qualified plan, it is exempt property and should be listed as such on

**SCHEDULE C—PROPERTY CLAIMED AS EXEMPT.** (see form 7, p.233.) In the second column, headed "SPECIFY LAW PROVIDING EACH EXEMPTION," type in: "11 U.S.C. §541(c)(2); 29 U.S.C. §1056(d)(1); and *Patterson v. Shumate*, 112 S.Ct. 2242 (1992)." These are the references to the federal law and the United Supreme Court decision making ERISA-qualified plans exempt. If your state also has a law exempting ERISA-qualified plans, also type in the reference to that law. (See your state's listing in Appendix A.)

If you *do not* have an ERISA-qualified plan, you need to see if your state exemptions cover your plan. (See your state's listing in Appendix A.) Some states only have such exemptions for pension plans of government employees, but some also have exemptions for any type of plan, including IRAs. If your plan is not covered by a state exemption, you may want to explore other options (such as cashing in your pension and using the money to acquire exempt property). If you are not yet at the required age, this may incur tax or other penalties for early withdrawal. It may also mean that you will have to start over growing a retirement plan after bankruptcy, which will reduce your benefits upon retirement. On the other hand, this will often still be better than losing all of the funds in your plan in the bankruptcy. In such cases, you may want to consult a bankruptcy attorney who can help you figure out the best possible course of action.

# After Your Discharge

Once you receive your discharge, you need to think about the future. The two main things you need to do are make sure that you do not get into financial trouble again and start rebuilding your credit.

## HANDLING YOUR FINANCES

From the **INCOME AND EXPENSES WORKSHEET** (worksheet 1), you have an idea of how to prepare a budget. Use the **MONTHLY BUDGET** in Appendix B to help keep your financial matters under control. (see worksheet 4, p.211.) Make additional copies of worksheet 4 to use in the months ahead. Your budgeting has three main goals, which include:

1. assuring that you are not spending more than you earn;

2. assuring that you will have the money available when a bill is due; and,

3. developing a savings plan.

You should have a checking account. If you do not, shop around for a bank with the lowest minimum balance for free checking or the lowest checking charges. If you are eligible to join a credit union, you will probably find that they have the best deal around. There are dozens of different checking account arrangements, so compare.

Use the top line of the first column of the **Monthly Budget** to write in the total amount in your checking account. (see worksheet 4, p.211.) Your job is to decide which of the debts listed needs to be paid before your next paycheck, and how much of the total needs to be assigned to each of those debts.

Use the other columns to allocate your next several paychecks to your debts. Hopefully, after deducting all of the debt payments from the amounts in the top column, something will be left over.

Ideally, experts say, you should save approximately 10% of each paycheck. For many people, this seems impossible, but that is no excuse for not trying to save something. If you have never saved, try it for awhile. You may be surprised to find out that the feeling you get from looking at a bank account balance with an emergency cushion of $200 or $1,000 is as good as the feeling you would get from spending that money.

The important thing is not to buy something unless you know exactly where you will get the money to pay for it when the bill is due. Whenever you think about buying on credit, look at your budget and ask yourself where the money will come from. It certainly cannot come from the rent money or from the food money. It should only come from the spending money, such as from next week's paycheck. If so, then subtract that amount from the "Spending" line in the column for next week's check, and write it on one of the lines for "Credit Payments," also writing in the name of the store or other credit card involved.

## OBTAINING CREDIT

One of the problems (or maybe it is a blessing in disguise) of going through a bankruptcy is that it will be difficult to obtain credit. During the bankruptcy you found out what life is like without the use of credit, and it is a good idea to do without credit until you are sure that you can keep your finances under control. However, in our society, credit is almost essential to improve one's standard of living.

Buying a home is frequently a better deal than renting one. Also, some essential items, such as cars, are very difficult to pay for in cash. It is a good idea to begin establishing some credit once you have things (including your spending habits) under control.

**Local Store Credit Cards**

One way to begin is to apply for a credit card from a local store. Almost every type of store now has its own credit cards, particularly local department stores and hardware stores. Many of these stores will issue a temporary card immediately upon filling out an application. Go into the store, fill out the application (which usually only asks your name, address, and where you work), then buy something immediately with the temporary card. Even if the application is later rejected, you still have an obligation to make the payments on the item you bought, and that repayment will be something positive in your new credit record. You can always do the same thing the next time you need to buy something at that store. Eventually, your timely payment will be noticed, and your application for a permanent card will be approved.

**Major Credit Cards**

Until you get a few local cards and establish a payment record on each, you should avoid applying for a major card (such as Visa or Mastercard), and avoid applying for a card at a major, nationwide department store (such as Sears or JCPenney). Such applications will almost certainly be rejected.

**Borrowing from Your Bank**

Another way to establish credit is to borrow against your own money. If you can accumulate some money in a savings account, the bank will probably allow you to borrow money against the savings account. Once you pay back the money, you have taken the first step toward establishing a positive credit history. You will have to pay a little interest, but the object here is to establish credit, not make a brilliant deal.

### Example:

Say you have $500 in a savings account. Borrow $250 against the account for a period of thirty days. Take the $250 and put it in your checking account. At the end of the thirty days, write a check to pay off the loan (even at an annual interest rate of 22%, this will mean writing a check for about $254.59). You will be paying $4.59 interest for the privilege of establishing some credit, which is not very expensive.

You are now ready to wisely deal with your financial situation and build a healthy credit history with your new credit. Your monthly budget will help keep you on track with your spending and your future financial health.

# Glossary

## A

**automatic stay.** A provision in the federal bankruptcy law that makes it illegal for creditors to make any attempt to collect a debt once a person files for bankruptcy. Creditors must then ask the bankruptcy court's permission to resume collection efforts.

## B

**blue book.** A common term for books that list the market value of various types of property, such as cars and boats.

## C

**Chapter 7 bankruptcy.** A chapter of the bankruptcy code providing for the discharge of debts.

**Chapter 11 bankruptcy.** A chapter of the bankruptcy code that was originally designed for corporations and partnerships, but may also be used by individuals with secured debts over $750,000; unsecured debts over $250,000; and, sufficient income to pay off a portion of these debts over several years.

**Chapter 13 bankruptcy.** A chapter of the bankruptcy code allowing a debtor to create a plan to repay some or all of his or her debts.

**Chapter 20 bankruptcy.** This is not an actual chapter of the bankruptcy code. It is a commonly used term for the situation where a debtor first files a Chapter 7 bankruptcy case, and once all dischargeable debts have been discharged, then files a Chapter 13 bankruptcy case to restructure payments on the debts that were not discharged in the Chapter 7 case. The terms derives from adding the numbers 7 and 13 from the two types of bankruptcy cases.

**codebtor.** A person who is jointly obligated with another to repay a debt.

**community property.** A type of property ownership, created by statute in some states, in which property is owned in common by a husband and wife as a kind of marital partnership.

**contingent debt.** A debt that will only be owed upon the occurence of some future event.

**co-signed debt.** A debt that a second party agrees to pay if the first party fails to pay.

**creditor.** One who is owed a debt.

# D

**discharge.** (1) The elimination of an obligation to repay a debt. (2) The release of a debtor from further oversight by the bankruptcy court at the end of a bankruptcy case.

**dischargeable debts.** Debts that may be discharged in a bankruptcy proceeding.

**disputed debts.** A debt that the debtor does not believe is owed or in which there is a disagreement over the amount owed.

# E

**executory contract.** A contract in which the obligations of either or both parties have not been completed.

**exempt property.** Property that may not be taken and sold to satisfy a debt.

# F

**foreclosure.** The legal process of taking real estate in order to satisfy a debt secured by a mortgage.

**future interest.** An interest in real property, whereby possession will occur in the future (such as after a life estate is completed).

# H

**homestead.** A person's primary home and place of residence, which, in most states, is wholly or partially exempt from the claims of creditors (unless the creditor holds a mortgage on the property).

# L

**lien avoidance.** A procedure, in certain cases and in certain states, whereby a debtor is allowed to keep property that would otherwise be subject to repossession.

**life estate.** An interest in land, whereby the person holding the life estate is allowed the use of the land during his or her life. Upon that person's death, the land goes to someone designated by the original owner.

# N

**nondischargeable debts.** Debts that may not be discharged in a bankruptcy proceeding.

**nonexempt property.** Property that is not exempt from the claims of creditors.

**nonpriority claim.** The claim of a creditor who is not the type of creditor given priority for payment by the bankruptcy code.

# P

**priority claim.** The claim of any creditor given priority for payment by the bankruptcy code.

# R

**reaffirmation.** When a debtor agrees that a debt will still be owed after bankruptcy, even though the debt could have been discharged.

**redemption.** When a debtor and creditor agree that the debtor will pay a certain sum and will be allowed to keep an item of property that secured the debt. In essence, the debtor is buying back the property.

**repossession.** The legal process of taking personal property (such as a car or household furniture) in order to satisfy a debt secured by the particular item of personal property.

# S

**secured debt.** A debt that is guaranteed by a particular piece of real or personal property, whereby the creditor may take the property if the debt is not repaid.

**setoff.** An amount owed by a creditor to a debtor, which is applied to reduce the amount of the debt owed.

# T

**tools of trade.** The legal term for items of property used in a person's business, trade, or profession.

**trustee.** The court-appointed person who oversees a bankruptcy case.

# U

**unliquidated debt.** A debt that is recognized by both debtor and creditor, but the exact amount owed is yet to be determined.

**unsecured debt.** A debt that is not guaranteed by any particular piece of real or personal property.

# W

**wage-earner plan.** A common name for a Chapter 13 bankruptcy.

# Exemptions (Federal and State)

This appendix can be used to find what exemptions are available to you. In addition to listing the exemptions available in each state, the federal exemptions are also listed. There are two types of federal exemptions. One is called *Federal Bankruptcy Exemptions* and the other is called *Federal Nonbankruptcy Exemptions*.

The Federal Bankruptcy Exemptions are not available in all states, so check the list at the beginning of the Federal Bankruptcy Exemption. If the Federal Bankruptcy Exemptions are allowed in your state, you will need to choose between the state exemptions and the Federal Bankruptcy Exemptions. You will need to compare the state exemptions to the Federal Bankruptcy Exemptions to determine which way will allow you to keep more property. In most cases, the state exemptions will be better for you, but make the comparison just to be sure.

The Federal Nonbankruptcy Exemptions are also available, along with your state's exemptions.

Under the listing for each state you will find a notation as to whether the Federal Bankruptcy Exemptions may be used. Under the heading

"MISCELLANEOUS," there is also a reminder for you to use any of the Federal Nonbankruptcy Exemptions that may apply to you.

The following listings give the section number for the applicable state law, and the exemption that relates to that section. At the beginning of each state's section, you will find information (with an example in parentheses) about how to write the statute reference in the second column of Schedule C.

If no amount is stated, the amount of that type of property you may claim is unlimited. Where an amount is stated, you may only claim up to that amount as exempt. If you want to be sure you understand the exemption, go to your library and look up the actual language in that section of your state's law.

Many states' law books have volume numbers on them. Where applicable, ignore the volume number because it is not part of the official manner of referring to the law in your state.

**NOTE:** *The symbol "§" or "§§" stands for "section" or "sections" of the statutes or code in your state. It refers to the particular part of the statutes of code listed here to the left of all references. A law librarian can help you.*

## DOUBLING EXEMPTIONS

Some states allow a husband and wife to each claim a separate exemption. This is referred to as *doubling* the exemption.

---

### Example:
If an automobile is exempt up to $3,000 in equity, the husband and wife may each claim an auto up to $3,000.

---

An asterisk (*) after an item indicates that doubling is specifically *prohibited* by law. Two asterisks (**) indicates that doubling is specifically *approved* by law. No notation indicates that the law does not state whether doubling is permitted, so you may want to list the exemption for both husband and wife, and see if the trustee accepts it.

## HOMESTEAD EXEMPTION

The 2005 changes to the bankruptcy law placed some limitation on the amount of exemption that may be claimed for a homestead. If you have not lived in the state in which you file for bankruptcy for at least forty months, your homestead exemption is limited to $125,000, unless that state's exemption is already less than $125,000. This was done to prevent people from moving to a state with a high or unlimited exemption for the purpose of sheltering assets. This law only applies in the following states: Arkansas, California, the District of Columbia, Florida, Iowa, Kansas, Louisiana, Massachusetts, Minnesota, Nevada, Oklahoma, Rhode Island, South Dakota, and Texas. If you have lived in one of these states for at least forty months before filing your petition, you can still use the state's homestead exemption in excess of $125,000.

## ERISA PENSION BENEFITS

These are benefits from retirement plans that qualify under the federal Employee Retirement Income Security Act (ERISA). Your employer or retirement plan administrator can tell you whether your plan is an ERISA-qualified plan.

Most states have laws providing for a bankruptcy exemption for ERISA-qualified retirement plan benefits. Whether the states can exempt such plans has been the source of much dispute in past years. The Supreme Court has said that ERISA-qualified pension plans may be exempted by the states.

You should check with a bankruptcy lawyer if you run into any problems with the trustee or judge regarding such a plan. Your retirement plan can be a vital asset, and you should take all necessary steps to preserve it and protect it from your creditors.

**– Warning –**

The exemption charts in this appendix are not guaranteed to be current, nor are they guaranteed to contain every possible exemption. These charts are designed to include the basic exemptions to cover the most usual situations. Legislatures may change the exemptions at any time, and there may be obscure exemptions applicable to very narrow situations. Your local public library or law library (usually found at your county courthouse) should have a current copy of your state's laws. Your law library should also have books about bankruptcy that contain the most recent exemptions. If you think you have a particular asset that may be entitled to an exemption not listed, or feel you need an exemption explained in more detail, you should consult an attorney.

## WEBSITES

You may find all states' statutes on the Internet, although they can vary dramatically in user-friendliness. Some of these sites are maintained by the state government, while others are maintained by private companies or law firms. For some states, the laws are also available by paying for a subscription service. A single site, **www.findlaw.com**, provides access to all of the states' websites.

Once you get to the Findlaw site, make sure you are on the tab labeled "For Legal Professionals" and click on "Cases & Codes." Then scroll down to the heading "U.S. State Laws" and click on the desired state. Next, click on the state's code or statutes.

# FEDERAL BANKRUPTCY EXEMPTIONS

The following Federal Bankruptcy Exemptions are available (as an alternative to the state exemptions) if you live in one of the following states:

| | | | |
|---|---|---|---|
| Arkansas | Massachusetts | New Mexico | Texas |
| Connecticut | Michigan | Pennsylvania | Vermont |
| District of Columbia | Minnesota | Rhode Island | Wisconsin |
| Hawaii | New Jersey | South Carolina | Washington |

If you use these exemptions, however, you cannot use the exemptions listed under your state. Be sure to compare these exemptions to those in the listing for your state, and use whichever allows you to keep more of your property. Remember, the Federal Bankruptcy Exemptions can be doubled by husband and wife.

The following section numbers relate to Title 11 of the United States Code, which is abbreviated "11 U.S.C." followed by the appropriate section ("§" is the symbol for section number, and "§§" is the symbol for sections (more than one).) An example is: "11 U.S.C. §522(d)(1)." Only the section number is used below on the left side listing.

**HOMESTEAD (\*\*)**
522(d)(1)    Real property, including mobile homes, co-ops, and burial plots, up to $15,000.

**PERSONAL PROPERTY (\*\*)**
522(d)(2)    Motor vehicle up to $2,400.
522(d)(3)    Animals, crops, clothing, appliances and furnishings, books, household goods, and musical instruments up to $400 per item, and up to $8,000 total.
522(d)(4)    Jewelry up to $1,000.
522(d)(5)    $800 of any property, and unused portion of homestead up to $7,500.
522(d)(9)    Professionally prescribed health aids.
522(d)(11)(B)    Wrongful death recovery for person you depended upon.
522(d)(11)(D)    Personal injury recovery up to $15,000, except for pain and suffering or for pecuniary loss.
522(d)(11)(E)    Lost earning payments.

**PENSIONS**
522(d)(10)(E)    ERISA-qualified benefits needed for support. Includes IRAs. *Rousey v. Jacoway*, 205 WL 742304 (April 4, 2005).

**PUBLIC BENEFITS**
522(d)(10)(A)    Public assistance, Social Security, Veteran's benefits, Unemployment Compensation.
522(d)(11)(A)    Crime victim's compensation.

**TOOLS OF TRADE (\*\*)**
522(d)(6)    Implements, books and tools of trade, up to $1,500.

**ALIMONY AND CHILD SUPPORT**
522(d)(10)(D)    Alimony and child support needed for support.

**INSURANCE**
522(d)(7)    Unmatured life insurance policy.
522(d)(8)    Life insurance policy with loan value up to $8,000 (\*\*).
522(d)(10)(C)    Disability, unemployment, or illness benefits.
522(d)(11)(C)    Life insurance payments for a person you depended on, which you need for support.

# FEDERAL NONBANKRUPTCY EXEMPTIONS

You may only use these exemptions if you choose the exemptions listed under your state. You may not use these if you choose to use the Federal Bankruptcy Exemptions listed on the previous page.

## RETIREMENT BENEFITS

| | |
|---|---|
| 5 U.S.C. §8346 | Civil Service employees. |
| 10 U.S.C. §1440 | Military service employees. |
| 22 U.S.C. §4060 | Foreign service employees. |
| 29 U.S.C. §1056 | ERISA benefits. |
| 31 U.S.C. §776 | Annuities for service in the General Accounting Office. |
| 38 U.S.C. §3101 | Veterans' benefits. |
| 38 U.S.C. §5301 | Veterans' benefits. |
| 42 U.S.C. §407 | Social Security benefits. |
| 45 U.S.C. §231m | Railroad workers. |
| 50 U.S.C. §403 | CIA employees. |

## SURVIVOR'S BENEFITS

| | |
|---|---|
| 10 U.S.C. §1450 | Military service. |
| 28 U.S.C. §376 | Judges, U.S. court directors. |
| 33 U.S.C. §775 | Lighthouse workers. |

## DEATH AND DISABILITY BENEFITS

| | |
|---|---|
| 5 U.S.C. §8130 | U.S. Government employees. |
| 33 U.S.C. §916 | Longshoremen, harbor workers. |
| 42 U.S.C. §1701 | Commpensation for war injury. |
| 42 U.S.C. §1717 | Military service. |
| 42 U.S.C. §3796 | Public safety officers. |

## MISCELLANEOUS

| | |
|---|---|
| 10 U.S.C. §1035 | Military deposits to savings accounts (while on permanent duty outside the U.S.). |
| 15 U.S.C. §1673 | 75% of earned but unpaid wages (judge may approve more). |
| 25 U.S.C. §543 & §545 | Klamath Indians tribe benefits. |
| 38 U.S.C. §770(g) | Military group life insurance. |
| 45 U.S.C. §352(e) | Railroad workers' unemployment. |
| 46 U.S.C. §11109 | Seamen's wages (except for support). |
| 46 U.S.C. §11110 | Seamen's clothing. |
| 46 U.S.C. §11111 | Seamen's wages (while on a voyage and pursuant to a written contract). |

# ALABAMA

Code of Alabama, Title 6, Chapter 10, Section 6-10-2 (Ala. Code §6-10-2).

## HOMESTEAD

| | |
|---|---|
| 6-10-2 & 6-10-20 | Real property or mobile home, up to $5,000. Property can't exceed 160 acres.(**) Must record homestead declaration. |

## PERSONAL PROPERTY

| | |
|---|---|
| 6-10-5 | A burial place and a church pew or seat. |
| 6-10-6 | Clothing, books, family portraits and pictures, and $3,000 of any other personal property (except life insurance). |

## WAGES

| | |
|---|---|
| 6-10-7 | 75% of earned but unpaid wages. Judge may approve more for low-income debtors. |

## PENSIONS

| | |
|---|---|
| 12-18-10 | Judges. |
| 16-25-23 | Teachers. |
| 36-21-77 | Law enforcement officers. |
| 36-27-28 | State employees. |

## PUBLIC BENEFITS

| | |
|---|---|
| 15-23-15 | Crime victims' compensation. |
| 25-4-140 | Unemployment compensation. |
| 25-5-86 | Workers' compensation. |
| 25-5-179 | Coal miners' pneumoconiosis benefits. |
| 31-7-2 | Southeast Asian War POW's benefits. |
| 38-4-8 | AFDC and aid to blind, aged, and disabled. |

## TOOLS OF TRADE

| | |
|---|---|
| 31-2-78 | Arms, uniforms, and equipment required to be kept by state military personnel. |

## INSURANCE

| | |
|---|---|
| 6-10-8 & 27-14-29 | Life insurance proceeds if beneficiary is spouse or child of the insured. |
| 27-14-31 | Disability proceeds up to an average of $250 per month. |
| 27-14-32 | Annuities up to $250 per month. |
| 27-15-26 | Life insurance, if policy prohibits use to pay creditors. |
| 27-30-25 | Mutual aid association benefits. |
| 27-34-27 | Fraternal benefit society benefits. |

## MISCELLANEOUS

| | |
|---|---|
| 10-8A-501 | Business partnership property. |
| Other | Add any applicable Federal Nonbankruptcy Exemptions. |

# ALASKA

Alaska Statutes, Title 9, Section 9.38.010 (Alaska Stat. §9.38.010). In *In re McNutt*, 87 B.R. 84 (9th Cir. 1988), the Federal Bankruptcy Exemptions were allowed.

## HOMESTEAD
9.38.010 (*)   Up to $54,000.

## PERSONAL PROPERTY
9.38.015      Burial plot; needed health aids; and tuition credits under advance college payment contract.
9.38.020      Motor vehicle up to $3,000, if market value is no more than $20,000; pets up to $1,000; jewelry up to $1,000; and household goods, clothing, books, musical instruments, and family portraits and heirlooms up to $3,000.
9.38.030      Personal injury and wrongful death recoveries, to the extent wages are exempt.
9.38.060      Proceeds from damaged exempt property.
34.35.105     Building materials.

## WAGES
9.38.030 &    Weekly net earnings up to $350, or up to $550 if sole wage earner in a household. If no regular pay, up to
9.38.050      $1,400 paid in any month, or $2,200 if sole wage earner in household.

## PENSIONS
9.38.015      Teachers, judicial & public employees, and elected officers, as to benefits accruing.
9.38.017      ERISA-qualified benefits, if deposited more than 120 days before filing.
9.38.030      Payments being received from other pensions.

## PUBLIC BENEFITS
9.38.015      Alaska longevity bonus, crime victims' compensation and federally exempt public benefits.
23.20.405     Unemployment compensation.
23.30.160     Workers' compensation.
43.23.065     45% of Permanent Fund dividends (this is income distributed to residents from the state's natural resources).
47.25.210     General relief assistance.
47.25.395     AFDC.
47.25.550     Assistance to blind, elderly and disabled adults.

## TOOLS OF TRADE
9.38.020      Implements, books or tools up to $2,800.

## ALIMONY AND CHILD SUPPORT
9.38.015      Child support if received from a collection agency.
9.38.030      Alimony, to extent wages are exempt.

## INSURANCE
9.38.015 &    Medical and disability benefits.
9.38.030
9.38.025      Life insurance or annuity contracts up to a $10,000 loan value.
9.38.030      Life insurance proceeds to a spouse or dependent, and personal injury insurance proceeds, to extent wages are exempt.
21.84.240     Fraternal benefit society benefits.

## MISCELLANEOUS
9.38.015      Liquor licenses; Alaska Fisheries limited entry permits.
9.38.015 &    Business partnership property.
32.06.501
Other         Add any applicable Federal Nonbankruptcy Exemptions.

# ARIZONA

Arizona Revised Statutes Annotated, Title 33, Section 33-1101 (Ariz. Rev. Stat. §33-1101).

## HOMESTEAD (*)
33-1101    Up to $150,000. Includes condos, co-ops, and mobile homes; and sale proceeds up to 18 months after sale, or new home purchased, whichever occurs first. Must record homestead declaration. §33-1102.

## PERSONAL PROPERTY (**)
33-1123    The following items up to $4,000 total: Two beds; one bed table, dresser and lamp for each bed; bedding; kitchen table and 4 chairs; dining table and 4 chairs; living room chair for each family member; couch; 3 living room tables and lamps; living room carpet or rug; refrigerator; stove; washer and dryer; one TV, radio or stereo (not one of each); radio alarm clock; vacuum cleaner; family portraits; and any pictures, oil paintings, and drawings created by the debtor. Additional bed, and dining chair, for each additional dependent if more than 4 persons in household.

33-1124    Food and fuel for 6 months.

33-1125    Motor vehicle up to $5,000 (or $10,000 if disabled); clothing to $500; pets, horses, milk cows and poultry to $500; books to $250; wedding and engagement rings to $1,000; musical instruments to $250; watch to $100; wheelchair and prostheses; and up to $500 total for bicycle, sewing machine, typewriter, burial plot, firearm and bible (only one of each may be kept).

33-1126    Proceeds for sold or damaged exempt property; prepaid rent or security deposit to lesser of $1,000 or 1.5 times rent (only if not claiming homestead); bank deposit to $150 in one account.

## WAGES
33-1126    Earnings of minor child, unless debt is for child.
33-1131    Minimum of 75% of unpaid net wages or pension payments. Judge may allow more.

## PENSIONS
9-931      Police officers.
9-968      Firefighters.
15-1628    Members of board of regents.
33-1126    ERISA-qualified benefits, if deposited more than 120 days before filing [IRAs included, *In re Herrscher*, 121 B.R. 29 (D. Ariz. 1990)].
38-762     State employees.
38-811     Elected officials.
38-850     Public safety personnel.
41-955     Rangers.

## PUBLIC BENEFITS
23-783     Unemployment compensation.
23-1068    Workers' compensation.
46-208     Welfare benefits.

## TOOLS OF TRADE
33-1127    Teaching aids of a teacher.
33-1130 (**)  Tools, equipment and books up to $2,500; farm machinery, utensils, instruments of husbandry, feed, seed, grain and animals up to a total value of $2,500; and arms, uniforms and equipment you are required by law to keep.

## INSURANCE
20-881     Fraternal benefit society benefits.
20-1131    Life insurance cash value up to $2,000 per dependent/$10,000 total.
20-1132    Group life insurance policy or proceeds.
33-1126 (**)  Life insurance proceeds if beneficiary is spouse or child, up to $20,000; life insurance cash value to $1,000 per dependent/$25,000 total; and health, accident or disability benefits.

## MISCELLANEOUS
29-1041    Business partnership property.
Other      Add any applicable Federal Nonbankruptcy Exemptions.

# ARKANSAS

Arkansas Code of 1987 Annotated, Title 16, Chapter 66, Section 16-66-210 (Ark. Code Ann. §16-66-210). Compare Federal Bankruptcy Exemptions.

**HOMESTEAD** (Choose one of the following)

16-66-210 (*)    *If you have lived in Arkansas for at least 40 months:* Head of family may claim up to $2,500 for up to 1 acre in city, town, or village; or up to 160 acres elsewhere; but in any event may claim an unlimited amount for up to 1/4 acre in a city, town, or village; or up to 80 acres elsewhere. (As a practical matter, except for property of little value, this means an unlimited exemption for up to 1/4 acre in a city, town, or village; or up to 80 acres elsewhere.) This exemption is also found in the Arkansas Constitution, and the reference to "Ark. Const. 9-3, 9-4 & 9-5" should also be used in your paperwork.

*If you have lived in Arkansas for less than 40 months:* The same provisions as above apply, except that the total amount is limited to $125,000 by federal law.

16-66-218    Real or personal property used as a residence, up to $800 if single or $1,250 if married. Also, $500 of any personal property, if married or head of household; $200 if single (cite "Ark. Const. 9-1; 9-2" also).

**PERSONAL PROPERTY (also see §16-66-218 under the homestead section above)**

16-66-218    Motor vehicle up to $1,200, and wedding bands provided that any diamonds can't exceed ½ carat.

16-66-207    Burial plot up to 5 acres, provided you don't use homestead exemption in section 16-66-218.

Ark. Const.    Clothing of unlimited value; and any personal property of up to $500 if married or head of family, or $200 otherwise. Use reference to "Ark. Const. 9-1 & 9-2."

**WAGES**

16-66-208    Earned but unpaid wages due for 60 days, but in not less than $25 per week.

**PENSIONS**

16-66-218    IRA deposits up to $20,000 if deposited over 1 year before filing for bankruptcy.

24-6-223    State police officers.

24-7-715    School employees.

24-10-616    Police officers and firefighters.

24-11-417    Disabled police officers.

24-11-814    Disabled firefighters.

**PUBLIC BENEFITS**

11-9-110    Workers' compensation.

11-10-109    Unemployment compensation.

16-90-716    Crime victims' compensation, unless you are seeking to discharge a debt for treatment of an injury incurred during the crime.

20-76-430    AFDC, and aid to blind, aged or disabled.

**TOOLS OF TRADE**

16-66-218    Tools, books and implements of trade to $750.

**INSURANCE**

16-66-209    Life, health, accident or disability proceeds, whether paid or due (case law limits to $500).

23-71-112    Stipulated insurance premiums.

23-72-114    Mutual assessment life or disability benefits up to $1,000.

23-74-119    Fraternal benefit society benefits.

23-79-131    Life insurance proceeds if beneficiary isn't the insured; life insurance proceeds if policy prohibits proceeds from being used to pay beneficiary's creditors.

23-79-132    Group life insurance.

23-79-133    Disability benefits.

23-79-134    Annuity contract.

**MISCELLANEOUS**

4-42-502    Business partnership property.

Other    Add any applicable Federal Nonbankruptcy Exemptions.

# CALIFORNIA

*West's* Annotated California Codes, Civil Procedure, Section 704.710 (Cal. Code Civ. Proc. §704.710). California has two separate systems of exemptions. You must select one, and cannot mix exemptions from the two systems. References are to the California Code of Civil Procedure unless otherwise stated. Be sure you are using the Code of Civil Procedure, not the Civil Code. "Gov't." refers to "Government."

## CALIFORNIA (SYSTEM 1)

**HOMESTEAD**

704.730 (*)   *If you have lived in California for at least 40 months:* Real or personal property occupied at time of filing for bankruptcy, including mobile home, boat, stock cooperative, community apartment, planned development or condominium, up to the following limits: $50,000 if single and not disabled; $75,000 if family and no other member has homestead; $150,000 if 65 or older or if physically or mentally disabled; $150,000 if creditors are seeking to force sale of your home and you are either (a)55 or older, single and earn under $15,000 per year, or (b)55 or older, married and earn under $20,000 per year. Sale proceeds are exempt for up to 6 months after sale.
*If you have lived in California for less than 40 months:* The same provisions as above apply, except that the total amount of any homestead exemption is limited to $125,000 by federal law.

**PERSONAL PROPERTY**

704.010 (*)   Motor vehicle or insurance if vehicle lost, destroyed or damaged up to $2,300.

704.020       Food, clothing, appliances and furnishings.

704.030 (*)   Building materials to repair or improve home up to $2,425.

704.040 (*)   Jewelry, heirlooms, and art up to $6,075 total.

704.050       Health aids.

704.080       Bank deposits from Social Security Administration up to $2,435 for single payee ($3,650 for huband and wife payees); proceeds from exempt property in form of cash or bank deposits.

704.090       Inmates trust funds up to $1,000.

704.140       Personal injury causes of action, and recoveries needed for support.

704.150       Wrongful death causes of action, and recoveries needed for support.

704.200       Burial plot.

**WAGES**

704.070       75% of wages paid within 30 days prior to filing bankruptcy.

704.113       Public employee vacation credits (75% minimum if receiving installment payments).

**PENSIONS**

704.110       Public retirement benefits.

704.115       Private retirements benefits to extent tax-deferred, including IRA and Keogh.

Gov't. 21201  Public employees.

Gov't. 31452  County employees.

Gov't. 31913  County peace officers.

Gov't. 32210  County firefighters.

**PUBLIC BENEFITS**

704.120       Unemployment benefits and union benefits due to labor dispute.

704.160       Workers' compensation.

704.170       AFDC and aid to blind, aged, and disabled.

704.180       Relocation benefits.

704.190       Financial aid to students.

**TOOLS OF TRADE**

704.060       Tools, implements, materials, books, uniforms, instruments, equipment, furnishings, motor vehicle, and vessels up to $6,075, or up to $12,150 if used by both spouses in the same occupation. Can't claim motor vehicle here if already claimed under 704.010.

**INSURANCE**

704.100 (**)  Matured life insurance benefits needed for support of unlimited value, or unmatured life insurance policy up to $9,700 in value.

704.120       Fraternal unemployment benefits and union benefits in a labor dispute.

| 704.130 | Disability or health benefits. |
| 704.720 | Homeowners' insurance proceeds for 6 months after received, up to amount of homestead. |
| Other | Fidelity bonds. Refer to as "Labor 404." |
| Other | Life insurance proceeds if policy prohibits use to pay creditors. Refer to as "Ins. 10132, 10170 & 10171." |

**MISCELLANEOUS**

| Corp. 16501 | Business partnership property. |
| Other | Add any applicable Federal Nonbankruptcy Exemptions. |

### CALIFORNIA (SYSTEM 2) [no doubling of any exemptions)

**HOMESTEAD**

| 703.140(b)(1) | Real or personal property (e.g., mobile home), including co-op, used as a residence up to $17,425. |

**PERSONAL PROPERTY**

| 703.140(b)(1) | Burial plot up to $17,425, instead of homestead. |
| 703.140(b)(2) | Motor vehicle up to $2,775. |
| 703.140(b)(3) | Clothing, household goods, appliances, furnishings, animals, books, musical instruments, and crops up to $450 per item. |
| 703.140(b)(4) | Jewelry up to $1,150. |
| 703.140(b)(5) | $15,000 of any property, less any claim for homestead or burial plot. |
| 703.140(b)(5) | $925 of any property. |
| 703.140(b)(9) | Health aids. |
| 703.140(b)(11) | Wrongful death recoveries needed for support. |
| 703.140(b)(11) | Personal injury recoveries up to $17,425, not to include pain, suffering or pecuniary loss. |

**PENSIONS**

| 703.140(b)(10) | ERISA-qualified benefits needed for support. |

**PUBLIC BENEFITS**

| 703.140(b)(10) | Unemployment compensation, Social Security, and public assistance. |
| 703.140(b)(10) | Veterans' benefits. |
| 703.140(b)(11) | Crime victims' compensation. |

**TOOLS OF TRADE**

| 703.140(b)(6) | Tools, books and implements of trade up to $1,750. |

**ALIMONY AND CHILD SUPPORT**

| 703.140(b)(10) | Alimony and child support needed for support. |

**INSURANCE**

| 703.140(b)(7) | Unmatured life insurance policy, other than credit. |
| 703.140(b)(8) | Unmatured life insurance contract accrued interest, dividends, loan, cash or surrender value up to $9,300. |
| 703.140(b)(10) | Disability benefits. |
| 703.140(b)(11) | Life insurance proceeds needed for support. |
| Other | Fidelity bonds. Refer to as "Labor 404." |

**MISCELLANEOUS**

| 695.060 | Business and professional licenses, except liquor licenses. |
| Other | Add any applicable Federal Nonbankruptcy Exemptions. |

# COLORADO

*West's* Colorado Revised Statutes Annotated, Title 13, Article 54, Section 13-54-102 (Colo. Rev. Stat. Ann. §13-54-102).

## HOMESTEAD
38-41-201     Real property up to $45,000. Property must be occupied at time petition is filed. Sale or insurance proceeds exempt for 1 year. Spouse or child of deceased owner can also qualify.

## PERSONAL PROPERTY
13-54-102     Motor vehicles to $3,000 (up to $6,000 if used by elderly or disabled debtor or dependent); clothing to $1,500 for debtor and each dependent; health aids; household goods to $3,000; food and fuel to $600; 1 burial site per person; watches, jewelry, and articles of adornment for debtor and each dependent to $1,000; family pictures and books to $1,500; utility and security deposits; proceeds for damaged exempt property; personal recoveries, unless debt related to the injury.

## WAGES
13-54-104     Minimum 75% of earned but unpaid wages, and pension payments. Judge may approve more for low-income debtors.

## PENSIONS
13-54-102     ERISA-qualified benefits, including IRAs and 401(k)s.
22-64-120     Teachers.
24-51-212     Public employees.
31-30.5-208   Police officers.
31-30-1117    Firefighters.

## PUBLIC BENEFITS
8-80-103      Unemployment compensation.
13-54-104     75% of workers' compensation.
13-54-102     Veterans' benefits for veteran, spouse or child if veteran served in war.
13-54-102 &   Crime victims' compensation.
24-4.1-114
26-2-131      AFDC, aid to blind, aged and disabled.

## TOOLS OF TRADE
13-54-102     Stock in trade, supplies, fixtures, maps, machines, tools, electronics, equipment, books, and business materials to $10,000; library of a professional to $3,000; livestock, poultry, or other animals, tractors, farm implements, trucks used in agriculture, harvesting equipment, seed, and agricultural machinery and tools to $25,000.

## ALIMONY AND CHILD SUPPORT
13-54-102.5   Child support if recipient does not mix with other funds, or if deposited in a separate account for the child's benefit.

## INSURANCE
10-7-106      Life insurance proceeds if policy prohibits use to pay creditors.
10-7-205      Group life insurance policy or proceeds.
13-54-104     75% of disability benefits.
10-14-403     Fraternal benefit society benefits.
13-54-102     Life insurance cash surrender value up to $50,000.
38-41-209     Homeowners' insurance proceeds for one year after received, up to homestead amount.

## MISCELLANEOUS
7-64-501      Business partnership property.
Other         Add any applicable Federal Nonbankruptcy Exemptions.

# CONNECTICUT

Connecticut General Statutes Annotated, Title 52, Section 52-352b (Conn. Gen. Stat. Ann. §52-352b). Compare Federal Bankruptcy Exemptions.

**HOMESTEAD**

| | |
|---|---|
| 52-352b | Real property, including mobile or manufactured home, up to $75,000. |

**PERSONAL PROPERTY**

| | |
|---|---|
| 52-352b | Motor vehicle up to $1,500; food, clothing and health aids; appliances, furniture and bedding; wedding and engagement rings; burial plot; residential utility and security deposits for 1 residence; proceeds for damaged exempt property; and $1,000 of any property. |

**WAGES**

| | |
|---|---|
| 52-361a | Minimum 75% of earned but unpaid wages. Judge may approve more for low-income debtors. |

**PENSIONS**

| | |
|---|---|
| 5-171;5-192w | State employees. |
| 10-183q | Teachers. |
| 52-352b | ERISA-qualified benefits, but only as to payments received and only to the extent wages are exempt. |

**PUBLIC BENEFITS**

| | |
|---|---|
| 7-446 | Municipal employees. |
| 27-140 | Vietnam veterans' death benefits. |
| 31-272 & 52-352b | Unemployment compensation. |
| 45-48 | Probate judges and employees. |
| 52-352b | Workers' compensation; veterans' benefits; Social Security; wages from earnings incentive programs; AFDC; aid to blind, aged and disabled. |
| 52-352b & 54-213 | Crime victims' compensation. |

**TOOLS OF TRADE**

| | |
|---|---|
| 52-352b | Arms, military equipment, uniforms and musical instruments of military personnel; tools, books, instruments and farm animals needed. Farm animals and livestock feed reasonably required, and monies due from insurance on such property, owned by a farm partnership where at least 50% of the partners are members of the same family. |

**ALIMONY AND CHILD SUPPORT**

| | |
|---|---|
| 52-352b | Alimony and child support, to extent wages are exempt. |

**INSURANCE**

| | |
|---|---|
| 38a-380 | Benefits under no-fault insurance law, to extent wages are exempt. |
| 38a-453 | Life insurance proceeds, dividends, interest, or cash or surrender value. |
| 38a-454 | Life insurance proceeds if policy prohibits use to pay creditors. |
| 38a-636 | Fraternal benefit society benefits. |
| 52-352b | Health and disability benefits; disability benefits paid by association for its members; unmatured life insurance policy dividends, interest, or loan value up to $4,000, if you or a person on whom you are dependent is the person whose life is insured. |

**MISCELLANEOUS**

| | |
|---|---|
| 34-346 | Business partnership property. |

# DELAWARE

Delaware Code Annotated, Title 10, Section 4902 (Del. Code Ann. tit. 10, §4902). In the books, ignore the volume number and look for the "title" numbers. For online research, you may need to know that the "49" in "4902" refers to Chapter 49.

## LIMITATION
10 §4914**    Total exemptions (in addition to retirement plans) may not exceed $5,000.

## HOMESTEAD
Tenancies by the entirety exempt without limitation as to debts of one spouse. [*In re Hovatter*, 25 B.R. 123 (D. Del. 1982)]; otherwise Del. Code Ann. tit. 10, §4901 says all real estate is subject to execution.

## PERSONAL PROPERTY
10 §4902 &    Clothing, including jewelry; books; family pictures; piano; leased organs and sewing machines; burial
10 §4903    plot; church pew or any seat in public place of worship. Also $500 of any other personal property if head of family (except tools of trade). School books and family library.

## WAGES
10 §4913    85% of earned but unpaid wages.

## PENSIONS
9 §4316    Kent County employees.
10 §4915    Retirement plans.
11 §8803    Police officers.
16 §6653    Volunteer firefighters.
29 §5503    State employees.

## PUBLIC BENEFITS
19 §2355    Workers' compensation.
19 §3374    Unemployment compensation.
31 §513    General assistance; AFDC; aid to aged and disabled.
31 §2309    Aid to blind.

## TOOLS OF TRADE
10 §4902    Tools, implements and fixtures, up to $75 in New Castle and Sussex counties, and up to $50 in Kent County.

## INSURANCE
12 §1901    Employee life insurance benefits.
18 §2726    Health or disability benefits.
18 §2727    Group life insurance policy or proceeds.
18 §2728    Annuity contract proceeds up to $350 per month.
18 §2729    Life insurance proceeds if policy prohibits use to pay creditors.
18 §6118    Fraternal benefit society benefits.

## MISCELLANEOUS
6 §1525    Business partnership property.
Other    Add any applicable Federal Nonbankruptcy Exemptions.

# DISTRICT OF COLUMBIA

D.C. Code, Title 15, Section 501 (D.C. Code §15-501). Compare Federal Bankruptcy Exemptions.

## HOMESTEAD
15-501    Unlimited interest in real property used as residence; can include co-op or burial plot.

## PERSONAL PROPERTY
15-501    *If you have lived in the District of Columbia for at least 40 months:* Motor vehicle to $2,575; household furnishings & goods, wearing apparel, appliances, books, animals, crops, or musical instruments, up to $425 per item and $8,625 total; health aids; family pictures; family library to $400; provisions for 3 months; and wrongful death payment for person debtor was a dependent upon, necessary for support; pain and suffering or compensation for pecuniary loss, pain and suffering, or loss of future earnings, of the debtor or person debtor is a dependent upon, to extent reasonably necessary for the support.

       *If you have lived in the District of Columbia for less than 40 months:* The same provisions as above apply, except that the total amount of any homestead exemption is limited to $125,000 by federal law.

42-1904.09   Residential condominium deposit.

## WAGES
15-503    Nonwage earning, including pensions, for 60 days, up to $200 per month for head of family; or $60 per month otherwise.

16-572    Minimum of 75% of earned but unpaid wages or pension payments.

## PENSIONS
1-507 & 16-571 DC government employees.

11-1570   Judges.

15-501    ERISA-qualified retirement plans, including IRAs. Stock bonus, pension, profit-sharing, annuity, or similar plan for illness, disability, death, age, or length of service, to the extent necessary for support (certain exceptions apply).

38-2001.17 &  DC public school teachers.
38-2021.17

## PUBLIC BENEFITS
4-215.01   Public assistance.

4-507    Violent crime victims compensation, unless claim is for products, services, or accommodations which are included in the compensation award.

15-501    Social Security benefit; veteran's benefit; disability, illness, or unemployment benefit; crime victim's reparation law.

51-118    Unemployment compensation.

## TOOLS OF TRADE
15-501    Implements, professional books, or tools of the trade up to $1,625; library, office furniture, and implements of a professional person or artist, up to $300.

15-501 &   Mechanic's tools, tools of trade or business, up to $200.
15-503

## ALIMONY AND CHILD SUPPORT
15-501    Alimony, support, or separate maintenance, necessary for support.

## INSURANCE
15-501    Other insurance proceeds to $200 per month, for a maximum of 2 months, for head of family; up to $60 per month otherwise. Unmatured life insurance (but not credit life insurance); payments under life insurance that insured the life of person debtor was dependent upon on the date of death, to extent necessary for support.

31-4716.01   Disability benefits.

31-4717    Group life insurance policy or proceeds.

31-5315    Fraternal benefit society benefits.

## MISCELLANEOUS
15-501    Any property up to $850, plus up to $8,075 of any unused amount of the homestead exemption.

33-105.01   Business partnership property.

Other     Add any applicable Federal Nonbankruptcy Exemptions.

# FLORIDA

Florida Statutes, Chapter 222, Section 222.05 (Fla. Stat. §222.05).

## HOMESTEAD

222.05    *If you have lived in the Florida for at least 40 months:* Real or personal property, including mobile or modular home and condominium, to unlimited value. Property cannot exceed ½ acre in a municipality, or 160 acres elsewhere. Spouse or child of deceased owner may claim exemption. (Also refer to Florida Constitution, as "Fla. Const. 10-4."). Also, tenancies by the entireties in real property are exempt as to debts of one spouse [*In re Avins*, 19 B.R. 736 (S.D.Fla. 1982)].
          *If you have lived in Florida for less than 40 months:* The same provisions as above apply, except that the total amount of any homestead exemption is limited to $125,000 by federal law.

## PERSONAL PROPERTY

220.20    All personal property owed in tenancy by the entirety, as to the debts of one spouse.
222.25    Motor vehicle up to $1,000; prescribed health aids.
Other     Any personal property up to $1,000 total. (Refer to as "Fla. Const. 10-4")(**).

## WAGES

222.11    For head of family, earnings up to $500 a week; also amounts greater than $500 unless debtor has agreed otherwise in writing. For head of family or others, exempt in any event up to amount allowed under the Consumer Credit Protection Act, 15 USC §1673. Applies to earned but unpaid wages, or wages paid and in a bank account.

## PENSIONS

112.215   Government employees' deferred compensation plans.
121.31    State and county officers and employees, and teachers, beginning service on or after 12/1/70; and highway patrol officers.
122.15    County officers and employees beginning service before 12/1/70, unless they elected to transfer to retirement system under Chapter 121.
175.241   Firefighters.
185.25    Police officers.
222.21    Federal government employees' pension payments needed for support and received 3 months before filing bankruptcy. Also, retirement plans under various sections of the Internal Revenue Code, including pension, profit sharing, and stock bonus plans under §401(a); annuity plans [§403(a)]; educational annuities [403(b)]; IRAs [§§408 & 408A]; and employee stock ownership plans [§409]. Also ERISA-qualified benefits.
238.15    Teachers beginning service before 12/1/70, unless they elected to transfer to retirement system under Chapter 121.

## PUBLIC BENEFITS

222.201   Public assistance and social security.
222.201 & Unemployment compensation.
443.051
222.201 & Veterans' benefits.
744.626
440.22    Workers' compensation.
769.05    Proceeds for job-related injuries under Chapter 769 relating to hazardous occupations.
960.14    Crime victims' compensation unless seeking to discharge debt for treatment of crime related injury.

## ALIMONY AND CHILD SUPPORT

222.201   Alimony and child support needed for support.

## INSURANCE

222.13    Death benefits payable to a specific beneficiary.
222.14    Annuity contract proceeds and life insurance cash surrender value.
222.18    Disability or illness benefits.
632.619   Fraternal benefit society benefits.

## MISCELLANEOUS

222.22    Funds paid to the Prepaid College Trust Fund or in a Medical Savings Account.
497.413   Funds the debtor may be entitled to from the Florida Department of Banking and Finance Preneed Funeral Contract Consumer Protection Trust Fund.
620.8501  Business partnership property.
Other     Add any applicable Federal Nonbankruptcy Exemptions.

# GEORGIA

Official Code of Georgia Annotated, Title 44, Chapter 13, Section 100 (Ga. Code Ann. §44-13-100). [Note: This is not the same set as the *Georgia Code*, which is a separate and outdated set of books.]

## HOMESTEAD
44-13-100(**) Real or personal property, including co-op, used as a residence, up to $10,000. Unused portion may be applied to any other property.

## PERSONAL PROPERTY
44-13-100     Motor vehicles up to $3,500; clothing, household goods, appliances, furnishings, books, musical instruments, animals, and crops up to $300 per item and $5,000 total; jewelry up to $500; health aids; lost future earnings recoveries needed for support; personal injury recoveries up to $10,000; wrongful death recoveries needed for support. Also, burial plot in lieu of homestead. Also, any property up to $600 plus any unused homestead amount.

## WAGES
18-4-20       Minimum 75% of earned but unpaid wages for private and federal government workers. Judge may approve more for low income debtors.

## PENSIONS
18-4-22       ERISA-qualified benefits.
47-2-332      Public employees.
44-13-100     Other pensions needed for support, and IRAs.

## PUBLIC BENEFITS
44-13-100     Unemployment compensation, veterans' benefits, social security, crime victims' compensation, and local public assistance.
49-4-35       Old age assistance.
49-4-58       Aid to blind.
49-4-84       Workers' compensation; aid to disabled.

## TOOLS OF TRADE
44-13-100     Tools, books, and implements of trade up to $1,500.

## ALIMONY AND CHILD SUPPORT
44-13-100     Alimony and child support needed for support.

## INSURANCE
44-13-100     Unmatured life insurance contract, unmatured life insurance dividends, interest, loan value or cash value up to $2,000 if you or someone you depend on is beneficiary, life insurance proceeds if policy is owned by someone you depend on and is needed for support.
33-15-20      Fraternal benefit society benefits.
33-25-11      Life insurance proceeds, dividends, interest, loan, cash or surrender value, provided that beneficiary is not the insured.
33-28-7       Annuity and endowment contract benefits.
33-27-7       Group insurance.
33-26-5       Industrial life insurance policy owned by someone you depend on for support.
33-29-15      Disability or health benefits up to $250 per month.

## MISCELLANEOUS
14-8-25       Business partnership property.
Other         Add any applicable Federal Nonbankruptcy Exemptions.

# HAWAII

Hawaii Revised Statutes Annotated, Chapter 36, Title 651, Section 36-651-91 (Haw. Rev. Stat. §36-651-91). Compare Federal Bankruptcy Exemptions.

## HOMESTEAD
| | |
|---|---|
| 36-651-91 & | Up to $30,000 if head of family or over 65; up to $20,000 otherwise. Property cannot exceed 1 |
| 36-651-92 | acre (includes long-term leased land). Sale proceeds are exempt for 6 months after sale. Tenancies by the entirety are exempt without limit as to debts of one spouse [*Security Pacific Bank v. Chang*, 818 F. Supp. (D. Haw. 1993)]. |

## PERSONAL PROPERTY
| | |
|---|---|
| 20-359-104 | Down payment for home in state project. |
| 36-651-121 | Motor vehicle up to wholesale value of $2,575; clothing; appliances and furnishings needed; books; jewelry, watches, and articles of adornment up to $1,000; proceeds for sold or damaged exempt property (sale proceeds exempt for 6 months after sale); burial plot up to 250 square feet, plus on-site tombstones, monuments, and fencing. |

## WAGES
| | |
|---|---|
| 20-353-22 | Prisoner's wages held by Dept. of Public Safety. |
| 36-651-121 & | Unpaid wages due for services of the past 31 days. If more than 31 days, 95% of first $100, 90%of |
| 36-652-1 | second $100, and 80% of balance. |

## PENSIONS
| | |
|---|---|
| 7-88-91 & 36-653-3 | Public officers and employees. |
| 36-651-124 | ERISA-qualified benefits, if deposited more than 3 years before filing. |
| 7-88-169 | Police officers and firefighters. |

## PUBLIC BENEFITS
| | |
|---|---|
| 20-346-33 | Public assistance paid by Dept. of Public Safety. |
| 21-383-163 | Unemployment compensation. |
| 21-386-57 | Workers' compensation. |
| 36-653-4 | Unemployment work relief up to $60 per month. |

## TOOLS OF TRADE
| | |
|---|---|
| 36-651-121 | Tools, books, uniforms, implements, instruments, furnishings, fishing boat, nets, motor vehicle, and other personal property needed for livelihood. |

## INSURANCE
| | |
|---|---|
| 24-431:10-231 | Disability benefits. |
| 24-431:10-232 | Annuity contract or endowment policy proceeds if beneficiary is insured spouse, child or parent. |
| 24-431:10-233 | Group life insurance policy or proceeds. |
| 24-431:10-234 | Life or health insurance policy for child. |
| 24-431:10-D:112 | Life insurance proceeds if policy prohibits use to pay creditors. |
| 24-432:2-403 | Fraternal benefit society benefits. |

## MISCELLANEOUS
| | |
|---|---|
| 23-425-126 | Business partnership property. |

# IDAHO

Idaho Code, Title 55, Chapter 10, Section 55-1003 (Idaho Code §55-1003).

## HOMESTEAD (*)

| | |
|---|---|
| 55-1003 | $50,000. Sale and insurance proceeds are exempt for 1 year (55-1008). If unimproved land, or improved land, or mobile home not yet occupied, must file homestead declaration (55-1004). |

## PERSONAL PROPERTY

| | |
|---|---|
| 11-603 | Health aids; burial plot. |
| 11-604 | Personal injury and wrongful death recoveries needed for support. |
| 11-605 | Motor vehicle up to $3,000; jewelry up to $1,000; clothing, pets, appliances, furnishings, books, musical instruments, family portraits, and sentimental heirlooms up to $500 per item and $5,000 total; 1 firearm up to $500; crops cultivated by the debtor on up to 50 acres (including water rights up to 160 inches) up to $1,000; any tangible personal property up to $800. |
| 11-606 | Proceeds for damaged exempt property, for up to 3 months after received. |
| 45-514 | Building materials. |

## WAGES

| | |
|---|---|
| 11-207 | Minimum of 75% of earned but unpaid wages and pension payments. Judge may approve more for low income debtors. |

## PENSIONS

| | |
|---|---|
| 11-604 | Payments being received from pensions needed for support, provided payments are not mixed with other money. |
| 11-604A | All employee benefit plans. |
| 50-1517 | Police officers. |
| 55-1011 | ERISA-qualified benefits. |
| 59-1325 | Public employees. |
| 72-1417 | Firefighters. |

## PUBLIC BENEFITS

| | |
|---|---|
| 11-603 | Unemployment compensation, Social Security, veterans' benefits, and federal, state, and local public assistance. |
| 56-223 | General assistance, AFDC, and aid to blind, aged, and disabled. |
| 72-802 | Workers' compensation. |
| 72-1020 | Crime victims' compensation, unless debt related to injury sustained during the crime. |

## TOOLS OF TRADE

| | |
|---|---|
| 11-605 | Tools, books and implements of trade up to $1,000; arms, uniforms, and accoutrements required to be kept by peace officer, national guard, or military personnel. |

## ALIMONY AND CHILD SUPPORT

| | |
|---|---|
| 11-604 | Alimony and child support needed for support. |

## INSURANCE

| | |
|---|---|
| 11-603 | Medical or hospital care benefits. |
| 11-604 & 41-1833 & 11-605 | Unmatured life insurance contract, other than credit life insurance contract; and dividend, interest, or loan value of any unmatured life insurance contract under which the insured is the debtor or the debtor's dependent, up to $5,000. |
| 41-1834 | Death and disability benefits; life insurance if insured in not the beneficiary. |
| 41-1830 | Life insurance policy if the beneficiary is a married woman. |
| 41-1833 | Life insurance proceeds, dividends, interest, loan, cash or surrender value if the insured is not the beneficiary. |
| 41-1835 | Group life insurance benefits. |
| 41-1836 | Annuity contract proceeds up to $1,250 per month. |
| 41-1930 | Life insurance proceeds if policy prohibits use to pay creditors. |
| 41-3218 | Fraternal benefit society benefits. |

## MISCELLANEOUS

| | |
|---|---|
| 53-3-501 | Business partnership property. |

# ILLINOIS

*West's* Smith-Hurd Illinois Compiled Statutes Annotated, Chapter 735, Act 5, Article 12, Section 5/12-901 (735 ILCS 5/12-901).

### HOMESTEAD (**)
735-5/12-901    Real or personal property, including a farm, lot and buildings, condominium, co-op, or mobile home, up to $7,500. Spouse or child of deceased owner can claim homestead (735-5/12-902). Sale proceeds up to 1 year (735-5/12-906).

### PERSONAL PROPERTY
625-45/3A-7(d)    Title certificate for a boat more than 12 feet in length.

735-5/12-1001    Motor vehicle up to $1,200; clothing needed; prescribed health aids; school books; family pictures; bible; personal injury recoveries up to $7,500; wrongful death recoveries needed for support; proceeds from sale of exempt property; any other personal property up to $2,000 (including wages).

### WAGES
740-170/4    Minimum 85% of earned but unpaid wages. Judge may approve more for low income debtor.

### PENSIONS
| | | | |
|---|---|---|---|
| 40-5/2-154 | General assembly members. | | |
| 40-5/3-144 & 40-5/5-218 | Police officers. | 40-5/18-161 | Judges. |
| 40-5/4-135 & 40-5/6-213 | Firefighters. | 40-5/19-117 | House of correction |
| 40-5/7-217 & 40-5/8-244 | Municipal employees. | | employees. |
| 40-5/9-228 | County employees. | 40-5/19-218 | Public library employees. |
| 40-5/11-223 | Civil service employees. | 40-5/22-230 | Disabled firefighters, and |
| 40-5/12-190 | Park employees. | | widows and children of |
| 40-5/13-808 | Sanitation district employees. | | firefighters. |
| 40-5/14-147 | State employees. | 735-5/12-1006 | ERISA-qualified benefits; |
| 50-5/15-185 | State university employees. | | and public employees. |
| 50-5/16-190 & 40-5/17-151 | Teachers. | | |

### PUBLIC BENEFITS
305-5/11-3    AFDC; aid to blind, aged, and disabled.

820-305-21    Workers' compensation.

820-310/21    Workers' occupational disease compensation.

735-5/12-1001    Veterans' benefits; Social Security; unemployment compensation; crime victims' compensation; restitution payments for World War II relocation of Japanese Americans and Aleuts under the federal Civil Liberties Act of 1988 and the Aleution and Pribilof Island Restitution Act.

### TOOLS OF TRADE
735-5/12-1001    Tools, books, and implements of trade up to $750.

### ALIMONY AND CHILD SUPPORT
735-5/12-1001    Alimony and child support needed for support.

### INSURANCE
215-5/238    Life insurance, annuity, or cash value if beneficiary is spouse, child, parent, or other dependent; life insurance proceeds if policy prohibits use to pay creditors.

215-5/299.1a    Fraternal benefit society benefits.

735-5/12-907    Homeowners' insurance proceeds for destroyed home, up to $7,500.

735-5/12-1001    Health and disability benefits, life insurance proceeds needed for support, and life insurance policy if beneficiary is spouse or child.

### MISCELLANEOUS
805-205/25    Business partnership property.

Other    Add any applicable Federal Nonbankruptcy Exemptions.

# INDIANA

*West's* Annotated Indiana Code, Title 34, Article 55, Chapter 10, Section 2 (Ind. Code Ann. §34-55-10-2).

## HOMESTEAD
| | |
|---|---|
| 34-55-10-2 | Real or personal property used as a residence up to $7,500 (LIMIT: Homestead plus personal property cannot exceed $10,000, not including health aids); tenancies by the entirety exempt without limit unless bankruptcy is seeking to discharge debts incurred by both spouses. |

## PERSONAL PROPERTY
| | |
|---|---|
| 34-55-10-2 | Health aids; up to $4,000 of real or tangible personal property; up to $100 of intangible personal property (except for money owed to you). |

## WAGES
| | |
|---|---|
| 24-4.5-5-105 | Minimum of 75% of earned but unpaid wages. Judge may approve more for low-income debtors. |

## PENSIONS
| | |
|---|---|
| 5-10.3-8-9 | Public employees. |
| 10-1-2-9 & 36-8-8-17 | Police officers, but only as to benefits accruing. |
| 21-6.1-5-17 | State teachers. |
| 34-55-10-2 | Public or private retirement benefits. |
| 36-8-7-22 & 36-8-8-17 | Firefighters. |
| 36-8-10-19 | Sheriffs, but only benefits accruing. |

## PUBLIC BENEFITS
| | |
|---|---|
| 16-7-3.6-15 | Crime victims' compensation, unless seeking to discharge debt for treatment of crime-related injury. |
| 22-3-2-17 | Workers' compensation. |
| 22-4-33-3 | Unemployment compensation. |

## TOOLS OF TRADE
| | |
|---|---|
| 10-2-6-3 | National guard arms, uniforms, and equipment. |

## INSURANCE
| | |
|---|---|
| 27-1-12-14 | Life insurance policy or proceeds if beneficiary is spouse or dependent. |
| 27-1-12-29 | Group life insurance policy. |
| 27-2-5-1 | Life insurance proceeds if policy prohibits use to pay creditors. |
| 27-8-3-23 | Mutual life or accident policy proceeds. |
| 27-11-6-3 | Fraternal benefit society benefits. |
| 34-55-10-2 | Medical care saving accounts. |

## MISCELLANEOUS
| | |
|---|---|
| 23-4-1-25 | Business partnership property. |
| Other | Add any applicable Federal Nonbankruptcy Exemptions. |

# IOWA

Iowa Code Annotated, Section 499A.18 (Iowa Code Ann. §499A-18).

## HOMESTEAD (*)

| 499A.18 & | *If you have lived in the Iowa for at least 40 months:* Real property or apartment, unlimited in value, |
|---|---|
| 561.2 & | but cannot exceed ½ acre in a city or town, or 40 acres elsewhere. |
| 561.16 | *If you have lived in Iowa for less than 40 months:* The same provisions as above apply, except that the total amount of any homestead exemption is limited to $125,000 by federal law. |

## PERSONAL PROPERTY

627.6    Motor vehicle, musical instruments and tax refunds up to $5,000 total (but tax refund portion limited to $1,000 of the total); clothing up to $1,000, plus receptacles to hold clothing; household goods, appliances, and furnishings up to $2,000 total; wedding and engagement rings; books, portraits, paintings and pictures up to $1,000; health aids; burial plot up to 1 acre; rifle or musket; shotgun; up to $100 of any other personal property including cash.

## WAGES

642.21    Minimum of 75% of earned but unpaid wages and pension payments. Judge may approve more for low income debtors.

## PENSIONS

97A-12    Peace officers.
97B-39    Public employees.
410.11    Disabled firefighters and police officers, but only for benefits being received.
411.13    Police officers and firefighters.
627.6     Pensions needed for support, but only as to payments being received, including IRAs.
627.8     Federal government pension, but only as to payments being received.

## PUBLIC BENEFITS

627.6     Unemployment compensation, veterans' benefits, Social Security, AFDC, and local public assistance.
627.13    Workers' compensation.
627.19    Adopted child assistance.

## TOOLS OF TRADE

627.6     Nonfarming equipment up to $10,000; farming equipment, including livestock and feed, up to $10,000; but not including a car.

## ALIMONY AND CHILD SUPPORT

627.6     Alimony and child support needed for support.

## INSURANCE

508.32    Life insurance proceeds if policy prohibits use to pay creditors.
509.12    Employee group insurance policy or proceeds.
627.6     Life insurance proceeds up to $10,000, (if acquired within two years prior to filing for bankruptcy); and accident, disability, health, illness, or life proceeds, dividends, interest, loan, cash, or surrender value up to $15,000; if beneficiary is spouse, child, or other dependent.

## MISCELLANEOUS

123.38    Liquor licenses.
486A.501  Business partnership property.
Other     Add any applicable Federal Non-Bankruptcy Exemptions.

# KANSAS

Kansas Statutes Annotated, Section 60-2301 (Kan. Stat. Ann. §60-2301). You may find either *"Vernon's* Kansas Statutes Annotated," or "Kansas Statutes Annotated, Official." The most recent law will be in the supplements, which is a pocket part in *"Vernon's"* and a separate soft-cover volume in the "Official." Both have a poor index.

## HOMESTEAD
60-2301      *If you have lived in Kansas for at least 40 months:* Real property, manufactured home, or mobile home of unlimited value, but can't exceed 1 acre in a city or town, or 160 acres on a farm. You must occupy or intend to occupy the property at the time you file for bankruptcy. (Also refer to "Const. 15-9").

         *If you have lived in Kansas for less than 40 months:* The same provisions as above apply, except that the total amount of any homestead exemption is limited to $125,000 by federal law.

## PERSONAL PROPERTY
60-2304      Motor vehicle up to $20,000 (no limit if equipped or designed for a disabled person); clothing to last 1 year; household equipment and furnishings; food and fuel to last 1 year; jewelry and articles of adornment up to $1,000; burial plot.

16-310      Funeral plan prepayments.

## WAGES
60-2310      Minimum of 75% of earned but unpaid wages. Judge may approve more for low income debtor.

## PENSIONS
12-5005 &      Police officers.
13-14a10

12-5005 &      Firefighters.
14-10a10

13-14,102      Elected and appointed officials in cities with populations of between 120,000 and 200,000.

60-2308      Federal government pension needed for support and received within 3 months prior to filing bankruptcy; ERISA-qualified benefits.

72-5526      State school employees.

74-2618      Judges.

74-4923 &      Public employees.
74-49,105

74-4989      State highway patrol officers.

## PUBLIC BENEFITS
39-717      AFDC; general assistance; social welfare.

44-514      Workers' compensation.

44-718      Unemployment compensation.

74-7313      Crime victims' compensation.

## TOOLS OF TRADE
48-245      National guard uniforms, arms, and equipment.

60-2304      Equipment, instruments, furniture, books, documents, breeding stock, seed, stock, and grain up to $7,500 total.

## INSURANCE
40-258      Life insurance proceeds up to $1,000, but only if payable to the decedent's estate.

40-414      Life insurance proceeds or cash value deposited into a bank account; life insurance forfeiture value, only if policy issued over 1 year prior to filing for bankruptcy; fraternal benefit society benefits.

40-414a      Life insurance proceeds if policy prohibits use to pay creditors.

## MISCELLANEOUS
41-326      Liquor licenses.

56a-501      Business partnership property.

Other      Add any applicable Federal Nonbankruptcy Exemptions.

# KENTUCKY

Kentucky Revised Statutes, Chapter 427, Section 427.060 (Ken. Rev. Stat. §427.060).

## HOMESTEAD
427.060      Real or personal property used as a family residence up to $5,000. Sale proceeds are also exempt.

## PERSONAL PROPERTY
304.39-260   Reparation benefits received and medical expenses paid under motor vehicle reparation law.
427.010      Motor vehicle up to $2,500; health aids; clothing, furniture, jewelry, and articles of adornment up to $3,000 total.
427.060      Burial plot up to $5,000, in lieu of homestead.
427.150      Lost earnings payments needed for support; wrongful death recoveries for person you depended upon for support; personal injury recoveries up to $7,500, but not including pain, suffering, or pecuniary loss.
427.160      $1,000 of any property.

## WAGES
427.101      Minimum of 75% of earned but unpaid wages. Judge may approve more for low income debtor, but judge may set different amount in Chapter 13 bankruptcy cases.

## PENSIONS
61.690       State employees.
67A.350      Urban county government employees.
67A.620 &   Police officers and firefighters.
95.878 &
427.120 &
427.125
161.700      Teachers.
427.150      Other pensions needed for support, including IRAs.

## PUBLIC BENEFITS
205.220      AFDC; aid to blind, aged, and disabled.
341.470      Unemployment compensation.
342.180      Workers' compensation.
427.110      Cooperative life or casualty insurance benefits; fraternal benefit society benefits.
427.150      Crime victims' compensation.

## TOOLS OF TRADE
427.010      Farmer's tools, equipment, livestock, and poultry up to $3,000.
427.030      Nonfarmer's tools up to $300; motor vehicle of mechanic, mechanical or electrical equipment servicer, minister, attorney, physician, surgeon, dentist, veterinarian, or chiropractor up to $2,500.
427.040      Library, office equipment, instruments and furnishings of a minister, attorney, physician, surgeon, dentist, veterinarian, or chiropractor up to $1,000.

## ALIMONY AND CHILD SUPPORT
427.150      Alimony and child support needed for support.

## INSURANCE
304.14-300   Life insurance proceeds or cash value if beneficiary is not the insured.
304.14-310   Health or disability benefits.
304.14-320   Group life insurance proceeds.
304.14-330   Annuity contract proceeds up to $350 per month.
304.14-340   Life insurance policy if the beneficiary is a married woman.
304.14-350   Life insurance proceeds if policy prohibits use to pay creditors.

## MISCELLANEOUS
362.270      Business partnership property.
Other        Add any applicable Federal Nonbankruptcy Exemptions.

# LOUISIANA

*West's* LSA Revised Statutes, Title 20, Section 1 (La. Rev. Stat. Ann. §20:1). Be sure to use the volumes marked "Revised Statutes," except for the item under PERSONAL PROPERTY marked "Civil 223," which will be found in a volume marked *"West's* LSA Civil Code." If searching online, use the "title" and "section" numbers.

## HOMESTEAD
20:1        *If you have lived in Louisiana for at least 40 months:* Up to $25,000, but cannot exceed 5 acres if the residence in a municipality, or 200 acres if not located in a municipality. As to obligations arising directly as a result of a catastrophic or terminal illness or injury, exemption is the full value of the based on value one year before seizure. Spouse or child of deceased owner, or spouse obtaining home in divorce may also claim the exemption. (*)
            *If you have lived in Louisiana for less than 40 months:* The same provisions as above apply, except that the total amount of any homestead exemption is limited to $125,000 by federal law.

## PERSONAL PROPERTY
8:313       Cemetery plot and monuments.
13:3881     Living room, dining room, and bedroom furniture; clothing; chinaware, glassware, utensils, and silverware (but not sterling); refrigerator, freezer, stove, washer and dryer; bedding and linens; family portraits; musical instruments; heating and cooling equipment; pressing irons and sewing machine; arms and military accoutrements; poultry, fowl and 1 cow; engagement and wedding rings up to $5,000; and equipment needed for therapy. Also, property of a minor child (also cite as "Civil 223").

## WAGES
13:3881     Minimum of 75% of earned but unpaid wages. Judge may approve more for low income debtor.

## PENSIONS
13:3881     ERISA-qualified benefit contributions, if deposited more than 1 year before filing.
20:33       Gratuitous payments to employee or heirs, whenever paid.

## PUBLIC BENEFITS
23:1205     Workers' compensation.
23:1693     Unemployment compensation.
46:111      AFDC; aid to blind, aged, and disabled.
46:1811     Crime victims' compensation.

## TOOLS OF TRADE
13:3881     Tools, books, instruments, nonluxury car, pickup truck (under 3 tons), and utility trailer needed for work.

## INSURANCE
22:558      Fraternal benefit society benefits.
22:646      Health, accident or disability proceeds, dividends, interest, loan, cash or surrender value.
22:647      Life insurance proceeds, dividends, interest, loan, cash or surrender value, if policy issued within 9 months of filing, up to $35,000.
22:649      Group insurance policies or proceeds.

## MISCELLANEOUS
Other       Add any applicable Federal Nonbankruptcy Exemptions.

# MAINE

Maine Revised Statutes Annotated, Title 14, Section 4422 (14 Me, Rev. Stat. Ann. §4422).

### HOMESTEAD (**)
14-4422    $35,000 (up to $70,000 if over 60 or disabled). Includes co-op and property owned by the debtor but used as a residence by a dependent of the debtor. Proceeds for 6 months (must be reinvested in new homestead within 6 months).

### PERSONAL PROPERTY
9-A-5-103    Balance due on repossessed goods, provided total amount financed is not more than $2,000.
14-4422    Motor vehicle up to $5,000; cooking stove; furnaces and stoves for heat; food to last 6 months; fuel not to exceed 5 tons of coal, 1,000 gallons of oil, or 10 cords of wood; health aids; 1 wedding ring & 1 engagement ring; other jewelry up to $750; up to $200 per item for each of the following: household goods & furnishings, clothing, appliances, books, animals, crops, and musical instruments; lost earnings payments needed for support; feed, seed, fertilizer, tools and equipment to raise and harvest food for 1 season; wrongful death recoveries needed for support; personal injury recoveries up to $12,500, not including pain and suffering; $400 of any property. Burial plot for the debtor or a dependent of the debtor, in lieu of homestead exemption.
37-B-262    Military arms, clothes, and equipment.

### PENSIONS
3-703    Legislators.
4-1203    Judges.
5-17054    State employees.
14-4422    ERISA-qualified benefits; IRA or other "illness, disability, death, age or length of service" plan up to $15,000, needed for support.

### PUBLIC BENEFITS
14-4422    Unemployment compensation, veterans' benefits, Social Security, and crime victims' compensation.
22-3753    AFDC.
39-67    Workers' compensation.

### TOOLS OF TRADE
14-4422    Books, materials, and stock up to $5,000; 1 of each type of farm implement necessary to raise and harvest crops; 1 boat not to exceed 5 tons used in commercial fishing.

### ALIMONY AND CHILD SUPPORT
14-4422    Alimony and child support needed for support.

### INSURANCE
14-4422    Unmatured life insurance policy; life insurance policy, dividends, interest, or loan value for person you depended upon up to $4,000.
24-A-2428    Life, annuity, accident, or endowment policy, proceeds, dividends, interest, loan, cash, or surrender value.
24-A-2429    Disability or health insurance proceeds, dividends, interest, loan, cash, or surrender value.
24-A-2430    Group life or health policy or proceeds.
24-A-2431    Annuity proceeds up to $450 per month.
24-A-4118    Fraternal benefit society benefits.

### MISCELLANEOUS
14-4422    Unused homestead to $6,000 total for tools of trade, personal injury recoveries, or household goods & furnishings, clothing, appliances, books, animals, crops, and musical instruments.
31-305    Business partnership property.
Other    Add any applicable Federal Non-Bankruptcy Exemptions.

# MARYLAND

References are to the Annotated Code of Maryland, which is divided into subjects. If you are looking in the books, the subject is printed on each volume. If you are searching online, you will first come upon a list of the various subjects. The subjects which relate to bankruptcy exemptions are listed below, using the following abbreviations: "Ct. & Jud. Proc." refers to "Courts and Judicial Procedure." "Comm." refers to "Commercial Law." "Corp." refers to "Corporations and Associations." "Insur." refers to "Insurance." "Labor & Employ." refers to "Labor and Employment." "St.Pers.Pen." refers to "State Personnel and Pensions." "Estates and Trusts" is not abbreviated. The numbers are the section numbers within the designated subject. Under the "Public Benefits" section is a reference to Article 88A §88A-73, which refers to a portion of the Code of Maryland that does not have any specific subject designated. Citation examples: "Md. Code Ann. §88A-73," or "Md. Ct. & Jud. Proc. Code Ann. §11-504."

**HOMESTEAD**

Tenancies by the entirety to unlimited amount as to debts of one spouse [*In re Sefren*, 41 B.R. 747 (D. Md. 1984)]. Also see the section below on "Personal Property."

**PERSONAL PROPERTY**

Ct. & Jud. Proc. 11-504    Clothing, household goods & furnishings, appliances, books, and pets up to $1,000 total; health aids; cash or property up to $6,000; lost future earnings recoveries; and any other real or personal property up to $5,000 total.

**WAGES**

Comm. 15-601.1    Earned but unpaid wages are exempt as follows: in Caroline, Kent, Queen Annes', and Worcester counties, the greater of 75% of actual wages or 30 times the federal minimum wage; in all other counties, the greater of 75% or $145 per week.

**PENSIONS**

St.Pers.Pen. 21-503    State employees.
Ct. & Jud. Proc. 11-504    ERISA-qualified benefits, except IRAs.

**PUBLIC BENEFITS**

Labor & Employ. 8-106    Unemployment compensation.
Labor & Employ. 9-732    Workers' compensation.
Article 88A, 88A-73    AFDC; general assistance.

**TOOLS OF TRADE**

Ct. & Jud. Proc. 11-504    Tools, books, instruments, appliances, and clothing needed for work (but cannot include car), up to $5,000.

**INSURANCE**

Estates & Trusts 8-115 &    Fraternal benefit society benefts; life insurance or annuity contract proceeds, dividends,
Insur. 8-431 & 16-111    interest, loan, cash, or surrender value if beneficiary is a dependent of the insured.
Comm. 15-601.1    Medical benefits deducted from wages.
Ct. & Jud. Proc. 11-504    Disability or health benefits.

**MISCELLANEOUS**

Corp. 9A-501    Business partnership property.
Other    Add any applicable Federal Nonbankruptcy Exemptions.

# MASSACHUSETTS

Although the set of books has the title *Annotated Laws of Massachusetts*, an online search will refer to *Massachsetts General Laws* and *General Laws of Massachusetts*. The most commonly used term is *Massachusetts General Laws*, or M.G.L., such as M.G.L., Chapter 188, Section 1 (M.G.L. §188-1). Compare Federal Bankruptcy Exemptions.

## HOMESTEAD
188-1 &    *If you have lived in Massachusetts for at least 40 months:* $500,000 in "land and buildings"; if over 65
188-1A    or disabled, also applies to "manufactured home."
   *If you have lived in Massachusetts for less than 40 months:* The same provisions as above apply, except that the total amount of any homestead exemption is limited to $125,000 by federal law.
209-1    Tenancies by the entirety, regardless of value, are exempt as to the debts of one spouse, unless the debt was "incurred on account of necessaries" for either spouse or a family member.

## PERSONAL PROPERTY
79-6A    Moving expenses for eminent domain (that is, if the government took your property).
235-34    Motor vehicle up to $750; furniture up to $3,000; clothing needed; beds and bedding; heating unit; books up to $200 total; cash up to $200 per month for rent, in lieu of homestead; cash for fuel, heat, water, or electricity up to $75 per month; bank deposits to $125; cash for food or food to $300; sewing machine to $200; burial plots and tombs; church pew; 2 cows, 2 swine, 12 sheep, and 4 tons of hay. Co-op shares up to $100.
246-28A    Bank, credit union, or trust company deposits up to $500 total.

## WAGES
246-28    Earned but unpaid wages up to $125 per week.

## PENSIONS
32-19    Public employees.
32-41    Private retirement benefits.
168-41 &    Savings bank employees.
168-44
235-34A &    ERISA-qualified benefits.
246-28

## PUBLIC BENEFITS
115-5    Veterans' benefits.
118-10    AFDC.
151A-36    Unemployment compensation.
152-47    Workers' compensation.
235-34    Public assistance.

## TOOLS OF TRADE
235-34    Tools, implements and fixtures up to $500 total; materials you designed and procured up to $500; boats, nets, and fishing tackle of fisherman up to $500; arms, uniforms, and accoutrements you are required to keep.

## INSURANCE
175-110A    Disability benefits up to $400 per week.
175-119A    Life insurance proceeds if policy prohibits use to pay creditors.
175-125    Life insurance annuity contract which states it is exempt; life or endowment policy, proceeds, dividends, interest, loan, cash, or surrender value.
175-126    Life insurance policy if beneficiary is a married woman.
175-132C    Group annuity policy or proceeds.
175-135    Group life insurance policy.
175F-15    Medical malpractice self-insurance.
176-22    Fraternal benefit society benefits.

## MISCELLANEOUS
108A-25    Business partnership property.
Other    Add any applicable Federal Non-Bankruptcy Exemptions.

# MICHIGAN

Michigan Compiled Laws Annotated, Section 600.6023 (M.C.L.A. §600.6023). [NOTE: You may come across an old set of books titled Michigan Statutes Annotated (M.S.A.), which uses a different numbering system. This set is no longer being used or updated.] Compare Federal Bankruptcy Exemptions.

## HOMESTEAD
600.6023      Real property, including condominium, up to $3,500; but may not exceed 1 lot in a city, town, or village, or 40 acres elsewhere. Spouse or child of deceased owner may claim the exemption. Tenancies by the entirety are exempt without limit as to debts of one spouse [*SNB Bank & Trust* v. *Kensey*, 378 N.W.2d 594 (Mich. App. 1985)].

## PERSONAL PROPERTY
128.112       Burial plots.
600.6023      Clothing; household goods, furniture, appliances, utensils and books up to $1,000 total; food and fuel to last 6 months if head of household; building and loan association shares up to $1,000 par value, in lieu of homestead exemption; family pictures; church pew, slip or seat; 2 cows, 5 swine, 10 sheep, 5 roosters, 100 hens, and hay and grain to last 6 months if head of household.

## WAGES
600.5311      60% of earned but unpaid wages for head of household; 40% for others; subject to following minimums: $15 per week plus $2 per week for each dependent other than spouse for head of household; $10 per week for others.

## PENSIONS
38.40         State employees.
38.559        Police officers and firefighters.
38.826        Judges.
38.927        Probate judges.
38.1057       Legislators.
38.1346       Public school employees.
600.6023      IRAs, to extent tax-deferred; ERISA-qualified benefits.

## PUBLIC BENEFITS
18.362        Crime victims' compensation.
35.1027       Vietnam veterans' benefits.
35.926        Veterans' benefits for WWII veterans.
35.977        Korean War veterans' benefits.
330.1158a     AFDC.
400.63        Social welfare benefits.
418.821       Workers' compensation.
421.30        Unemployment compensation.

## TOOLS OF TRADE
600.6023      Tools, implements, materials, stock, apparatus, motor vehicle, horse, team and harness up to $1,000 total; arms and accoutrements you are required to keep.

## INSURANCE
500.2207      Life insurance proceeds, dividends, interest, loan, cash, or surrender value; life or endowment proceeds if beneficiary is spouse or child of insured.
500.2209      Life insurance proceeds up to $300 per year if the beneficiary is a married woman or a husband.
500.4054      Life, annuity, or endowment proceeds if policy or contract prohibits use to pay creditors.
500.8046      Fraternal benefit society benefits.
600.6023      Disability, mutual life, or health benefits.

## MISCELLANEOUS
449.25        Business partnership property.
Other         Add any applicable Federal Nonbankruptcy Exemptions.

# MINNESOTA

Minnesota Statutes Annotated, Section 510.01 (Minn. Stat. Ann. §510.01). [NOTE: Some courts have held "unlimited" exemptions invalid as state constitution only allows for "reasonable" exemptions; see *In re Tveten*, 402 N.W.2d 551 (Minn. 1987).] Be sure to check the Cumulative Annual Pocket Part, as amounts are required to be adjusted periodically. Compare Federal Bankruptcy Exemptions.

## HOMESTEAD

| | |
|---|---|
| 510.01 &<br>510.02 &<br>550.37 | *If you have lived in Minnesota for at least 40 months:* Real property, mobile or manufacturer home up to $200,000 ($500,000 if used primarily for agriculture), but cannot exceed ½ acre in "the laid out or platted portion of" a city or 160 acres elsewhere. Sale and insurance proceeds for 1 year.<br>*If you have lived in Minnesota for less than 40 months:* The same provisions as above apply, except that the total amount of any homestead exemption is limited to $125,000 by federal law. |

## PERSONAL PROPERTY

| | |
|---|---|
| 550.37 | Motor vehicle up to $2,000 ($20,000 if modified for disability at a cost of at least $1,500); clothing, including watch; furniture, appliances, radio, TV, and phonographs, up to $4,500 total; food and utensils; books and musical instruments; burial plot; church pew or seat; proceeds for damaged or destroyed exempt property; personal injury lost earnings, and wrongful death recoveries. |

## WAGES

| | |
|---|---|
| 550.37 | Wages deposited into bank accounts for 20 days after deposit; earned but unpaid wages paid within 6 months of returning to work if you previously received welfare; wages of released inmates paid received within 6 months of release. |
| 571.55 | Minimum of 75% of earned but unpaid wages. Judge may approve more for low income debtor. |
| 550.37 | Earnings of a minor child. |

## PENSIONS

| | | | |
|---|---|---|---|
| 181B.16 | Private retirement benefits accruing. | 550.37 | ERISA-qualified benefits, including IRAs, needed for support, up to $51,000 present value. |
| 352.15 | State employees. | | |
| 352B.071 | State troopers. | | |
| 353.15 | Public employees. | | |
| 354.10 &<br>354A.11 | Teachers. | | |

## PUBLIC BENEFITS

| | |
|---|---|
| 176.175 | Workers' compensation. |
| 268.17 | Unemployment compensation. |
| 550.37 | AFDC, supplemental security income (SSI), general assistance, supplemental assistance. |
| 550.38 | Veterans' benefits. |
| 611A.60 | Crime victims' compensation. |

## TOOLS OF TRADE

| | |
|---|---|
| 550.37 | Tools, library, furniture, machines, instruments, implements and stock in trade up to $5,000; farm machines, implements, livestock, produce and crops of farmers up to $13,000. (Total of these cannot exceed $13,000.) Teaching materials of a school teacher, including books and chemical apparatus, of unlimited value and not subject to $13,000 limit. |

## INSURANCE

| | |
|---|---|
| 61A.04 | Life insurance proceeds if policy prohibits use to pay creditors. |
| 61A.12 | Life insurance or endowment proceeds, dividends, interest, loan, cash, or surrender value if the insured is not the beneficiary. |
| 64B.18 | Fraternal benefit society benefits. |
| 550.37 | Life insurance proceeds if beneficiary is spouse or child, up to $20,000 plus additional $5,000 per dependent; unmatured life insurance contract dividends, interest, loan, cash, or surrender value if insured is the debtor or someone the debtor depends upon up to $4,000; police, fire, or beneficiary association benefits. |
| 550.39 | Accident or disability proceeds. |

## MISCELLANEOUS

| | |
|---|---|
| 323A.0501 | Business partnership property. |
| Other | Add any applicable Federal Nonbankruptcy Exemptions. |

# MISSISSIPPI

Mississippi Code 1972 Annotated, Title 85, Section 85-3-21 (Miss. Code Ann. §85-3-21).

## HOMESTEAD
| | |
|---|---|
| 85-3-21 & 85-3-23 | $75,000, but cannot exceed 160 acres. Must occupy at time of filing bankruptcy, unless you are wid owed or over 60 and married or widowed. Sale proceeds are also exempt. |

## PERSONAL PROPERTY
| | |
|---|---|
| 85-3-1 | Clothing, furniture, appliances, 1 radio and 1 television, 1 firearm, 1 lawn mower, linens, china, crockery, kitchenware, and personal effects (including wedding rings) of the debtor and depend ents, but not works of art, other electronic entertainment equipment, jewelry (other than wedding rings), and items acquired as antiques; books; animals; crops; motor vehicles; cash on hand; health aids; and any item of tangible personal property worth less than $200; proceeds from exempt property. |
| 85-3-17 | Personal injury judgments up to $10,000. |

## WAGES
| | |
|---|---|
| 85-3-4 | Earned but unpaid wages owed for 30 days, 75% after 30 days. |

## PENSIONS
| | |
|---|---|
| 21-29-257 | Police officers and firefighters. |
| 25-11-129 | Public employees retirement and disability benefits. |
| 25-11-201-23 | Teachers. |
| 25-13-31 | Highway patrol officers. |
| 25-14-5 | State employees. |
| 71-1-43 | Private retirement benefits. |
| 85-3-1 | IRAs, Keoghs, and ERISA-qualified benefits, if deposited more than 1 year before filing. |

## PUBLIC BENEFITS
| | |
|---|---|
| 25-11-129 | Social Security. |
| 43-3-71 | Assistance to blind. |
| 43-9-19 | Assistance to aged. |
| 43-29-15 | Assistance to disabled. |
| 71-3-43 | Workers' compensation. |
| 71-5-539 | Unemployment compensation. |
| 99-41-23 | Crime victims' compensation. |

## INSURANCE
| | |
|---|---|
| 83-7-5 | Life insurance proceeds if policy prohibits use to pay creditors. |
| 83-29-39 | Fraternal benefit society benefits. |
| 85-3-1 | Disability benefits. |
| 85-3-11 | Life insurance policy or proceeds up to $50,000. |
| 85-3-13 | Life insurance proceeds if beneficiary is the decedent's estate, up to $5,000. |
| 85-3-23 | Homeowners' insurance proceeds up to $75,000. |

## MISCELLANEOUS
| | |
|---|---|
| 79-12-49 | Business partnership property. |
| Other | Add any applicable Federal Nonbankruptcy Exemptions. |

# MISSOURI

*Vernon's* Annotated Missouri Statutes, Chapter 513, Section 513.430 (Mo. Rev. Stat. §513.430).

## HOMESTEAD
| | |
|---|---|
| 513.430 & | Real property up to $15,000, or mobile home up to $1,000. Tenancies by the entirety are exempt without |
| 513.475 | limit as to debts of one spouse [*In re Anderson*, 12 B.R. 483 (W.D. Mo. 1981)].(*) |

## PERSONAL PROPERTY
| | |
|---|---|
| 214.190 | Burial grounds up to $100 or 1 acre. |
| 513.430 | Motor vehicle up to $1,000; clothing, household goods, appliances, furnishings, books, animals, musical instruments and crops up to $1,000 total; health aids; jewelry up to $500; wrongful death recoveries for a person you depended upon. |
| 513.430 & 513.440 | Any property up to $1,250 plus $250 per child for head of family; up to $400 for others. |
| Other | Personal injury causes of action. Refer to as: "*In re Mitchell*, 73 B.R. 93". |

## WAGES
| | |
|---|---|
| 513.470 | Wages of a servant or common laborer up to $90. |
| 525.030 | Minimum of 75% of earned but unpaid wages. Judge may approve more for low income debtor. 90% for head of family. |

## PENSIONS
| | |
|---|---|
| 70.695 | Public officers and employees. |
| 71.207 | Employees of cities with more than 100,000 population. |
| 86.190 & 86.353 & 86.493 & 86.780 | Police department employees. |
| 87.090 & 87.365 & 87.485 | Firefighters. |
| 104.250 | Highway and transportation employees. |
| 104.540 | State employees. |
| 169.090 | Teachers. |
| 513.430 | ERISA-qualified benefits needed for support; life insurance dividends, loan value, or interest, up to $5,000, if bought more than 6 months before filing. |

## PUBLIC BENEFITS
| | |
|---|---|
| 287.260 | Workers' compensation. |
| 288.380 & 513.430 | Unemployment compensation. |
| 513.430 | Social Security, veterans' benefits, and AFDC. |

## TOOLS OF TRADE
| | |
|---|---|
| 513.430 | Tools, books, and implements to $2,000. |

## ALIMONY AND CHILD SUPPORT
| | |
|---|---|
| 513.430 | Alimony and child support up to $500 per month. |

## INSURANCE
| | |
|---|---|
| 376.530 & 376.560 | Life insurance proceeds if policy owned by woman insuring her husband. |
| 376.550 | Life insurance proceeds if policy owned by an unmarried woman and beneficiary is her father or brother. |
| 377.090 | Fraternal benefit society benefits, up to $5,000, if bought more than 6 months before filing. |
| 377.330 | Assessment or stipulated premium proceeds. |
| 513.430 | Death, disability, or illness benefits needed for support; unmatured life insurance policy. |

## MISCELLANEOUS
| | |
|---|---|
| 358.250 | Business partnership property. |
| Other | Add any applicable Federal Nonbankruptcy Exemptions. |

# MONTANA

Montana Code Annotated, Title 70, Chapter 32, Part 1, Section 70-32-101 (Mont. Code Ann. §70-32-101).

## HOMESTEAD
70-32-101 &   Real property or mobile home up to $100,000. Must occupy at time of filing for bankruptcy, and must
70-32-104 &   record a homestead declaration before filing (70-32-106 & 107). Proceeds for 18 months (70-32-216).
70-32-201

## PERSONAL PROPERTY
25-13-608    Health aids; burial plot.
25-13-609    Motor vehicle up to $2,500; clothing, household goods and furnishings, appliances, jewelry, books, animals and feed, musical instruments, firearms, sporting goods, and crops up to $600 per item and $4,500 total.
25-13-610    Proceeds for damaged or lost exempt property for 6 months after receipt.
35-15-404    Cooperative association shares up to $500 value.

## WAGES
25-13-614    Minimum of 75% of earned but unpaid wages. Judge may approve more for low income debtor.

## PENSIONS
| | | | |
|---|---|---|---|
| 19-3-105 | Public employees. | 19-9-1006 & 19-10-504 | Police officers. |
| 19-4-706 | Teachers. | 19-11-612 & 19-13-1004 | Firefighters. |
| 19-5-704 | Judges. | 19-21-212 | University system employees. |
| 19-6-705 | Highway patrol officers. | 31-2-106 | ERISA-qualified benefits in excess of |
| 19-7-705 | Sheriffs. | | 15% of annual income, if deposited at |
| 19-8-805 | Game wardens. | | least 1 year before filing. |

## PUBLIC BENEFITS
25-13-608    Social Security, veterans', & local public assistance benefits.
39-71-743    Workers' compensation.
39-73-110    Silicosis benefits.
39-51-3105    Unemployment compensation.
53-2-607    AFDC, aid to aged and disabled, vocational rehabilitation to the blind, subsidized adoption payments.
53-9-129    Crime victims' compensation.

## TOOLS OF TRADE
25-13-609    Tools, books, and instruments of trade up to $3,000.
25-13-613    Arms, uniforms, and accoutrements needed to carry out government functions.

## ALIMONY AND CHILD SUPPORT
25-13-608    Alimony and child support.

## INSURANCE
25-13-608 &   Disability or illness proceeds, benefits, dividends, interest, loan, cash, or surrender value, and medical or
33-15-513    hospital benefits.
25-13-609    Unmatured life insurance contracts up to $4,000.
33-7-511    Fraternal benefit society benefits.
33-15-511    Life insurance proceeds, dividends, interest, loan, cash, or surrender value.
33-15-512    Group life insurance policy or proceeds.
33-15-514    Annuity contract proceeds up to $350 per month.
33-20-120    Life insurance proceeds if policy prohibits use to pay creditors.
80-2-245    Hail insurance benefits.

## MISCELLANEOUS
35-10-508    Business partnership property.
Other    Add any applicable Federal Nonbankruptcy Exemptions.

# NEBRASKA

Revised Statutes of Nebraska, Chapter 40, Section 101 (Neb. Rev. Stat. §40-101).

## HOMESTEAD
| | |
|---|---|
| 40-101 | $12,500, but cannot exceed 2 lots in a city or 160 acres elsewhere. Sale proceeds are exempt for 6 months (40-113). |

## PERSONAL PROPERTY
| | |
|---|---|
| 12-511 | Perpetual care funds. |
| 12-517 | Burial plot. |
| 12-605 | Tombs, crypts, lots, niches, and vaults. |
| 25-1552 | $2,500 of any property except wages, in lieu of homestead. |
| 25-1556 | Personal possessions; clothing needed; furniture and kitchen utensils up to $1,500; food and fuel to last 6 months. |
| 25-1563 | Recovery for personal injuries. |

## WAGES
| | |
|---|---|
| 25-1558 | Minimum of 85% of earned but unpaid wages or pension payments for head of family; 75% for others. Judge may approve more for low income debtor. |

## PENSIONS
| | |
|---|---|
| 23-2322 | County employees. |
| 25-1559 | Military disability benefits up to $2,000. |
| 25-1563-01 | ERISA-qualified benefits needed for support. |
| 79-1060 & 79-1552 | School employees. |
| 84-1324 | State employees. |

## PUBLIC BENEFITS
| | |
|---|---|
| 48-149 | Workers' compensation. |
| 48-647 | Unemployment compensation. |
| 68-1013 | AFDC; aid to blind, aged, and disabled. |

## TOOLS OF TRADE
| | |
|---|---|
| 25-1556 | Tools or equipment up to $2,400. (**) (Can include motor vehicle used for work or to commute to and from workplace.) |

## INSURANCE
| | |
|---|---|
| 44-371 | Life insurance or annuity contract proceeds up to $10,000 loan value. |
| 44-754 | Disability benefits to $200 per month. |
| 44-1089 | Fraternal benefit society benefits up to loan value of $10,000. |

## MISCELLANEOUS
| | |
|---|---|
| 67-427 | Business partnership property. |
| Other | Add any applicable Federal Nonbankruptcy Exemptions. |

# NEVADA

Nevada Revised Statutes Annotated, Chapter 21, Section 21-090(m) [Nev. Rev. Stat. §21-090(m)].

## HOMESTEAD (*)

21.090(m) & *If you have lived in Nevada for at least 40 months:* Real property or mobile home up to $200,000. Must
115.010    record a homestead declaration before filing for bankruptcy (115.020).

*If you have lived in Nevada for less than 40 months:* The same provisions as above apply, except that the total amount of any homestead exemption is limited to $125,000 by federal law.

## PERSONAL PROPERTY

21.090    Motor vehicle up to $15,000 (no limit if equipped for the disabled); household goods, furniture, home and yard equipment up to $10,000 total; books up to $1,500 total; pictures and keepsakes; health aids; 1 gun.

21.100    Metal-bearing ores, geological specimens, paleontological remains or art curiosities (must be arranged, classified, catalogued, and numbered in reference books).

452.550    Burial plot purchase money held in trust.

689.700    Funeral service contract money held in trust.

## WAGES

21.090    Minimum of 75% of earned but unpaid wages. Judge may approve more for low income debtor.

## PENSIONS

21.090    Up to $500,000 in an IRA, or retirement plans under various sections of the Internal Revenue Code, including simplified employee pension plan under 26 USC §408, cash or deferred arrangement plan, or a trust forming part of a stock bonus, pension, or profit-sharing plan under 26 USC §§401 et seq.

286.670    Public employees.

## PUBLIC BENEFITS

422.291    AFDC; aid to blind, aged and disabled.

612.710    Unemployment compensation.

615.270    Vocational rehabilitation benefits.

616.550    Industrial insurance (worker's compensation).

## TOOLS OF TRADE

21.090    Tools, materials, library, equipment, and supplies up to $4,500; farm trucks, equipment, tools, stock and seed up to $4,500; cabin or dwelling of a miner or prospector, cars, implements and appliances for mining and a mining claim you work up to $4,500; arms, uniforms, and accoutrements you are required to keep.

## INSURANCE

21.090    Life insurance policy or proceeds if premiums don't exceed $1,000 per year.

687B.260    Life insurance proceeds if you are not insured.

687B.270    Health insurance proceeds, dividends, interest, loan, cash, or surrender value.

687B.280    Group life or health policy or proceeds.

687B.290    Annuity contract proceeds up to $350 per month.

695A.220    Fraternal benefit society benefits.

## MISCELLANEOUS

87.250    Business partnership property.

Other    Add any applicable Federal Nonbankruptcy Exemptions.

# NEW HAMPSHIRE

New Hampshire Revised Statutes Annotated, Chapter 480, Section 480:1 (N.H. Rev. Stat. Ann. §480:1).

## HOMESTEAD
480:1         Real property, or manufactured home, up to $100,000.

## PERSONAL PROPERTY
511:2         (1) clothing; (2) beds, bedsteads, and bedding; (3) furniture up to $3,500; (4) one refrigerator, cooking stove, and heating stove, and utensils for each; (5) sewing machine; (6) provisions and fuel up to $400; (7) books up to $800; (8) 1 hog and 1 pig, or pork if already slaughtered; (9) 6 sheep and their fleeces; (10) 1 cow, 1 yoke of oxen or a horse (if needed for farming, etc.), and hay up to 4 tons; (11) domestic fowls up to $300; (12) church pew; (13) automobile up to $4,000; (14) jewelry up to $500; and (15) any property up to $1,000. Also up to $7,000 in any property for any unused amounts allowed for items (3), (6), (7), (13), (14), and tools of trade.
512:21        Proceeds for lost or destroyed exempt property.

## WAGES
512:21        Earned but unpaid wages of debtor and spouse (judge determines amount exempt based on percent of federal minimum wage, so claim all); jury and witness fees; wages of a minor child.

## PENSIONS
100A:26       Public employees.
102:23        Firefighters.
103:18        Police officers.
512:21        Federally created pensions accruing.

## PUBLIC BENEFITS
167:25        AFDC; aid to blind, aged, and disabled.
281A:52       Workers' compensation.
282A:159      Unemployment compensation.

## TOOLS OF TRADE
511:2         Tools of trade up to $5,000; arms, uniforms, and equipment of a military member; 1 yoke of oxen or horse needed for farming or teaming.

## ALIMONY AND CHILD SUPPORT
161C:11       Child support only.

## INSURANCE
402:69        Firefighters' aid insurance.
408:1         Life insurance or endowment proceeds if beneficiary is a married woman.
408:2         Life insurance or endowment proceeds if you are not the insured.
418:24        Fraternal benefit society benefits.
512:21        Homeowners' insurance proceeds up to $5,000.

## MISCELLANEOUS
304A:25       Business partnership property.
Other         Add any applicable Federal Nonbankruptcy Exemptions.

# NEW JERSEY

New Jersey Statutes Annotated, Title 2A, Chapter 17, Section 2A-17-19 (N.J. Stat. Ann. §2A-17-19). Compare Federal Bankruptcy Exemptions.

## PERSONAL PROPERTY
| | |
|---|---|
| 2A:17-19 | Clothing; goods, personal property, and stock or interest in corporations up to $1,000 total. |
| 2A:26-4 | Household good and furniture up to $1,000. |
| 8A:5-10 | Burial plots. |

## WAGES
| | |
|---|---|
| 2A:17-56 | 90% of earned but unpaid wages if your income is less than $7,500; otherwise judge may exempt less. |
| 38A:4-8 | Military personnel wages and allowances. |

## PENSIONS
| | |
|---|---|
| A:057.6 | Civil defense workers. |
| 18A:66-51 | Teachers. |
| 18A:66-116 | School district employees. |
| 43:6A-41 | Judges. |
| 43:7-13 | Prison employees. |
| 43:8A-20 | Alcohol beverage control officers. |
| 43:10-57 & 43:10-105 | County employees. |
| 43-13-9 | ERISA-qualified benefits. |
| 43:13-44 | Municipal employees. |
| 43:15A-55 | Public employees. |
| 43:16-7 & 43:16A-17 | Police officers, firefighters, and traffic officers. |
| 43:18-12 | City boards of health employees. |
| 43:19-17 | Street and water department employees. |
| 53:5A-45 | State police. |

## PUBLIC BENEFITS
| | |
|---|---|
| 34:15-29 | Workers' compensation. |
| 43:21-53 | Unemployment compensation. |
| 44:7-35 | Old-age, permanent disability assistance. |
| 52:4B-30 | Crime victims' compensation. |

## INSURANCE
| | |
|---|---|
| A:9-57.6 | Civil defense workers' disability, death, medical, or hospital benefits. |
| 17:18-12 & 17B:24-8 | Health and disability benefits. |
| 17:44A-19 | Fraternal benefit society benefits. |
| 17B:24-6 | Life insurance proceeds, dividends, interest, loan, cash, or surrender value, if insured. |
| 17B:24-7 | Annuity contract proceeds up to $500 per month. |
| 17B:24-9 | Group life or health policy or proceeds. |
| 17B:24-10 | Life insurance proceeds if policy prohibits use to pay creditors. |
| 38A:4-8 | Military member disability or death benefits. |

## MISCELLANEOUS
| | |
|---|---|
| 42:1A-27 | Business partnership property. |
| Other | Add any applicable Federal Nonbankruptcy Exemptions. |

# NEW MEXICO

New Mexico Statutes 1978 Annotated, Chapter 42, Section 42-10-9 (N.M. Stat. Ann. §42-10-9). Compare Federal Bankruptcy Exemptions.

**HOMESTEAD** (\*\*)

| | |
|---|---|
| 42-10-9 | $30,000; includes "dwelling house" being purchased or leased (even if land on which it sits is owned by another). |

**PERSONAL PROPERTY**

| | |
|---|---|
| 42-10-1 | Motor vehicle up to $4,000; $500 of any property. |
| 42-10-1 & 42-10-2 | Clothing; jewelry up to $2,500; books, furniture, and health equipment. |
| 42-10-10 | $2,000 of any property, in lieu of homestead. |
| 48-2-15 | Building materials. |
| 53-4-28 | Minimum amount of shares needed for membership in cooperative association. |
| 70-4-12 | Tools, machinery and materials needed to dig, drill, torpedo, complete, operate or repair an oil line, gas well or pipeline. |

**WAGES**

| | |
|---|---|
| 35-12-7 | Minimum of 75% of earned but unpaid wages. Judge may approve more for low income debtor. |

**PENSIONS**

| | |
|---|---|
| 22-11-42 | Public school employees. |
| 42-10-1 & 42-10-2 | Pension or retirement benefits. |

**PUBLIC BENEFITS**

| | |
|---|---|
| 27-2-21 | AFDC; general assistance. |
| 31-22-15 | Crime victims' compensation (this will be repealed effective 7/1/06). |
| 51-1-37 | Unemployment compensation. |
| 52-1-52 | Workers' compensation. |
| 52-3-37 | Occupational disease disablement benefits. |

**TOOLS OF TRADE**

| | |
|---|---|
| 42-10-1 & 42-10-2 | $1,500. |

**INSURANCE**

| | |
|---|---|
| 42-10-3 | Life, accident, health or annuity benefits or cash value, if beneficiary is a citizen of New Mexico. |
| 42-10-4 | Benevolent association benefits up to $5,000. |
| 42-10-5 | Life insurance proceeds. |
| 59A-44-18 | Fraternal benefit society benefits. |

**MISCELLANEOUS**

| | |
|---|---|
| 53-10-2 | Ownership in an unincorporated association. |
| 54-1A-501 | Business partnership property. |
| Other | Add any applicable Federal Nonbankruptcy Exemptions. |

# NEW YORK

References of numbers only are to *McKinney's* Consolidated Laws of New York, Civil Practice Law and Rules, Section 5206 (C.P.L.R. §5206). Other references are to "Debtor & Creditor" (D&C); "Estates, Powers & Trusts" (Est, Pow & Tr.); "Insurance" (Insur.); "Retirement & Social Security" (Ret. & Soc. Sec.); "Partnership" (Part.); and "Unconsolidated" (Unc.).

### HOMESTEAD

| | |
|---|---|
| 5206 | Real property, including mobile home, condominium, or co-op, up to $10,000.(**) |

### PERSONAL PROPERTY

| | |
|---|---|
| 5205 | Clothing, furniture, refrigerator, television, radio, sewing machine, security deposits with landlord or utility company, tableware, cooking utensils and crockery, stoves with food and fuel to last 60 days, health aids (including animals with food), church pew or seat, wedding ring, bible, schoolbooks, pictures; books up to $50; burial plot without a structure to ¼ acre; domestic animals with food to $450; watch to $35; trust fund principal; 90% of trust fund income. |
| D & C282 | Motor vehicle up to $2,400; lost earnings recoveries needed for support; personal injury recoveries up to $7,500, not including pain and suffering; wrongful death recoveries for a person you depended upon for support. |
| D & C283 | IN LIEU OF HOMESTEAD: Cash in the lesser amount of $2,500, or an amount when added to an annuity equals $5,000. |

### WAGES

| | |
|---|---|
| 5205 | 90% of earned but unpaid wages received within 60 days of filing for bankruptcy; 90% of earnings from milk sales to milk dealers; 100% for a few militia members. |

### PENSIONS

| | |
|---|---|
| 5205 & D & C 282 | ERISA-qualified plans, Keoghs and IRAs needed for support. |
| Insur. 4607 | Public retirement benefits. |
| Ret. & Soc. Sec. 110 | State employees. |
| Unc. 5711-o | Village police officers. |

### PUBLIC BENEFITS

| | |
|---|---|
| D & C 282 | Unemployment benefits; veterans' benefits; Social Security; AFDC; aid to blind, aged, and disabled; crime victims' compensation; home relief; local public assistance. |

### TOOLS OF TRADE

| | |
|---|---|
| 5205 | Professional furniture, books, instruments, farm machinery, team and food for 60 days, up to $600 total; arms, swords, uniforms, equipment, horse, emblem and medal of a military member. |

### ALIMONY AND CHILD SUPPORT

| | |
|---|---|
| D & C282 | Alimony and child support needed for support. |

### INSURANCE

| | |
|---|---|
| 5205 | Insurance proceeds for damaged exempt property. |
| 5205; D & C 283 | Annuity contract benefits up to $5,000, if purchased within 6 months of filing for bankruptcy and not tax-deferred. |
| Est, Pow & Tr. 7-1.5 | Life insurance proceeds if policy prohibits use to pay creditors. |
| Insur. 3212 | Fraternal benefit society benefits; disability or illness benefits up to $400 per month; life insurance proceeds, dividends, interest, loan, cash, or surrender value if beneficiary is not the insured. |

### MISCELLANEOUS

| | |
|---|---|
| Part. 51 | Business partnership property. |
| Other | Add any applicable Federal Nonbankruptcy Exemptions. |

# NORTH CAROLINA

General Statutes of North Carolina, Chapter 1C, Section 1C-1601 (N.C. Gen. Stat. §1C-1601).

## HOMESTEAD
1C-1601    Real or personal property used as a residence, including co-op, up to $10,000. Tenancies by the entirety exempt without limit as to debts of one spouse [*In re Crouch*, 33 B.R. 271 (E.D. N.C. 1983)].

## PERSONAL PROPERTY
1C-1601    Motor vehicle up to $1,500; health aids; clothing, household goods, furnishings, appliances, books, animals, musical instruments and crops up to $3,500 total, plus additional $750 per dependent up to $3,000 total; personal injury and wrongful death recoveries for a person you depended upon; $3,500 of any property, less any amount claimed for homestead or burial plot.
1C-1601    Burial plot up to $10,000, in lieu of homestead.
1C-1601    $3,500 of any property, less any amount claimed for homestead or burial plot.

## WAGES
1-362    Earned but unpaid wages received 60 days before filing for bankruptcy.

## PENSIONS
58-86-90    Firefighters and rescue squad workers.
120-4.29    Legislators.
128-31    Municipal, city, and county employees.
135-9 & 135-95    Teachers and state employees.
143-166.30    Law enforcement officers.

## PUBLIC BENEFITS
15B-17    Crime victims' compensation.
96-17    Unemployment compensation.
97-21    Workers' compensation.
108A-36    AFDC; special adult assistance.
111-18    Aid to blind.

## TOOLS OF TRADE
1C-1601    Tools, books, and implements of trade up to $750.

## INSURANCE
Const.10-5    Life insurance policy if beneficiary is insured spouse or child.
58-58-115    Life insurance proceeds, dividends, interest, loan, cash, or surrender value.
58-58-165    Group life insurance policy or proceeds.
58-58-165    Employee group life policy or proceeds.
58-24-85    Fraternal benefit society benefits.

## MISCELLANEOUS
59-55    Business partnership property.
Other    Add any applicable Federal Nonbankruptcy Exemptions.

# NORTH DAKOTA

North Dakota Century Code Annotated, Chapter 28-22, Section 28-22-02 (N.D. Cent. Code §28-22-02).

## HOMESTEAD
28-22-02      Real property, mobile home, or house trailer up to $80,000.
47-18-01

## PERSONAL PROPERTY
The following list applies to all debtors:

28-22-02      Clothing; fuel to last 1 year; bible; books up to $100; family pictures; church pew; burial plots; crops or grain raised on the debtor's tract of land, limited to 1 tract of 160 acres.

28-22-03.1      Motor vehicle up to $1,200 ($32,000 if modified for a physically disabled person at a cost of at least $1,500); personal injury recoveries not including pain and suffering, up to $7,500; wrongful death recoveries up to $7,500.

28-22-03.1      IN LIEU OF HOMESTEAD: cash to $7,500.

The following list applies to the head of household, not claiming crops or grain:

28-22-03      $5,000 of any personal property; OR

28-22-04      Furniture and bedding up to $1,000; books and musical instruments up to $1,500; tools and library of a professional up to $1,000; tools of a mechanic and stock in trade up to $1,000; and farm implements and livestock up to $4,500.

The following list applies to a non-head of household not claiming crops:

28-22-05      $2,500 of any personal property.

## WAGES
32-09.1-.03      Minimum of 75% of earned but unpaid wages. Judge may approve more for low income debtor.

## PENSIONS
28-22-03.1      Disabled veterans' benefits (does not include military retirement pay); annuities, pensions, IRAs, Keoghs, simplified employee plans (together with the insurance exemption under this section total may not exceed $200,000, although no limit if needed for support).

28-22-19      Public employees.

## PUBLIC BENEFITS
28-22-03.1      Social Security.
28-22-19      AFDC; crime victims' compensation.
37-25-07      Vietnam veterans' adjustment compensation.
52-06-30      Unemployment compensation.
65-05-29      Workers' compensation.

## TOOLS OF TRADE
     See Personal Property section.

## INSURANCE
26.1-15.1-18 &      Fraternal benefit society benefits.
26.1-33-40

26.1-33-40      Life insurance proceeds payable to the decedent's estate.

28-22-03.1      Life insurance surrender value to $100,000 per policy if beneficiary is relative of the insured and policy was owned for more than 1 year before filing for bankruptcy. Together with pension exemption in this section, total cannot exceed $200,000, or $100,000 per plan, but no limit if needed for support.

## MISCELLANEOUS
45-17-01      Business partnership property.
Other      Add any applicable Federal Nonbankruptcy Exemptions.

# OHIO

*Page's* Ohio Revised Code, Title 23, Section 2329.66 (Ohio Rev. Code §2329.66).

**HOMESTEAD**

| | |
|---|---|
| 2329.66 | Real or personal property used as a residence up to $5,000. Tenancies by the entirety are exempt without limit as to debts of one spouse [*In re Thomas*, 14 B.R. 423 (N.D. Ohio 1981)]. |

**PERSONAL PROPERTY**

| | |
|---|---|
| 517.09 & 2329.66 | Burial plot. |
| 2329.66 | (1) motor vehicle up to $1,000; (2) clothing, beds and bedding up to $200 per item; (3) cooking unit and refrigerator up to $300 each; (4) cash, bank, and security deposits, tax refund and money due within 90 days up to $400 total (may include earnings not otherwise exempt); (5) household goods, furnishings, appliances, jewelry, books, animals, musical instruments, firearms, hunting and fishing equipment and crops up to $200 per item (see LIMIT below); (6) jewelry, up to $400 for one piece and up to $200 for each other piece (see LIMIT below); (7) health aids; (8) wrongful death recoveries for person you depended upon for support; (9) compensation for lost future earnings needed for support; (10) personal injury recoveries not including pain and suffering up to $5,000; and (11) $400 of any property. LIMIT: If homestead is not claimed, items under (5) and (6) may not exceed $2,000 total ($1,500 if homestead is claimed). **NOTE:** Section 2329.66 is relatively detailed and complex, so be sure to read it. |

**WAGES**

| | |
|---|---|
| 2329.66 | Minimum of 75% of earned but unpaid wages. Judge may approve more for low income debtor. |

**PENSIONS**

| | |
|---|---|
| 145.56 | Public employees. |
| 146.13 | Volunteer firefighters' dependents. |
| 742.47 | Police officers and firefighters. |
| 2329.66 | Police officers' and firefighters' death benefits; ERISA-qualified benefits, IRAs and Keoghs needed for support. |
| 3307.71 & 3309.66 | Public school employees. |
| 5505.22 | State highway patrol employees. |

**PUBLIC BENEFITS**

| | | | |
|---|---|---|---|
| 2329.66 & 4123.67 | Workers' compensation. | 2329.66 & 5115.07 | Disability assistance. |
| 2329.66 & 4141.32 | Unemployment compensation. | 2743.66 | Crime victims' compensation. |
| 2329.66 & 5107.12 | AFDC. | 3304.19 | Vocational rehabilitation benefits. |

**TOOLS OF TRADE**

| | |
|---|---|
| 147.04 | Seal and official register of a notary public. |
| 2329.66 | Tools, books, and implements of trade up to $750. |

**ALIMONY AND CHILD SUPPORT**

| | |
|---|---|
| 2329.66 | Alimony and child support needed for support. |

**INSURANCE**

| | |
|---|---|
| 2329.63 & 2329.66 | Benevolent society benefits to $5,000. |
| 2329.66 & 3917.05 | Group life insurance policy or proceeds. |
| 2329.66 & 3921.18 | Fraternal benefit society benefits. |
| 2329.66 & 3923.19 | Disability benefits to $600 per month. |
| 3911.10 | Life, endowment or annuity contract dividends, interest, loan, cash, or surrender value for your spouse, child or other dependent. |
| 3911.12 | Life insurance proceeds for spouse. |
| 3911.14 | Life insurance proceeds if policy prohibits use to pay creditors. |

**MISCELLANEOUS**

| | |
|---|---|
| 1775.24 & 2329.66 | Business partnership property. |
| Other | Add any applicable Federal Nonbankruptcy Exemptions. |

# OKLAHOMA

Oklahoma Statutes Annotated, Title 31, Section 2 (Okla. Stat. tit 31, §2).

## HOMESTEAD

31-2    *If you have lived in Oklahoma for at least 40 months:* Real property or manufactured home of unlimited value, but cannot exceed 160 acres if not in a city or town, or 1 acre in a city or town. Can be 160 acres if property was annexed by a city or town on or after 11/1/97. Can be more than one parcel. You do not need to occupy the home as long as you do not acquire another. May be limited to $5,000 if more than 25% of area of improvements is used for business purposes.
*If you have lived in Oklahoma for less than 40 months:* The same provisions as above apply, except that the total amount of any homestead exemption is limited to $125,000 by federal law.

## PERSONAL PROPERTY

8-7     Burial plots.
31-1    Motor vehicle up to $3,000; clothing up to $4,000; furniture, books, portraits, pictures, gun and health aids; food to last 1 year; 2 bridles and 2 saddles; 100 chickens, 20 sheep, 10 hogs, 5 cows and calves under 6 months, 2 horses and forage for livestock to last 1 year; personal injury, workers' compensation and wrongful death recoveries (not to include punitive damages) up to $50,000 total.

## WAGES

12-1171.1 &    75% of wages earned within 90 days prior to filing bankruptcy. Judge may approve more if you can show
31-1           hardship.

## PENSIONS

| | | | |
|---|---|---|---|
| 11-49-126 | Firefighters. | 31-7 | Disabled veterans. |
| 11-50-124 | Police officers. | 47-2-303.3 | Law enforcement employees. |
| 19-959 | County employees. | 60-328 | Tax exempt benefits. |
| 31-1 | ERISA-qualified benefits. | 70-17-109 | Teachers. |

## PUBLIC BENEFITS

21-142.13    Crime victims' compensation.
40-2-303     Unemployment compensation.
56-173       AFDC; Social Security.
85-48        Workers' compensation.

## TOOLS OF TRADE

31-1    Tools, books, apparatus of trade, and husbandry implements to farm homestead, up to $5,000 total.

## ALIMONY AND CHILD SUPPORT

31-1    Alimony and child support.

## INSURANCE

36-2410    Assessment or mutual benefits.
36-2510    Limited stock insurance benefits.
36-2720    Fraternal benefit society benefits.
36-3631    Life insurance policy or proceeds if you are not the insured.
36-3632    Group life insurance policy or proceeds if you are not the insured.
36-6125    Funeral benefits if pre-paid and placed in trust.

## MISCELLANEOUS

54-1-501    Business partnership property.
Other       Add any applicable Federal Nonbankruptcy Exemptions.

# OREGON

Oregon Revised Statutes Annotated, Chapter 18, Section 18.428 (Or. Rev. Stat. §18.428). All exemptions may be doubled by husband and wife [*In re Wilson*, 22 B.R. 146 (D. Ore. 1982)].

**HOMESTEAD**

| | |
|---|---|
| 18.428 & | Real property, houseboat, or mobile home on land you own up to $25,000 ($33,000 if joint owners). Mobile |
| 18.402 & | home on land you don't own, $23,000 ($30,000 if joint). Property may not exceed 1 block in a city or town, |
| 18.395160 | or acres elsewhere. Must occupy or intend to at time of filing. Sale proceeds exempt 1 year if plan to purchase another home. |

**PERSONAL PROPERTY**

| | |
|---|---|
| 18.345 | Motor vehicle to $1,700(**); clothing, jewelry, personal items to $1,800 total(**); household items, furniture, utensils, TVs and radios to $3,000 total; health aids; cash for sold exempt property; books, pictures & musical instruments to $600 total(**); food & fuel to last 60 days if debtor is householder; domestic animals & poultry with food to last 60 days to $1,000; lost earnings payments for debtor or someone debtor depended upon needed for support(**); personal injury recoveries (not pain and suffering) to $7,500(**); $400 of any personal property (can't be used to increase an existing exemption). |
| 18.348 | Bank deposits up to $7,500, and cash for sold exempt items. |
| 18.364 | Pistol; rifle or shotgun if owned by person over the age of 16, up to $1,000. |
| 65.870 | Burial plot. |

**WAGES**

| | |
|---|---|
| 18.385 | Minimum of 75% of earned but unpaid wages. Judge may approve more for low income debtor. |
| 292.070 | Wages withheld in a state employee's bond saving account. |

**PENSIONS**

| | |
|---|---|
| 18.358 | Federal, state or local government employees. ERISA-qualified benefits, if deposited at least 1 year before filing (IRAs, but not Keoghs). |
| 237.201 | Public officers and employees. |
| 239.261 | School district employees. |

**PUBLIC BENEFITS**

| | | | |
|---|---|---|---|
| 18.345 & 147.325 | Crime victims' compensation (**). | 413.610 | Old-age assistance. |
| 344.580 | Vocational rehabilitation. | 414.095 | Medical assistance. |
| 401.405 | Civil and disaster relief. | 418.040 | AFDC. |
| 411.760 | General assistance. | 655.530 | Injured inmates benefits. |
| 412.115 | Aid to blind. | 656.234 | Workers' compensation. |
| 412.610 | Aid to disabled. | 657.855 | Unemployment compensation. |

**TOOLS OF TRADE**

| | |
|---|---|
| 18.345 | Tools, implements, apparatus, team, harness, or library, up to $3,000 total (**). |

**ALIMONY AND CHILD SUPPORT**

| | |
|---|---|
| 18.345 | Alimony and child support needed to support. |

**INSURANCE**

| | |
|---|---|
| 732.240 | Life insurance proceeds if policy prohibits use to pay creditors. |
| 743.046 | Life insurance proceeds or cash value if you are not the insured. |
| 743.047 | Group life insurance policy or proceeds. |
| 743.049 | Annuity contract benefits up to $500 per month. |
| 743.050 | Health or disability insurance proceeds, dividends, interest, loan, cash, or surrender value. |
| 748.225 | Fraternal benefit society benefits. |

**MISCELLANEOUS**

| | |
|---|---|
| 67.190 | Business partnership property. |
| 471.301 | Liquor licenses. |
| Other | Add any applicable Federal Nonbankruptcy Exemptions. |

# PENNSYLVANIA

*Purdon's* Pennsylvania Consolidated Statutes Annotated, Title 42, Section 8123 (42 Pa. Cons. Stat. Ann. §8123). Compare Federal Bankruptcy Exemptions.

### HOMESTEAD
None, but tenancies by the entirety are exempt without limit as to debts of one spouse [*In re McCormick*, 18 B.R. 911 (W.D. Pa. 1982)].

### PERSONAL PROPERTY
| | |
|---|---|
| 42-8123 | $300 of any property. |
| 42-8124 | Clothing, bibles, school books, sewing machines, uniform, and accoutrements. |
| 42-8125 | Tangible personal property at an international exhibition sponsored by the U.S. government. |

### WAGES
| | |
|---|---|
| 42-8127 | Earned but unpaid wages. |

### PENSIONS
| | |
|---|---|
| 16-4716 | County employees. |
| 24-8533 & 42-8124 | Public school employees. |
| 42-8124 | Private retirement benefits if plan provides benefits are not assignable; and self-employment retirement or annuity funds. Also plans under the following sections of the Internal Revenue Code: §401(a); annuity plans [§403(a)]; educational annuities [§403(b)]; IRAs [§408]; and employee stock ownership plans [§409]; upto $15,000 per year deposited and if deposited at least 1 year before filing. |
| 53-764 & 53-776 & 53-23666 | Police officers. |
| 42-8124 & 53-881.115 | Municipal employees. |
| 53-13445 & 53-23572 & 53-39383 | City employees. |
| 42-8124 & 71-5953 | State employees. |

### PUBLIC BENEFITS
| | |
|---|---|
| 42-8124 | Workers' compensation. |
| 43-863 | Unemployment compensation. |
| 51-20012 | Veterans' benefits. |
| 51-20098 | Korean conflict veterans' benefits. |
| 71-180-7.10 | Crime victims' compensation. |

### INSURANCE
| | |
|---|---|
| 42-8124 | Fraternal benefit society benefits; insurance or annuity payments up to $100 per month; annuity or life insurance proceeds retained by insurer at maturity or otherwise if policy provides such proceeds are not assignable; group insurance policy or proceeds; annuity or life insurance proceeds if beneficiary is decedent's spouse, child, or other dependent relative; accident or disability insurance proceeds; no-fault automobile insurance proceeds. |

### MISCELLANEOUS
| | |
|---|---|
| 15-8342 | Business partnership property. |
| Other | Add any applicable Federal Nonbankruptcy Exemptions. |

# RHODE ISLAND

General Laws of Rhode Island, Title 9, Section 9-26-4.1 (R.I. Gen. Laws §9-26-4.1). Compare Federal Bankruptcy Exemptions.

## HOMESTEAD

9-26-4.1    *If you have lived in Rhode Island for at least 40 months:* $150,000.

            *If you have lived in Rhode Island for less than 40 months:* Homestead exemption is limited to $125,000 by federal law.

## PERSONAL PROPERTY

7-8-25     Consumer cooperative association holdings up to $50.

9-26-3     Body of a deceased person.

9-26-4     All motor vehicles up to $10,000 total; clothing needed; furniture and family stores of a housekeeper, beds and bedding, up to $8,600 total; jewelry up to $1,000 total; books up to $300 total; burial plot; debt owed to you which is secured by a promissory note or bill of exchange; and prepaid tuition accounts.

## WAGES

9-26-4     Earned but unpaid wages up to $50; wages of spouse; earned but unpaid wages of a seaman, or if you have received welfare during the year prior to filing for bankruptcy; wages paid to the poor by a charitable organization; earnings of a minor child.

30-7-9     Earned but unpaid wages of a military member on active duty.

## PENSIONS

9-26-4     ERISA-qualified benefits.

9-26-5     Police officers and firefighters.

28-17-4    Private employees.

36-10-34   State and municipal employees.

## PUBLIC BENEFITS

28-33-27   Workers' compensation.

28-41-32   State disability benefits.

28-44-58   Unemployment compensation.

30-7-9     Veterans' disability or survivor benefits.

40-6-14    AFDC; general assistance; aid to blind, aged, and disabled.

## TOOLS OF TRADE

9-26-4     Working tools up to $1,200; library of a professional in practice.

## INSURANCE

27-4-11    Life insurance proceeds, dividends, interest, loan, cash or surrender value if beneficiary is not the insured.

27-4-12    Life insurance proceeds if policy prohibits use to pay creditors.

27-18-24   Accident or illness proceeds, benefits, dividends, interest, loan, cash, or surrender value.

27-25-18   Fraternal benefit society benefits.

28-41-32   Temporary disability insurance.

## MISCELLANEOUS

7-12-36    Business partnership property.

Other      Add any applicable Federal Nonbankruptcy Exemptions.

# SOUTH CAROLINA

Code of Laws of South Carolina, Title 15, Section 15-41-30 (S.C. Code §15-41-30).

## HOMESTEAD
15-41-30    Real property, personal property used as homestead (mobile home), or co-op, up to $5,000. (**)

## PERSONAL PROPERTY
15-41-30    Motor vehicle up to $1,200; clothing, household goods, furnishings, appliances, books, musical instruments, animals and crops up to $2,500 total; jewelry up to $500; health aids; personal injury and wrongful death recoveries.

15-41-30    IN LIEU OF HOMESTEAD: Burial plot up to $5,000.(**)

15-41-30    IN LIEU OF HOMESTEAD AND BURIAL PLOT: Cash and other liquid assets up to $1,000.

## PENSIONS
9-1-1680    Public employees.
9-8-190    Judges and solicitors.
9-9-180    General assembly members.
9-11-270    Police officers.
9-13-230    Firefighters.
15-41-30    ERISA-qualified benefits.

## PUBLIC BENEFITS
15-41-30    Unemployment compensation; Social Security; veterans' benefits.
15-41-30 &    Crime victims' compensation.
16-3-1300
42-9-360    Workers' compensation.
43-5-190    AFDC; general relief; aid to blind, aged, and disabled.

## TOOLS OF TRADE
15-41-30    Tools, books, and implements of trade up to $750 total.

## ALIMONY AND CHILD SUPPORT
15-41-30    Alimony and child support.

## INSURANCE
15-41-30    Unmatured life insurance contract (but a credit insurance policy is not exempt); disability or illness benefits; life insurance proceeds from a policy for a person you depended upon which is needed for support; life insurance dividends, interest, loan, cash, or surrender value from a policy for a person you depended upon up to $4,000.

38-37-870    Fraternal benefit society benefits.
38-63-40    Life insurance proceeds for a spouse or child up to $25,000.
38-63-50    Life insurance proceeds if policy prohibits use to pay creditors.

## MISCELLANEOUS
33-41-720    Business partnership property.
Other    Add any applicable Federal Nonbankruptcy Exemptions.

# SOUTH DAKOTA

South Dakota Codified Laws, Title 43, Chapter 31, Section 43-31-1 (S.D. Codified Laws §43-31-1).

## HOMESTEAD
43-31-1 &
43-31-2 &
43-31-5

*If you have lived in South Dakota for at least 40 months:* Real property, including mobile home if larger than 240 square feet and registered in the State at least 6 months prior to filing bankruptcy, of unlimited value; but cannot exceed 1 acre in a town or 160 acres elsewhere. Sale proceed sare exempt for 1 year after sale up to $30,000 (of unlimited value if you are an unmarried widow or widower, or are over 70). Spouse or child of a deceased owner may also claim exemption. Cannot include gold or silver mine, mill, or smelter.

*If you have lived in South Dakota for less than 40 months:* The same provisions as above apply, except that the total amount of any homestead exemption is limited to $125,000 by federal law.

## PERSONAL PROPERTY
43-45-2      All debtors may claim clothing; food and fuel to last 1 year; bible; books up to $200; pictures; church pew; burial plot; all property in South Dakota if judgment is in favor of any state for failure to pay that state's income tax on benefits received from a pension or other retirement plan while the judgment debtor was a resident of South Dakota.

43-45-4      $4,000 of any personal property; $6,000 if head of family.

## WAGES
15-20-12     Earned wages owing 60 days prior to filing for bankruptcy, needed for support.

24-8-10      Wages of prisoners in work programs.

## PENSIONS
3-12-115     Public employees.

9-16-47      City employees.

## PUBLIC BENEFITS
28-7-16      AFDC.

61-6-28      Unemployment compensation.

62-4-42      Workers' compensation.

## TOOLS OF TRADE
See Personal Property.

## INSURANCE
43-45-6      Life insurance proceeds if beneficiary is surviving spouse or child up to $10,000.

58-12-4      Health benefits up to $20,000; endowment or life insurance policy, proceeds or cash value up to $20,000 (*).

58-12-8      Annuity contract proceeds up to $250 per month.

58-15-70     Life insurance proceeds if policy prohibits use to pay creditors.

58-37-68     Fraternal benefit society benefits.

## MISCELLANEOUS
48-7A-501    Business partnership property.

Other        Add any applicable Federal Nonbankruptcy Exemptions.

# TENNESSEE

Tennessee Code Annotated, Title 26, Section 26-2-301 (Tenn. Code Ann. §26-2-301).

## HOMESTEAD
26-2-301      $5,000; $7,500 for joint owners. Tenancies by the entirety are exempt without limit as to debts of one spouse [*In re Arango*, 136 B.R. 740; affirmed 992 F.2d 611 (6th Cir. 1993)]. Spouse or child of deceased owner may claim. May also claim a life estate or a 2 to 15 year lease.

## PERSONAL PROPERTY
26-2-103      $4,000 of any personal property.

26-2-104      Clothing and storage containers; schools books, pictures, portraits, and bible.

26-2-111      Health aids; lost earnings payments for yourself or a person you depended upon; personal injury recoveries, not including pain and suffering, up to $7,500; wrongful death recoveries up to $10,000 (LIMIT: total of personal injury claims, wrongful death claims, and crime victims' compensation cannot exceed $15,000).

26-2-305 &    Burial plot up to 1 acre.
46-2-102

## WAGES
26-2-106 &    Minimum of 75% of earned but unpaid wages, plus $2.50 per week per child. Judge may approve more
26-2-107      for low income debtor.

## PENSIONS
8-36-111      Public employees.

26-2-105      State and local government employees.

26-2-111      ERISA-qualified benefits.

45-9-909      Teachers.

## PUBLIC BENEFITS
26-2-111      Unemployment compensation; veterans' benefits; Social Security; local public assistance, and Families First program benefits.

26-2-111 &    Crime victims' compensation up to $5,000, but see" LIMIT" under Personal Property above.
29-13-111

50-6-223      Workers' compensation.

71-2-216      Old-age assistance.

71-3-121      AFDC.

71-4-117      Aid to blind.

71-4-1112     Aid to disabled.

## TOOLS OF TRADE
26-2-111      Tools, books, and implements of trade up to $1,900.

## ALIMONY AND CHILD SUPPORT
26-2-111      Alimony and child support which is owed for at least 30 days prior to filing for bankruptcy.

## INSURANCE
26-2-110      Disability, accident or health benefits, for a resident and citizen of Tennessee.

26-2-111      Disability or illness benefits.

26-2-304      Homeowners' insurance proceeds up to $5,000.

56-7-201      Life insurance proceeds or cash value if beneficiary is the debtor's spouse, child, or other dependent.

56-25-208     Fraternal benefit society benefits.

## MISCELLANEOUS
61-1-501      Business partnership property.

Other         Add any applicable Federal Nonbankruptcy Exemptions.

# TEXAS

There are two sets of books that contain the Texas laws. One is called *Vernon's* Texas Civil Statutes, and is arranged by section number. The other is called *Vernon's* Texas Codes Annotated, and is divided into subjects, such as "Property," Insurance," "Human Resources," etc. The references given below that begin with just a number are references to the Civil Statutes (such as "110B-21.005"). The references that begin with a word are references to the subject volume or volumes of the Codes (such as "Prop. 41.001"). Compare Federal Bankruptcy Exemptions.

## HOMESTEAD

| | |
|---|---|
| Prop. 41.001 & Prop. 41.002 | *If you have lived in Texas for at least 40 months:* Unlimited amount, but cannot exceed 1 acre in a city, town, or village, or 100 acres (200 acres for family) elsewhere. Sale proceeds are exempt for 6 months after sale. You need not occupy at filing, as long as you do not acquire another home. |
| | *If you have lived in Texas for less than 40 months:* The same provisions as above apply, except that the total amount of any homestead exemption is limited to $125,000 by federal law. |

## PERSONAL PROPERTY

| | |
|---|---|
| Prop. 41.001 | Burial plots. |
| Prop. 42.001 | Prescribed health aids. |
| Prop. 42.002 | Home furnishings, including family heirlooms; food; clothing; jewelry up to 25% of the "SPECIAL LIMIT" stated below; 2 firearms; athletic & sporting equipment (includes bicycles); 1 motor vehicle for each adult with drivers license or who relies on another to operate a vehicle; 2 horses, mules, or donkeys, with saddle, blanket & bridle for each; 12 head cattle; 60 head other livestock; 120 fowl; food on hand for these animals; and household pets. SPECIAL LIMIT: Total of all items under Property 42.002 (including tools of trade and cash value of life insurance) cannot exceed $30,000 total ($60,000 for head of family). |

## WAGES

| | |
|---|---|
| Prop. 42.001 | Current wages for personal services; and unpaid commissions for personal services up to 25% of the "SPECIAL LIMIT" stated above. |

## PENSIONS

| | | | |
|---|---|---|---|
| 110B-21.005 | State employees. | 6243d-1 & 6243j & 6243g-1 | Police officers. |
| 110B-31.005 | Teachers. | 6243e & 6243e.1 & 6243e.2 | Firefighters. |
| 110B-41.004 | Judges. | 6243g & 110B-61.006 | Municipal employees. |
| 110B-51.006 | County and district employees. | Prop. 42.0021 | Church benefits; ERISA-qualified retirement benefits to extent tax-deferred, including IRAs, Keoghs, and simplified employee plans. |
| 6228f | Law enforcement officers' survivors. | | |

## PUBLIC BENEFITS

| | | | |
|---|---|---|---|
| 5221b-13 | Unemployment compensation. | Hum.Res. 31.040 | AFDC. |
| 8306-3 | Workers' compensation. | Hum.Res. 32.036 | Medical assistance. |
| 8309-1 | Crime victims' compensation. | | |

## TOOLS OF TRADE

| | |
|---|---|
| Prop. 42.002 | Tools, books, and equipment, including motor vehicles and boats used in trade or profession; and farming or ranching vehicles and implements. |

## INSURANCE

| | |
|---|---|
| Insur. 3.50-2 | Texas employee uniform group insurance. |
| Insur. 3.50-3 | Texas state college or university employee benefits. |
| Insur. 3.50-4 | Retired public school employees group insurance. |
| Insur. 10.28 | Fraternal benefit society benefits. |
| Insur. 21.22 | Life, health, accident or annuity benefits; life insurance proceeds if policy prohibits use to pay creditors. |
| Prop. 42.002 | Life insurance cash value if beneficiary is debtor or family member. |

## MISCELLANEOUS

| | |
|---|---|
| 6132b-2.04 | Business partnership property. |
| Other | Add any applicable Federal Nonbankruptcy Exemptions. |

# UTAH

Utah Code Annotated 1953, Title 78, Chapter 23, Section 78-23-3 (Utah Code Ann. §78-23-3).

## HOMESTEAD(**)
78-23-3     Real property or mobile home (land may not exceed 1 acre), up to $5,000 if some or all of property is not debtor's primary personal residence; up to $20,000 if all of property is debtor's primary personal residence. May be claimed on more than one parcel. Proceeds of sale exempt for 1 year. Water rights and interests, in the form of corporate stock or otherwise, are exempt to extent they are necessarily employed in supplying water to the homestead for domestic and irrigating purposes.

## PERSONAL PROPERTY
78-23-5     Clothing, except furs and jewelry; refrigerator, freezer, stove, microwave oven, washer, dryer, and sewing machine; health aids; food to last 12 months; beds and bedding; carpets; artwork done by, or depicting, a family member, if not part of trade or business; burial plot; personal injury recoveries for yourself or a person you depend upon; wrongful death recoveries for a person you depended upon; any form of disability, illness or unemployment benefits.
78-23-8     Sofas, chairs, and related furnishings for one household up to $500; dining and kitchen tables and chairs for one household up to $500; animals, books, and musical instruments up to $500; heirlooms or other items of sentimental value up to $500.
78-23-9     Proceeds for damaged personal property.

## WAGES
70C-7-103     Minimum of 75% of earned but unpaid wages. Judge may approve more for low income debtor.

## PENSIONS
49-1-609     Public employees.
78-23-5     ERISA-qualified benefits.
78-23-6     Any pension needed for support.

## PUBLIC BENEFITS
35-1-80     Workers' compensation.
35-2-35     Occupational disease disability benefits.
35-4-18     Unemployment compensation.
55-15-32     AFDC; general assistance.
63-63-21     Crime victims' compensation.
78-23-5     Veterans' benefits.

## TOOLS OF TRADE
39-1-47     Military property of a national guard member.
78-23-8     Motor vehicle used in business or trade up to $2,500 (does not qualify if only used for transportation to and from work); tools, books, and implements of trade up to $3,500.

## ALIMONY AND CHILD SUPPORT
78-23-5     Child support.
78-23-6     Alimony needed for support.

## INSURANCE
31A-9-603     Fraternal benefit society benefits.
78-23-5     Disability, illness, medical or hospital benefits.
78-23-6     Life insurance proceeds if beneficiary is insured's spouse or other dependent, needed for support.
78-23-7     Life insurance policy cash surrender value up to $5,000.

## MISCELLANEOUS
48-1-22     Business partnership property.
Other     Add any applicable Federal Nonbankruptcy Exemptions.

# VERMONT

Vermont Statutes Annotated, Title 27, Section 101 (27 V.S.A. §101). [Note: Online, you will find laws listed first by Title, then Chapter, then Section. You will need to use trial and error to figure the "Chapter" number that contains the section you want. For example you will find section 27 V.S.A. §101 under "Chapter 3," 12 V.S.A. §2740 under "Chapter 111," and 11 V.S.A. §3241 under "Chapter 22."] Compare Federal Bankruptcy Exemptions.

## HOMESTEAD

27-101     $75,000. May include outbuildings, rents, issues, and profits. Spouse of deceased owner may claim (27 V.S.A. §105). Tenancies by the entirety are exempt without limit as to debts of one spouse [*In re McQueen*, 21 B.R. 736 (D. Ver. 1982)].

## PERSONAL PROPERTY

12-2740     Motor vehicles up to $2,500; clothing, goods, furnishings, appliances, books, musical instruments, animals and crops up to $2,500 total; refrigerator, stove, freezer, water heater, heating unit and sewing machines; health aids; bank deposits up to $700; wedding ring; jewelry up to $500; 500 gallons of oil, 5 tons of coal or 10 cords of firewood; 500 gallons of bottled gas; lost future earnings for yourself or a person you depended upon; personal injury and wrongful death recoveries for a person you depended upon; 1 cow, 10 sheep, 10 chickens, 3 swarms of bees, and feed to last 1 winter; 1 yoke of oxen or steers, 2 horses, 2 harnesses, 2 halters, 2 chains, 1 plow and 1 ox yoke; growing crops up to $5,000.

12-2740     $400 of any property; plus $7,000, less any amount claimed for clothing, goods, furnishings, appliances, books, musical instruments, animals, crops, motor vehicle, jewelry, tools of trade and growing crops, of any property.

## WAGES

12-3170     Minimum of 75% of earned but unpaid wages (judge may approve more for low income debtor); all wages if you received welfare during the 2 months prior to filing for bankruptcy.

## PENSIONS

3-476     State employees.
12-2740     Self-directed accounts, including IRAs and Keoghs, up to $10,000; other pensions.
16-1946     Teachers.
24-5066     Municipal employees.

## PUBLIC BENEFITS

12-2740     Veterans' benefits, Social Security, and crime victims' compensation needed for support.
21-681     Workers' compensation.
21-1376     Unemployment compensation.
33-2575     AFDC; general assistance; aid to blind, aged, and disabled.

## TOOLS OF TRADE

12-2740     Tools and books of trade up to $5,000.

## ALIMONY AND CHILD SUPPORT

12-2740     Alimony and child support needed for support.

## INSURANCE

8-3705     Life insurance proceeds if policy prohibits use to pay creditors.
8-3706     Life insurance proceeds if insured is not the beneficiary.
8-3708     Group life or health benefits.
8-3709     Annuity contract benefits up to $350 per month.
8-4086     Health benefits up to $200 per month.
8-4478     Fraternal benefit society benefits.
12-2740     Unmatured life insurance contract (but not credit insurance policy); disability or illness benefits needed for support; life insurance proceeds for a person you depended upon.

## MISCELLANEOUS

11-3241     Business partnership property.
Other     Add any applicable Federal Nonbankruptcy Exemptions.

# VIRGINIA

Code of Virginia 1950, Title 34, Section 34-4 (Va. Code. §34-4).

## HOMESTEAD (**)

34-4    $5,000 [$7,000 for veterans with a 40% V.A.-rated service connected disability (34-4.1)], plus $500 per dependent. Tenancies by the entirety are exempt without limitation as to debts of one spouse [*In re Harris*, 155 B.R. 948 (E.D.Va. 1993)]. Includes rents and profits (34-18). Sale proceeds are exempt (34-20). Must file homestead declaration prior to filing for bankruptcy (34-6).

## PERSONAL PROPERTY

34-4.1    $2,000 of any property of a disabled veteran who is a householder.

34-13    Unused homestead.

34-26    ONLY IF YOU ARE A HOUSEHOLDER YOU MAY CLAIM: Motor vehicle up to $2,000; wearing apparel up to $1,000; household furnishings up to $5,000; family portraits and heirlooms up to $5,000; burial plot and preneed funeral contract up to $5,000; wedding and engagement rings, family Bible; animals owned as pets, provided they are not raised for sale or profit; and medically prescribed health aids.

34-13    IN LIEU OF HOMESTEAD: $5,000 of any personal property.

## WAGES

34-29    Minimum of 75% of earned but unpaid wages or pension payments. Judge may approve more for low income debtor.

## PENSIONS

51-111.15    State employees.

51-127.7    County employees.

51-180    Judges.

## PUBLIC BENEFITS

19.2-368.12    Crime victims' compensation, unless seeking to discharge debt for treatment of crime-related injury.

60.2-600    Unemployment compensation.

63.1-88    AFDC; general relief; aid to blind, aged, and disabled.

65.1-82    Workers' compensation.

## TOOLS OF TRADE

Anyone May Claim:

44-96    Arms, uniforms and equipment of a military member.

If You Are a Householder You May Also Claim:

34-26    Tools, books, instruments, implements, equipment, and machines, including motor vehicles, vessels, and aircraft, necessary for use in occupation or trade up to $10,000.

34-27    For farmer: tractor, wagon, cart, horses, pair of mules with gear up to $3,000; fertilizer, 2 plows, harvest cradle, 2 iron wedges, pitchfork and rake, up to $1,000.

## INSURANCE

38.2-3122    Life insurance proceeds, dividends, interest, loan, cash, or surrender value if beneficiary is not the insured.

38.2-3123    If you are a householder, life insurance cash values up to $10,000.

38.2-3339    Group life insurance policy or proceeds.

38.2-3549    Accident, sickness or industrial sick benefits.

38.2-3811    Cooperative life insurance benefits.

38.2-4021    Burial society benefits.

38.2-4118    Fraternal benefit society benefits.

51-111.67:8    Group life or accident insurance for government officials.

## MISCELLANEOUS

50-73.105    Business partnership property.

Other    Add any applicable Federal Nonbankruptcy Exemptions.

# WASHINGTON

*West's* Revised Code of Washington Annotated, Title 6, Chapter 6.13, Section 6.13.010 (Wash. Rev. Code Ann. §6-13-010). Compare Federal Bankruptcy Exemptions.

**HOMESTEAD** (*)

6.13.010    Real property or mobile home up to $40,000 [no limit on exemption if you are seeking to discharge a debt based on another state's claim of failure to pay that state income tax on pension or retirement benefits you received while a resident of Washington (6.13.030)]. If property is unimproved or unoccupied at time of filing bankruptcy, you must file a homestead declaration.

**PERSONAL PROPERTY**

6.15.010    2 motor vehicles up to $2,500 (**); clothing, but furs, jewelry & ornaments limited to $1,000 per individual; household goods, furniture, appliances, food, fuel, home and yard equipment up to $2,700 ($3,000 for husband and wife); pictures and keepsakes; private libraries up to $1,500; health aids; $2,000 of any other personal property, but not more than $200 of it in cash, bank deposits, stocks, bonds, or other securities; and personal injury awards up to $16,150.

68.20.120    Burial plots if sold by a nonprofit cemetery association.

**WAGES**

6.27.150    Minimum of 75% of earned but unpaid wages. Judge may approve more for low income debtor.

**PENSIONS**

6.15.020    Federal employees; ERISA-qualified benefits, including IRAs.
41.24.240    Volunteer firefighters.
41.28.200    City employees.
41.40.380    Public employees.
43.43.310    State patrol officers.

**PUBLIC BENEFITS**

7.68.070 &    Crime victims' compensation.
51.32.040
50.40.020    Unemployment compensation.
51.32.040    Industrial insurance (workers' compensation).
74.04.280    General assistance.
74.08.210    Old-age assistance.
74.13.070    AFDC.

**TOOLS OF TRADE**

6.15.010    Tools and materials used in another person's trade up to $5,000; library, office furniture, equipment and supplies of a physician, surgeon, attorney, clergyman or other professional up to $5,000; farm trucks, tools, equipment, supplies, stock and seed of a farmer up to $5,000.

**ALIMONY AND CHILD SUPPORT**

6.15.010    Past due, current, or future child support.

**INSURANCE**

6.15.030    Insurance proceeds for destroyed exempt property.
46.18.400    Disability benefits, proceeds, dividends, interest, loan, cash, or surrender value.
46.18.410    Life insurance proceeds, dividends, interest, loan, cash, or surrender value if the insured is not the beneficiary.
46.18.420    Group life insurance policy or proceeds.
46.18.430    Annuity contract proceeds up to $250 per month.
48.36A.180    Fraternal benefit society benefits.

**MISCELLANEOUS**

25.05.200    Business partnership property.
Other    Add any applicable Federal Nonbankruptcy Exemptions.

# WEST VIRGINIA

West Virginia Code, Chapter 38, Article 10, Section 38-10-4 (W.Va. Code §38-10-4).

## HOMESTEAD
| | |
|---|---|
| 38-10-4 | Real or personal property used as a residence up to $25,000. Unused portion may be applied to any other property. For physicians in certain circumstances limit is $250,000. |

## PERSONAL PROPERTY
| | |
|---|---|
| 38-10-4 | Motor vehicle up to $2,400; clothing, household goods, furnishings, appliances, books, musical instruments, animals and crops up to $400 per item, and $8,000 total; jewelry up to $1,000; health aids; lost earnings payments needed for support; personal injury recoveries, not including pain and suffering, up to $7,500; wrongful death recoveries for a person you depended upon needed for support; $800 of any property. |
| 38-10-4 | $7,900, less amount of homestead claimed, of any property. |
| 38-10-4 | Burial plot up to $25,000, in lieu of homestead. |

## WAGES
| | |
|---|---|
| 38-5A-3 | 80% of earned but unpaid wages. Judge may approve more for low income debtor. |

## PENSIONS
| | |
|---|---|
| 5-10-46 | Public employees. |
| 18-7A-30 | Teachers. |
| 38-10-4 | ERISA-qualified benefits needed for support. |

## PUBLIC BENEFITS
| | |
|---|---|
| 9-5-1 | AFDC; general assistance; aid to blind, aged, and disabled. |
| 14-2A-24 & 38-10-4 | Crime victims' compensation. |
| 23-4-18 | Workers' compensation. |
| 38-10-4 | Unemployment compensation; veterans' benefits; Social Security. |

## TOOLS OF TRADE
| | |
|---|---|
| 38-4-10 | Tools, books and implements of trade up to $1,500. |

## ALIMONY AND CHILD SUPPORT
| | |
|---|---|
| 38-10-4 | Alimony and child support needed for support. |

## INSURANCE
| | |
|---|---|
| 33-6-27 | Life insurance proceeds unless you are policy owner and beneficiary. |
| 33-6-28 | Group life insurance policy and proceeds. |
| 33-23-21 | Fraternal benefit society benefits. |
| 38-10-4 | Unmatured life insurance contract (except for credit life insurance contract); health or disability benefits; life insurance dividends, interest, loan, cash, or surrender value for person you depended upon up to $4,000. |
| 48-3-23 | Life insurance proceeds or cash value if the beneficiary is a married woman. |

## MISCELLANEOUS
| | |
|---|---|
| 47B-5-1 | Business partnership property. |
| Other | Add any applicable Federal Nonbankruptcy Exemptions. |

# WISCONSIN

*West's* Wisconsin Statutes Annotated, Section 815.20 (Wis. Stat. Ann. §815.20). Compare Federal Bankruptcy Exemptions.

**HOMESTEAD**

815.20      $40,000. Sale proceed exempt for 2 years after sale provided you intend to acquire another home. Must occupy or intend to occupy at time of filing for bankruptcy.

**PERSONAL PROPERTY**

815.18      Automobile up to $1,200 (plus any of the $5,000 household furnishings exemption that is unused); household goods and furnishings; wearing apparel, keepsakes, jewelry and other articles of adornment, appliances, books, musical instruments, firearms, sporting goods, animals or other items for family use up to $5,000 total; burial plot, monument, tombstone, etc.; and bank deposits up to $1,000; wrongful death proceeds and lost earnings compensation for debtor or person on whom debtor was dependent, to extent necessary to support debtor or family; and personal injury payments for debtor or person upon whom debtor depended, up to $25,000.

**WAGES**

815.18      75% of net wages, but limited to amount necessary for support, and no less that 30 times the state or federal minimum wage, whichever is greater.

**PENSIONS**

40.08       Public employees.

66.81       Certain municipal employees in a city of more 150,000 or more in population.

815.18      Police officers, firefighters, military pensions, and public and private retirement benefits (including plans for self-employed persons).

**PUBLIC BENEFITS**

| | | | |
|---|---|---|---|
| 45.35 | Veterans' benefits. | 108.13 | Unemployment compensation. |
| 49.41 | AFDC; other social service payments. | 949.07 | Crime victims' compensation. |
| 102.27 | Workers' compensation. | | |

**TOOLS OF TRADE**

815.18      Equipment, inventory, farm products, and professional books used in the business of the debtor or a dependent, up to $7,500.

**ALIMONY AND CHILD SUPPORT**

815.18      Alimony and child support needed for support.

**INSURANCE**

614.96      Fraternal benefit society benefits.

632.42      Life insurance proceeds if policy prohibits use to pay creditors.

815.18      Unmatured life insurance contracts, and up to $4,000 in value in accrued dividends, interest or loan value (except for credit life contracts) if owned by debtor and insuring debtor, dependent, or person debtor is dependent upon; federal disability benefits; life insurance proceeds if debtor was dependent upon insured, to extent necessary to support debtor or family; and fire insurance proceeds received during prior two years for destroyed exempt property.

**MISCELLANEOUS**

178.21      Business partnership property.

Other       Add any applicable Federal Nonbankruptcy Exemptions.

# WYOMING

Wyoming Statutes Annotated, Title 1, Chapter 20, Section 1-20-101 (Wyo. Stat. Ann. §1-20-101).

## HOMESTEAD (**)

1-20-101 &    Real property up to $10,000; house trailer up to $6,000. Tenancies by the entirety are exempt without
1-20-104      limit as to debts of one spouse [*In re Anselmi*, 52 B.R. 479 (D. Wyo. 1985)]. Spouse or child of deceased
              owner may claim; must occupy at time of filing for bankruptcy.

## PERSONAL PROPERTY

1-20-105      Clothing and wedding rings up to $1,000 total.
1-20-106      Household articles, furniture, bedding and food up to $2,000 per person in the home; school books,
              pictures, and bible; motor vehicle up to $2,400.
1-20-106 &    Burial plot.
35-8-104
26-32-102     Prepaid funeral contracts.

## WAGES

1-15-511      Minimum of 75% of earned but unpaid wages. Judge may approved more for low income debtor.
17-16-308     Wages of inmates on work release.
19-2-501      Earnings of national guard members.

## PENSIONS

1-20-110      Private or public retirement funds or accounts.
9-3-426       Public employees.
9-3-620       Highway officers, criminal investigators, and game and fish wardens.
15-5-209      Payments being received by police officers and firefighters.

## PUBLIC BENEFITS

| | | | |
|---|---|---|---|
| 1-40-113 | Crime victims' compensation. | 27-14-702 | Workers' compensation. |
| 27-3-319 | Unemployment compensation. | 42-2-113 | AFDC; general assistance. |

## TOOLS OF TRADE

1-20-106      Motor vehicle, tools, implements, team and stock in trade to $2,000; library and implements of a pro-
              fessional up to $2,000.

## INSURANCE

1-20-111      Funds in a qualified medical savings account.
26-15-129     Life insurance proceeds if insured is not the beneficiary.
26-15-130     Disability benefits if policy prohibits use to pay creditors.
26-15-131     Group life or disability policy or proceeds.
26-15-132     Annuity contract proceeds up to $350 per month.
26-15-133     Life insurance proceeds if policy prohibits use to pay creditors.
26-29-116     Fraternal benefit society benefits.

## MISCELLANEOUS

12-4-604      Liquor licenses and malt beverage permits.
17-21-501     Business partnership property.
Other         Add any applicable Federal Nonbankruptcy Exemptions.

# Checklists and Worksheets

This appendix has checklists for filing a bankruptcy case under either Chapter 7 or Chapter 13 of the Bankruptcy Code and the worksheets referred to throughout this book.

The checklists include all of the items required for the initial filing of your case. Use them to ensure that you bring the appropriate forms and materials with you to the bankruptcy court clerk. (Local court rules may require additional forms or materials, and additional forms may also be needed as your case progresses.)

Follow the instructions in the various sections of this book when filing in the worksheets. To use them, first tear them out and make photocopies of the ones you will need, in case you make a mistake.

## TABLE OF CHECKLISTS

## TABLE OF WORKSHEETS

# IF YOU ARE FILING FOR CHAPTER 7 BANKRUPTCY, YOU SHOULD BRING:

❑ **Voluntary Petition** (form 1)

❑ **Summary of Schedules** (form 4)

❑ **Schedule A—Real Property** (form 5)

❑ **Schedule B—Personal Property** (form 6)

❑ **Schedule C—Property Claimed as Exempt** (form 7)

❑ **Schedule D—Creditors Holding Secured Claims** (form 8)

❑ **Schedule E—Creditors Holding Unsecured Priority Claims** (form 9)

❑ **Schedule F—Creditors Holding Unsecured Nonpriority Claims** (form 10)

❑ **Schedule G—Executory Contracts and Unexpired Leases** (form 11)

❑ **Schedule H—Codebtors** (form 12)

❑ **Schedule I—Current Income of Individual Debtor(s)** (form 13)

❑ **Schedule J—Current Expenditures of Individual Debtor(s)** (form 14)

❑ **Declaration Concerning Debtor's Schedules** (form 15)

❑ **Statement of Financial Affairs** (form 16)

❑ **Chapter 7 Debtor's Statement of Intention** (form 17)

❑ **Statement of Current Monthly Income and Means Test Calculation** (form 18)

❑ **Debtor's Certification of Completion of Instructional Course Concerning Personal Financial Management** (form 21)

❑ Master Address List (either using the **Mailing Matrix** (form 22) or other format as required by the court in which you file your case)

❑ Last year's federal income tax return

❑ Current paystub or other evidence of current income

❑ Check or money order for the filing fee

❑ Note pad and pen, for writing down any information or instructions the court clerk may give you

Other forms you may need, depending upon your situation:

❑ **Application to Pay Filing Fee in Installments** (form 2) (if you are filing this form, your check or money order should be for the amount of the first payment listed on the form)

❑ **Application for Waiver of the Chapter 7 Filing Fee** (form 3)

# IF YOU ARE FILING FOR CHAPTER 13 BANKRUPTCY, YOU SHOULD BRING:

❑ **VOLUNTARY PETITION** (form 1)
❑ **SUMMARY OF SCHEDULES** (form 4)
❑ **SCHEDULE A—REAL PROPERTY** (form 5)
❑ **SCHEDULE B—PERSONAL PROPERTY** (form 6)
❑ **SCHEDULE C—PROPERTY CLAIMED AS EXEMPT** (form 7)
❑ **SCHEDULE D—CREDITORS HOLDING SECURED CLAIMS** (form 8)
❑ **SCHEDULE E—CREDITORS HOLDING UNSECURED PRIORITY CLAIMS** (form 9)
❑ **SCHEDULE F—CREDITORS HOLDING UNSECURED NONPRIORITY CLAIMS** (form 10)
❑ **SCHEDULE G—EXECUTORY CONTRACTS AND UNEXPIRED LEASES** (form 11)
❑ **SCHEDULE H—CODEBTORS** (form 12)
❑ **SCHEDULE I—CURRENT INCOME OF INDIVIDUAL DEBTOR(S)** (form 13)
❑ **SCHEDULE J—CURRENT EXPENDITURES OF INDIVIDUAL DEBTOR(S)** (form 14)
❑ **DECLARATION CONCERNING DEBTOR'S SCHEDULES** (form 15)
❑ **STATEMENT OF FINANCIAL AFFAIRS** (form 16)
❑ **STATEMENT OF CURRENT MONTHLY INCOME AND DISPOSABLE INCOME CALCULATION** (form 19)
❑ **CHAPTER 13 PLAN** (form 20)
❑ **DEBTOR'S CERTIFICATION OF COMPLETION OF INSTRUCTIONAL COURSE CONCERNING PERSONAL FINANCIAL MANAGEMENT** (form 21)
❑ Master Address List (either using the **MAILING MATRIX** (form 22) or other format as required by the court in which you file your case
❑ Last year's federal income tax return
❑ Current paystub or other evidence of current income
❑ Check or money order for the filing fee
❑ Note pad and pen, for writing down any information or instructions the court clerk may give you

Depending upon your situation, you may also need:
❑ **APPLICATION TO PAY FILING FEE IN INSTALLMENTS** (form 2) (if you are filing this form, your check or money order should be for the amount of the first payment listed on the form)

# INCOME AND EXPENSES WORKSHEET

INCOME (Monthly):

    Take-Home Pay (wages, salary, commissions)     _____

    Self-Employment Income     _____

    Interest and Dividends     _____

    Income From Real Estate     _____

    Retirement Income     _____

    Alimony or Support Payments     _____

    Other: _____     _____

    _____     _____

TOTAL MONTHLY INCOME     _____

EXPENSES (Monthly):

    Mortgage or Rent     _____

    Homeowners/Renters Insurance     _____

    Real Estate Taxes     _____

    Electricity     _____

    Gas     _____

    Water     _____

    Telephone     _____

    Garbage Pick-up     _____

    Other: _____     _____

    Home Repair/Maintenance     _____

    Auto Loan     _____

    Other Installment Loan Payments:

    _____     _____

    _____     _____

    _____     _____

    _____     _____

    Auto Insurance     _____

    Gasoline     _____

    Auto Repairs/Maintenance     _____

    Food     _____

    Clothing     _____

    Medical, Dental, and Medicines     _____

    Life Insurance     _____

    Laundry     _____

    Recreation/Travel/Entertainment     _____

    Education     _____

    License Fees, Dues, Memberships     _____

    Other Taxes     _____

    Other: _____     _____

    _____     _____

    _____     _____

    _____     _____

TOTAL MONTHLY EXPENSES     _____

DEFICIT (Total Income - Total Expenses)     _____

# PROPERTY WORKSHEET

| (1) Property | (2) Value | (3) Amount Owed | (4) Equity | (5) Exempt | (6) Secured |
|---|---|---|---|---|---|
| Real Estate: | | | | | |
| Autos, etc.: | | | | | |
| Boats, etc.: | | | | | |
| Cash on Hand: | | | | | |
| Bank Accounts: | | | | | |
| Clothing: | | | | | |
| Jewlery: | | | | | |
| Household Goods: | | | | | |
| Collections: | | | | | |
| Sports Equipment: | | | | | |
| Business Goods or Trade Tools: | | | | | |
| Investments: | | | | | |
| Insurance: | | | | | |
| Other Property: | | | | | |
| TOTALS: | | | | | |

# DEBT WORKSHEET

| (1) Debt | (2) Lender | (3) Item | (4) Balance | (5) Secured | (6) Dischargeable |
|----------|-----------|----------|-------------|-------------|-------------------|
| Real Estate: | | | | | |
| Autos, etc.: | | | | | |
| Boats, etc.: | | | | | |
| Credit Cards: | | | | | |
| Student Loans: | | | | | |
| Taxes Owed: | | | | | |
| Other Debts: | | | | | |
| TOTALS: | | | | | |

# MONTHLY BUDGET

TOTAL  —————  —————  —————  —————
Mortgage or Rent  —————  —————  —————  —————
Homeowners/Renters Insurance  —————  —————  —————  —————
Real Estate Taxes  —————  —————  —————  —————
Electricity  —————  —————  —————  —————
Gas/Heating Oil  —————  —————  —————  —————
Water  —————  —————  —————  —————
Telephone  —————  —————  —————  —————
Cell Phone  —————  —————  —————  —————
Cable Television  —————  —————  —————  —————
Internet Access  —————  —————  —————  —————
Garbage Pickup  —————  —————  —————  —————
Lawn Service  —————  —————  —————  —————
Other: _____  —————  —————  —————  —————
Home Repair/Maintenance  —————  —————  —————  —————
Auto Loan  —————  —————  —————  —————
Other Installment Loans:

_____  —————  —————  —————  —————
_____  —————  —————  —————  —————
_____  —————  —————  —————  —————
_____  —————  —————  —————  —————

Auto Insurance  —————  —————  —————  —————
Gasoline  —————  —————  —————  —————
Auto Repairs/Maintenance  —————  —————  —————  —————
Food  —————  —————  —————  —————
Clothing  —————  —————  —————  —————
Health Insurance  —————  —————  —————  —————
Medical, Dental, and Medicines  —————  —————  —————  —————
Day Care/Baby-sitting  —————  —————  —————  —————
Laundry  —————  —————  —————  —————
Education  —————  —————  —————  —————
Recreation/Travel/Entertainment  —————  —————  —————  —————
License Fees/Dues/Memberships  —————  —————  —————  —————
Gifts  —————  —————  —————  —————
Other Taxes  —————  —————  —————  —————
Other: _____  —————  —————  —————  —————

_____  —————  —————  —————  —————
_____  —————  —————  —————  —————
_____  —————  —————  —————  —————
_____  —————  —————  —————  —————

# Blank Forms

This appendix contains all of the forms necessary for you to file your own bankruptcy. They are explained in detail throughout the text.

**NOTE:** *Some of the Bankruptcy Court forms, such as the* STATEMENT OF FINANCIAL AFFAIRS *(form 16), have independent page numbers issued by the Bankruptcy Court. Forms with two sets of page numbers are numbered by the court (lower number) and by this book (top number).*

## TABLE OF FORMS

(Official Form 1) (10/05)

| United States Bankruptcy Court<br>District of_____ | **Voluntary Petition** |
|---|---|

| Name of Debtor (if individual, enter Last, First, Middle): | Name of Joint Debtor (Spouse) (Last, First, Middle): |
|---|---|
| All Other Names used by the Debtor in the last 8 years<br>(include married, maiden, and trade names): | All Other Names used by the Joint Debtor in the last 8 years<br>(include married, maiden, and trade names): |
| Last four digits of Soc. Sec./Complete EIN or other Tax I.D. No. (if more than one, state all): | Last four digits of Soc. Sec./Complete EIN or other Tax I.D. No. (if more than one, state all): |
| Street Address of Debtor (No. & Street, City, and State):<br><br>ZIPCODE | Street Address of Joint Debtor (No. & Street, City, and State):<br><br>ZIPCODE |
| County of Residence or of the Principal Place of Business: | County of Residence or of the Principal Place of Business: |
| Mailing Address of Debtor (if different from street address):<br><br>ZIPCODE | Mailing Address of Joint Debtor (if different from street address):<br><br>ZIPCODE |
| Location of Principal Assets of Business Debtor (if different from street address above):<br>ZIPCODE | |

**Type of Debtor** (Form of Organization)
(Check **one** box.)

☐ Individual (includes Joint Debtors)
☐ Corporation (includes LLC and LLP)
☐ Partnership
☐ Other (If debtor is not one of the above entities, check this box and provide the information requested below.)

State type of entity: _____
_____

**Nature of Business**
(Check **all** applicable boxes.)

☐ Health Care Business
☐ Single Asset Real Estate as defined in 11 U.S.C. § 101 (51B)
☐ Railroad
☐ Stockbroker
☐ Commodity Broker
☐ Clearing Bank
☐ Nonprofit Organization qualified under 15 U.S.C. § 501(c)(3)

**Chapter of Bankruptcy Code Under Which the Petition is Filed** (Check one box)

☐ Chapter 7     ☐ Chapter 11     ☐ Chapter 15 Petition for Recognition of a Foreign Main Proceeding
☐ Chapter 9     ☐ Chapter 12     ☐ Chapter 15 Petition for Recognition of a Foreign Nonmain Proceeding
☐ Chapter 13

**Nature of Debts** (Check one box)

☐ Consumer/Non-Business     ☐ Business

**Chapter 11 Debtors**

**Check one box:**

☐ Debtor is a small business debtor as defined in 11 U.S.C. § 101(51D).
☐ Debtor is not a small business debtor as defined in 11 U.S.C. § 101(51D).

**Check if:**

☐ Debtor's aggregate noncontingent liquidated debts owed to non-insiders or affiliates are less than $2 million.

**Filing Fee** (Check one box)

☐ Full Filing Fee attached

☐ Filing Fee to be paid in installments (Applicable to individuals only) Must attach signed application for the court's consideration certifying that the debtor is unable to pay fee except in installments. Rule 1006(b). See Official Form 3A.

☐ Filing Fee waiver requested (Applicable to chapter 7 individuals only). Must attach signed application for the court's consideration. See Official Form 3B.

**Statistical/Administrative Information**

☐ Debtor estimates that funds will be available for distribution to unsecured creditors.

☐ Debtor estimates that, after any exempt property is excluded and administrative expenses paid, there will be no funds available for distribution to unsecured creditors.

THIS SPACE IS FOR COURT USE ONLY

Estimated Number of Creditors

| 1-49 | 50-99 | 100-199 | 200-999 | 1,000-5,000 | 5,001-10,000 | 10,001-25,000 | 25,001-50,000 | 50,001-100,000 | OVER 100,000 |
|---|---|---|---|---|---|---|---|---|---|
| ☐ | ☐ | ☐ | ☐ | ☐ | ☐ | ☐ | ☐ | ☐ | ☐ |

Estimated Assets

| $0 to $50,000 | $50,001 to $100,000 | $100,001 to $500,000 | $500,001 to $1 million | $1,000,001 to $10 million | $10,000,001 to $50 million | $50,000,001 to $100 million | More than $100 million |
|---|---|---|---|---|---|---|---|
| ☐ | ☐ | ☐ | ☐ | ☐ | ☐ | ☐ | ☐ |

Estimated Debts

| $0 to $50,000 | $50,001 to $100,000 | $100,001 to $500,000 | $500,001 to $1 million | $1,000,001 to $10 million | $10,000,001 to $50 million | $50,000,001 to $100 million | More than $100 million |
|---|---|---|---|---|---|---|---|
| ☐ | ☐ | ☐ | ☐ | ☐ | ☐ | ☐ | ☐ |

| Voluntary Petition<br>*(This page must be completed and filed in every case)* | Name of Debtor(s): |
|---|---|

| **Prior Bankruptcy Case Filed Within Last 8 Years** (If more than one, attach additional sheet) | | |
|---|---|---|
| Location<br>Where Filed: | Case Number: | Date Filed: |

| **Pending Bankruptcy Case Filed by any Spouse, Partner or Affiliate of this Debtor** (If more than one, attach additional sheet) | | |
|---|---|---|
| Name of Debtor: | Case Number: | Date Filed: |
| District: | Relationship: | Judge: |

| Exhibit A | Exhibit B |
|---|---|
| (To be completed if debtor is required to file periodic reports (e.g., forms 10K and 10Q) with the Securities and Exchange Commission pursuant to Section 13 or 15(d) of the Securities Exchange Act of 1934 and is requesting relief under chapter 11.)<br><br>☐ Exhibit A is attached and made a part of this petition. | (To be completed if debtor is an individual whose debts are primarily consumer debts.)<br>I, the attorney for the petitioner named in the foregoing petition, declare that I have informed the petitioner that [he or she] may proceed under chapter 7, 11, 12, or 13 of title 11, United States Code, and have explained the relief available under each such chapter. I further certify that I delivered to the debtor the notice required by § 342(b) of the Bankruptcy Code.<br>X _____<br>Signature of Attorney for Debtor(s)          Date |

| Exhibit C | Certification Concerning Debt Counseling by Individual/Joint Debtor(s) |
|---|---|
| Does the debtor own or have possession of any property that poses or is alleged to pose a threat of imminent and identifiable harm to public health or safety?<br><br>☐ Yes, and Exhibit C is attached and made a part of this petition.<br>☐ No | ☐ I/we have received approved budget and credit counseling during the 180-day period preceding the filing of this petition.<br><br>☐ I/we request a waiver of the requirement to obtain budget and credit counseling prior to filing based on exigent circumstances. (Must attach certification describing.) |

### Information Regarding the Debtor (Check the Applicable Boxes)

**Venue** (Check any applicable box)

☐ Debtor has been domiciled or has had a residence, principal place of business, or principal assets in this District for 180 days immediately preceding the date of this petition or for a longer part of such 180 days than in any other District.

☐ There is a bankruptcy case concerning debtor's affiliate, general partner, or partnership pending in this District.

☐ Debtor is a debtor in a foreign proceeding and has its principal place of business or principal assets in the United States in this District, or has no principal place of business or assets in the United States but is a defendant in an action or proceeding [in a federal or state court] in this District, or the interests of the parties will be served in regard to the relief sought in this District.

### Statement by a Debtor Who Resides as a Tenant of Residential Property
*Check all applicable boxes.*

☐ Landlord has a judgment against the debtor for possession of debtor's residence. (If box checked, complete the following.)

_____
(Name of landlord that obtained judgment)

_____
(Address of landlord)

☐ Debtor claims that under applicable nonbankruptcy law, there are circumstances under which the debtor would be permitted to cure the entire monetary default that gave rise to the judgment for possession, after the judgment for possession was entered, and

☐ Debtor has included in this petition the deposit with the court of any rent that would become due during the 30-day period after the filing of the petition.

| (Official Form 1) (10/05) | FORM B1, Page 3 |
|---|---|
| **Voluntary Petition**<br>*(This page must be completed and filed in every case)* | Name of Debtor(s): |

## Signatures

| **Signature(s) of Debtor(s) (Individual/Joint)** | **Signature of a Foreign Representative** |
|---|---|

**Signature(s) of Debtor(s) (Individual/Joint)**

I declare under penalty of perjury that the information provided in this petition is true and correct.

[If petitioner is an individual whose debts are primarily consumer debts and has chosen to file under chapter 7] I am aware that I may proceed under chapter 7, 11, 12 or 13 of title 11, United States Code, understand the relief available under each such chapter, and choose to proceed under chapter 7.

[If no attorney represents me and no bankruptcy petition preparer signs the petition] I have obtained and read the notice required by § 342(b) of the Bankruptcy Code.

I request relief in accordance with the chapter of title 11, United States Code, specified in this petition.

X_____
  Signature of Debtor

X_____
Signature of Joint Debtor

_____
Telephone Number (If not represented by attorney)

_____
Date

**Signature of a Foreign Representative**

I declare under penalty of perjury that the information provided in this petition is true and correct, that I am the foreign representative of a debtor in a foreign proceeding, and that I am authorized to file this petition.

(Check only one box.)

☐ I request relief in accordance with chapter 15 of title 11, United States Code. Certified copies of the documents required by § 1515 of title 11 are attached.

☐ Pursuant to § 1511 of title 11, United States Code, I request relief in accordance with the chapter of title 11 specified in this petition. A certified copy of the order granting recognition of the foreign main proceeding is attached.

X_____

(Signature of Foreign Representative)

_____

(Printed Name of Foreign Representative)

_____
Date

**Signature of Attorney**

X_____
Signature of Attorney for Debtor(s)

_____
Printed Name of Attorney for Debtor(s)

_____
Firm Name

_____
Address

_____
Telephone Number

_____
Date

**Signature of Non-Attorney Bankruptcy Petition Preparer**

I declare under penalty of perjury that: (1) I am a bankruptcy petition preparer as defined in 11 U.S.C. § 110; (2) I prepared this document for compensation and have provided the debtor with a copy of this document and the notices and information required under 11 U.S.C. §§ 110(b), 110(h), and 342(b); and, (3) if rules or guidelines have been promulgated pursuant to 11 U.S.C. § 110(h) setting a maximum fee for services chargeable by bankruptcy petition preparers, I have given the debtor notice of the maximum amount before preparing any document for filing for a debtor or accepting any fee from the debtor, as required in that section. Official Form 19B is attached.

_____
Printed Name and title, if any, of Bankruptcy Petition Preparer

_____
Social Security number (If the bankrutpcy petition preparer is not an individual, state the Social Security number of the officer, principal, responsible person or partner of the bankruptcy petition preparer.)(Required by 11 U.S.C. § 110.)

**Signature of Debtor (Corporation/Partnership)**

I declare under penalty of perjury that the information provided in this petition is true and correct, and that I have been authorized to file this petition on behalf of the debtor.

The debtor requests relief in accordance with the chapter of title 11, United States Code, specified in this petition.

X_____
Signature of Authorized Individual

_____
Printed Name of Authorized Individual

_____
Title of Authorized Individual

_____
Date

Address

_____

X_____

_____
Date

Signature of Bankruptcy Petition Preparer or officer, principal, responsible person, or partner whose social security number is provided above.

Names and Social Security numbers of all other individuals who prepared or assisted in preparing this document unless the bankruptcy petition preparer is not an individual:

If more than one person prepared this document, attach additional sheets conforming to the appropriate official form for each person.

*A bankruptcy petition preparer's failure to comply with the provisions of title 11 and the Federal Rules of Bankruptcy Procedure may result in fines or imprisonment or both 11 U.S.C. §110; 18 U.S.C. §156.*

*This page intentionally blank.*

Form 3A
(10/05)

# United States Bankruptcy Court

_____ District Of _____

In re _____,                    Case No. _____
                        Debtor

                                                          Chapter _____

## APPLICATION TO PAY FILING FEE IN INSTALLMENTS

1.      In accordance with Fed. R. Bankr. P. 1006, I apply for permission to pay the filing fee amounting to $_____ in installments.

2.      I am unable to pay the filing fee except in installments.

3.      Until the filing fee is paid in full,  I will not make any additional payment or transfer any additional property to an attorney or any other person for services in connection with this case.

4.      I propose the following terms for the payment of the Filing Fee.*

        $ _____     Check one ☐     With the filing of the petition, or
                                          ☐     On or before _____

        $ _____     on or before _____

        $ _____     on or before _____

        $ _____     on or before _____

*       The number of installments proposed shall not exceed four (4), and the final installment shall be payable not later than 120 days after filing the petition.  For cause shown, the court may extend the time of any installment, provided the last installment is paid not later than 180 days after filing the petition. Fed. R. Bankr. P. 1006(b)(2).

5.      I understand that if I fail to pay any installment when due, my bankruptcy case may be dismissed and I may not receive a discharge of my debts.

_____                          _____
Signature of Attorney          Date                      Signature of Debtor                Date
                                                         (In a joint case, both spouses must sign.)

_____                          _____
Name of Attorney                                         Signature of Joint Debtor (if any)      Date

--------------------------------------------------------------------------------------------------------------------

### DECLARATION AND SIGNATURE OF NON-ATTORNEY BANKRUPTCY PETITION PREPARER (See 11 U.S.C. § 110)

   I declare under penalty of perjury that: (1) I am a bankruptcy petition preparer as defined in 11 U.S.C. § 110; (2) I prepared this document for compensation and have provided the debtor with a copy of this document and the notices and information required under 11 U.S.C. §§ 110(b), 110(h), and 342(b); (3) if rules or guidelines have been promulgated pursuant to 11 U.S.C. § 110(h) setting a maximum fee for services chargeable by bankruptcy petition preparers, I have given the debtor notice of the maximum amount before preparing any document for filing for a debtor or accepting any fee from the debtor, as required under that section; and (4) I will not accept any additional money or other property from the debtor before the filing fee is paid in full.

_____                          _____
Printed or Typed Name and Title, if any, of Bankruptcy Petition Preparer   Social Security No. (Required by 11 U.S.C. § 110.)
_If the bankruptcy petition preparer is not an individual, state the name, title (if any), address, and social security number of the officer, principal, responsible person, or partner who signs the document._

_____

Address

x_____                         _____
Signature of Bankruptcy Petition Preparer                Date

Names and Social Security numbers of all other individuals who prepared or assisted in preparing this document, unless the bankruptcy petition preparer is not an individual:

_If more than one person prepared this document, attach additional signed sheets conforming to the appropriate Official Form for each person.
A bankruptcy petition preparer's failure to comply with the provisions of title 11 and the Federal Rules of Bankruptcy Procedure may result in fines or imprisonment or both.  11 U.S.C. § 110; 18 U.S.C. § 156._

Form 3A Contd.
(10/05)

# United States Bankruptcy Court

_____ District Of _____

In re _____,      Case No. _____
                          Debtor

                                                      Chapter _____

**ORDER APPROVING PAYMENT OF FILING FEE IN INSTALLMENTS**

☐      IT IS ORDERED that the debtor(s) may pay the filing fee in installments on the terms proposed in the foregoing application.

☐      IT IS ORDERED that the debtor(s) shall pay the filing fee according to the following terms:

$ _____      Check one  ☐   With the filing of the petition, or
                                        ☐   On or before _____

$ _____ on or before _____

$ _____ on or before _____

$ _____ on or before _____

☐      IT IS FURTHER ORDERED that until the filing fee is paid in full the debtor(s) shall not make any additional payment or transfer any additional property to an attorney or any other person for services in connection with this case.

BY THE COURT

Date: _____                    _____
                                               _United States Bankruptcy Judge_

Form B3B
(10/05)

In re: _____          Case No. _____
        Debtor(s)                              (if known)

## APPLICATION FOR WAIVER OF THE CHAPTER 7 FILING FEE
## FOR INDIVIDUALS WHO CANNOT PAY THE FILING FEE IN FULL OR IN INSTALLMENTS

### Part A.  Family Size and Income

1.  Including yourself, your spouse, and dependents you have listed or will list on Schedule I (Current Income of Individual Debtors(s)), how many people are in your family? (Do not include your spouse if you are separated AND are not filing a joint petition.) _____

2.  Restate the following information that you provided, or will provide, on Line 16 of Schedule I. Attach a completed copy of Schedule I, if it is available.

    Total Combined Monthly Income (Line 16 of Schedule I):        $_____

3.  State the monthly net income, if any, of dependents included in Question 1 above. Do not include any income already reported in Item 2. If none, enter $0.

                                                                  $_____

4.  Add the "Total Combined Monthly Income" reported in Question 2 to your dependents' monthly net income from Question 3.

                                                                  $_____

5.  Do you expect the amount in Question 4 to increase or decrease by more than 10% during the next 6 months? Yes ___ No ___

    If yes, explain.

### Part B: Monthly Expenses

6.  EITHER (a) attach a completed copy of Schedule J (Schedule of Monthly Expenses), and state your total monthly expenses reported on Line 18 of that Schedule, OR (b) if you have not yet completed Schedule J, provide an estimate of your total monthly expenses.

                                                                  $ _____

7.  Do you expect the amount in Question 6 to increase or decrease by more than 10% during the next 6 months? Yes ___ No ___
    If yes, explain.

### Part C.  Real and Personal Property

EITHER (1) attach completed copies of Schedules A (Real Property) and Schedule B (Personal Property), OR (2) if you have not yet completed those schedules, answer the following questions.

8.  State the amount of cash you have on hand:                    $ _____

9.  State below any money you have in savings, checking, or other accounts in a bank or other financial institution.

| Bank or Other Financial Institution: | Type of Account such as savings, checking, CD: | Amount: |
|---|---|---|
| | | $ _____ |
| _____ | _____ | $ _____ |
| _____ | _____ | |

Form B3B Cont.
(10/05)

10. State below the assets owned by you. **Do not list ordinary household furnishings and clothing**.

Home     Address:

_____

_____

Value: $ _____

Amount owed on mortgages and liens: $ _____

Other real estate     Address:

_____

_____

Value: $ _____

Amount owed on mortgages and liens: $ _____

Motor vehicle     Model/Year: _____

_____

Value: $ _____

Amount owed: $ _____

Motor vehicle     Model/Year: _____

_____

Value: $ _____

Amount owed: $ _____

Other     Description_____

_____

Value: $ _____

Amount owed: $ _____

11. State below any person, business, organization, or governmental unit that owes you money and the amount that is owed.

Name of Person, Business, or Organization that Owes You Money

_____

_____

Amount Owed

$ _____

$ _____

## Part D. Additional Information.

12. Have you paid an **attorney** any money for services in connection with this case, including the completion of this form, the bankruptcy petition, or schedules? Yes ___ No ___
If yes, how much have you paid? $ _____

13. Have you promised to pay or do you anticipate paying an **attorney** in connection with your bankruptcy case? Yes ___ No ___
If yes, how much have you promised to pay or do you anticipate paying? $ _____

14. Have you paid **anyone other than an attorney** (such as a bankruptcy petition preparer, paralegal, typing service, or another person) any money for services in connection with this case, including the completion of this form, the bankruptcy petition, or schedules? Yes ___ No ___
If yes, how much have you paid? $ _____

15. Have you promised to pay or do you anticipate paying **anyone other than an attorney** (such as a bankruptcy petition preparer, paralegal, typing service, or another person) any money for services in connection with this case, including the completion of this form, the bankruptcy petition, or schedules?
Yes ___ No ___
If yes, how much have you promised to pay or do you anticipate paying? $ _____

16. Has anyone paid an attorney or other person or service in connection with this case, on your behalf?
Yes ___ No ___

If yes, explain.

Form B3B Cont.
(10/05)

17. Have you previously filed for bankruptcy relief during the past eight years? Yes \_\_\_ No \_\_\_

| Case Number (if known) | Year filed | Location of filing | Did you obtain a discharge? (if known) |
|---|---|---|---|
| _____ | _____ | _____ | Yes \_\_\_\_  No \_\_\_\_  Don't know \_\_\_\_ |
| _____ | _____ | _____ | Yes \_\_\_\_  No \_\_\_\_  Don't know \_\_\_\_ |

18. Please provide any other information that helps to explain why you are unable to pay the filing fee in installments.

19. I (we) declare under penalty of perjury that I (we) cannot currently afford to pay the filing fee in full or in installments and that the foregoing information is true and correct.

Executed on: _____          _____
                         Date                                                    Signature of Debtor

_____          _____
                         Date                                                    Signature of Co-debtor

--------------------------------------------------------------------------------

### DECLARATION AND SIGNATURE OF BANKRUPTCY PETITION PREPARER (See 11 U.S.C. § 110)

I declare under penalty of perjury that: (1) I am a bankruptcy petition preparer as defined in 11 U.S.C. § 110; (2) I prepared this document for compensation and have provided the debtor with a copy of this document and the notices and information required under 11 U.S.C. §§ 110(b), 110(h), and 342(b); and (3) if rules or guidelines have been promulgated pursuant to 11 U.S.C. § 110(h) setting a maximum fee for services chargeable by bankruptcy petition preparers, I have given the debtor notice of the maximum amount before preparing any document for filing for a debtor or accepting any fee from the debtor, as required under that section.

_____          _____
Printed or Typed Name and Title, if any, of Bankruptcy Petition Preparer          Social Security No. (Required by
                                                                                                                11 U.S.C. §110.)

*If the bankruptcy petition preparer is not an individual, state the name, title (if any), address, and social security number of the officer, principal, responsible person, or partner who signs the document.*

_____

_____
Address

x_____          _____
Signature of Bankruptcy Petition Preparer                                        Date

Names and Social Security numbers of all other individuals who prepared or assisted in preparing this document, unless the bankruptcy petition preparer is not an individual:

*If more than one person prepared this document, attach additional signed sheets conforming to the appropriate Official Form for each person.*

*A bankruptcy petition preparer's failure to comply with the provisions of title 11 and the Federal Rules of Bankruptcy Procedure may result in fines or imprisonment or both.* 11 U.S.C. § 110; 18 U.S.C. § 156.

Form B3B
(10/05)

United State Bankruptcy Court
_____ District of _____

In re: _____          Case No. _____
    Debtor(s)

**ORDER ON DEBTOR'S APPLICATION FOR WAIVER OF THE CHAPTER 7 FILING FEE**

Upon consideration of the debtor's "Application for Waiver of the Chapter 7 Filing Fee," the court orders that the application be:

[   ] GRANTED.

    This order is subject to being vacated at a later time if developments in the administration of the bankruptcy case demonstrate that the waiver was unwarranted.

[   ] DENIED.

    The debtor shall pay the chapter 7 filing fee according to the following terms:

    $ _____ on or before _____

    $ _____ on or before _____

    $ _____ on or before _____

    $ _____ on or before _____

    Until the filing fee is paid in full, the debtor shall not make any additional payment or transfer any additional property to an attorney or any other person for services in connection with this case.

    IF THE DEBTOR FAILS TO TIMELY PAY THE FILING FEE IN FULL OR TO TIMELY MAKE INSTALLMENT PAYMENTS, THE COURT MAY DISMISS THE DEBTOR'S CHAPTER 7 CASE.

[   ] SCHEDULED FOR HEARING.

    A hearing to consider the debtor's "Application for Waiver of the Chapter 7 Filing Fee" shall be held on _____ at _____ am/pm at _____.
                                       (address of courthouse)

    IF THE DEBTOR FAILS TO APPEAR AT THE SCHEDULED HEARING, THE COURT MAY DEEM SUCH FAILURE TO BE THE DEBTOR'S CONSENT TO THE ENTRY OF AN ORDER DENYING THE FEE WAIVER APPLICATION BY DEFAULT.

                                      BY THE COURT:

DATE: _____

                                      _____
                                      United States Bankruptcy Judge

Form 6-Summary
(10/05)

# United States Bankruptcy Court

_____ District Of _____

In re _____,          Case No. _____
                    Debtor

                                                 Chapter _____

## SUMMARY OF SCHEDULES

Indicate as to each schedule whether that schedule is attached and state the number of pages in each.  Report the totals from Schedules A, B, D, E, F, I, and J in the boxes provided.  Add the amounts from Schedules A and B to determine the total amount of the debtor's assets.  Add the amounts of all claims from Schedules D, E, and F to determine the total amount of the debtor's liabilities. Individual debtors must also complete the "Statistical Summary of Certain Liabilities."

**AMOUNTS SCHEDULED**

| NAME OF SCHEDULE | ATTACHED (YES/NO) | NO. OF SHEETS | ASSETS | LIABILITIES | OTHER |
|---|---|---|---|---|---|
| A - Real Property | | | $ | | |
| B - Personal Property | | | $ | | |
| C - Property Claimed as Exempt | | | | | |
| D - Creditors Holding Secured Claims | | | | $ | |
| E - Creditors Holding Unsecured Priority Claims | | | | $ | |
| F - Creditors Holding Unsecured Nonpriority Claims | | | | $ | |
| G - Executory Contracts and Unexpired Leases | | | | | |
| H - Codebtors | | | | | |
| I - Current Income of Individual Debtor(s) | | | | | $ |
| J - Current Expenditures of Individual Debtors(s) | | | | | $ |
| TOTAL | | | $ | $ | |

Form 6-Summ2
(10/05)

# United States Bankruptcy Court

_____ District Of _____

In re _____,
                Debtor

Case No. _____

Chapter _____

## STATISTICAL SUMMARY OF CERTAIN LIABILITIES (28 U.S.C. § 159)
### [Individual Debtors Only]

Summarize the following types of liabilities, as reported in the Schedules, and total them.

| Type of Liability | Amount |
|---|---|
| Domestic Support Obligations (from Schedule E) | $ |
| Taxes and Certain Other Debts Owed to Governmental Units (from Schedule E) | $ |
| Claims for Death or Personal Injury While Debtor Was Intoxicated (from Schedule E) | $ |
| Student Loan Obligations (from Schedule F) | $ |
| Domestic Support, Separation Agreement, and Divorce Decree Obligations Not Reported on Schedule E | $ |
| Obligations to Pension or Profit-Sharing, and Other Similar Obligations (from Schedule F) | $ |
| TOTAL | $ |

**The foregoing information is for statistical purposes only under 28 U.S.C. § 159.**

Form B6A
(10/05)

In re _____,     Case No. _____
          **Debtor**                                      **(If known)**

# SCHEDULE A - REAL PROPERTY

Except as directed below, list all real property in which the debtor has any legal, equitable, or future interest, including all property owned as a co-tenant, community property, or in which the debtor has a life estate. Include any property in which the debtor holds rights and powers exercisable for the debtor's own benefit. If the debtor is married, state whether husband, wife, or both own the property by placing an "H," "W," "J," or "C" in the column labeled "Husband, Wife, Joint, or Community." If the debtor holds no interest in real property, write "None" under "Description and Location of Property."

**Do not include interests in executory contracts and unexpired leases on this schedule. List them in Schedule G - Executory Contracts and Unexpired Leases.**

If an entity claims to have a lien or hold a secured interest in any property, state the amount of the secured claim. See Schedule D. If no entity claims to hold a secured interest in the property, write "None" in the column labeled "Amount of Secured Claim."

If the debtor is an individual or if a joint petition is filed, state the amount of any exemption claimed in the property only in Schedule C - Property Claimed as Exempt.

| DESCRIPTION AND LOCATION OF PROPERTY | NATURE OF DEBTOR'S INTEREST IN PROPERTY | HUSBAND, WIFE, JOINT, OR COMMUNITY | CURRENT VALUE OF DEBTOR'S INTEREST IN PROPERTY, WITHOUT DEDUCTING ANY SECURED CLAIM OR EXEMPTION | AMOUNT OF SECURED CLAIM |
|---|---|---|---|---|
|  |  |  |  |  |

Total▶

(Report also on Summary of Schedules.)

*This page intentionally blank.*

Form B6B
(10/05)

**In re** _____,          **Case No.** _____
          **Debtor**                                              **(If known)**

# SCHEDULE B - PERSONAL PROPERTY

Except as directed below, list all personal property of the debtor of whatever kind. If the debtor has no property in one or more of the categories, place an "x" in the appropriate position in the column labeled "None." If additional space is needed in any category, attach a separate sheet properly identified with the case name, case number, and the number of the category. If the debtor is married, state whether husband, wife, or both own the property by placing an "H," "W," "J," or "C" in the column labeled "Husband, Wife, Joint, or Community." If the debtor is an individual or a joint petition is filed, state the amount of any exemptions claimed only in Schedule C - Property Claimed as Exempt.

**Do not list interests in executory contracts and unexpired leases on this schedule. List them in Schedule G - Executory Contracts and Unexpired Leases.**

If the property is being held for the debtor by someone else, state that person's name and address under "Description and Location of Property." In providing the information requested in this schedule, do not include the name or address of a minor child. Simply state "a minor child."

| TYPE OF PROPERTY | N O N E | DESCRIPTION AND LOCATION OF PROPERTY | HUSBAND, WIFE, JOINT, OR COMMUNITY | CURRENT VALUE OF DEBTOR'S INTEREST IN PROPERTY, WITHOUT DEDUCTING ANY SECURED CLAIM OR EXEMPTION |
|---|---|---|---|---|
| 1. Cash on hand. | | | | |
| 2. Checking, savings or other financial accounts, certificates of deposit, or shares in banks, savings and loan, thrift, building and loan, and homestead associations, or credit unions, brokerage houses, or cooperatives. | | | | |
| 3. Security deposits with public utilities, telephone companies, landlords, and others. | | | | |
| 4. Household goods and furnishings, including audio, video, and computer equipment. | | | | |
| 5. Books; pictures and other art objects; antiques; stamp, coin, record, tape, compact disc, and other collections or collectibles. | | | | |
| 6. Wearing apparel. | | | | |
| 7. Furs and jewelry. | | | | |
| 8. Firearms and sports, photographic, and other hobby equipment. | | | | |
| 9. Interests in insurance policies. Name insurance company of each policy and itemize surrender or refund value of each. | | | | |
| 10. Annuities. Itemize and name each issuer. | | | | |
| 11. Interests in an education IRA as defined in 26 U.S.C. § 530(b)(1) or under a qualified State tuition plan as defined in 26 U.S.C. § 529(b)(1). Give particulars. (File separately the record(s) of any such interest(s). 11 U.S.C. § 521(c); Rule 1007(b)). | | | | |

Form B6B-Cont.
(10/05)

In re _____,    Case No. _____
              **Debtor**                                              **(If known)**

# SCHEDULE B - PERSONAL PROPERTY
## (Continuation Sheet)

| TYPE OF PROPERTY | N O N E | DESCRIPTION AND LOCATION OF PROPERTY | HUSBAND, WIFE, JOINT, OR COMMUNITY | CURRENT VALUE OF DEBTOR'S INTEREST IN PROPERTY, WITH-OUT DEDUCTING ANY SECURED CLAIM OR EXEMPTION |
|---|---|---|---|---|
| 12. Interests in IRA, ERISA, Keogh, or other pension or profit sharing plans. Give particulars. | | | | |
| 13. Stock and interests in incorporated and unincorporated businesses. Itemize. | | | | |
| 14. Interests in partnerships or joint ventures. Itemize. | | | | |
| 15. Government and corporate bonds and other negotiable and non-negotiable instruments. | | | | |
| 16. Accounts receivable. | | | | |
| 17. Alimony, maintenance, support, and property settlements to which the debtor is or may be entitled. Give particulars. | | | | |
| 18. Other liquidated debts owed to debtor including tax refunds. Give particulars. | | | | |
| 19. Equitable or future interests, life estates, and rights or powers exercisable for the benefit of the debtor other than those listed in Schedule A – Real Property. | | | | |
| 20. Contingent and noncontingent interests in estate of a decedent, death benefit plan, life insurance policy, or trust. | | | | |
| 21. Other contingent and unliquidated claims of every nature, including tax refunds, counterclaims of the debtor, and rights to setoff claims. Give estimated value of each. | | | | |

Form B6B-cont.
(10/05)

In re _____,     Case No. _____
          **Debtor**                                                                  **(If known)**

# SCHEDULE B -PERSONAL PROPERTY
(Continuation Sheet)

| TYPE OF PROPERTY | N O N E | DESCRIPTION AND LOCATION OF PROPERTY | HUSBAND, WIFE, JOINT, OR COMMUNITY | CURRENT VALUE OF DEBTOR'S INTEREST IN PROPERTY, WITH-OUT DEDUCTING ANY SECURED CLAIM OR EXEMPTION |
|---|---|---|---|---|
| 22. Patents, copyrights, and other intellectual property. Give particulars. | | | | |
| 23. Licenses, franchises, and other general intangibles. Give particulars. | | | | |
| 24. Customer lists or other compilations containing personally identifiable information (as defined in 11 U.S.C. § 101(41A)) provided to the debtor by individuals in connection with obtaining a product or service from the debtor primarily for personal, family, or household purposes. | | | | |
| 25. Automobiles, trucks, trailers, and other vehicles and accessories. | | | | |
| 26. Boats, motors, and accessories. | | | | |
| 27. Aircraft and accessories. | | | | |
| 28. Office equipment, furnishings, and supplies. | | | | |
| 29. Machinery, fixtures, equipment, and supplies used in business. | | | | |
| 30. Inventory. | | | | |
| 31. Animals. | | | | |
| 32. Crops - growing or harvested. Give particulars. | | | | |
| 33. Farming equipment and implements. | | | | |
| 34. Farm supplies, chemicals, and feed. | | | | |
| 35. Other personal property of any kind not already listed. Itemize. | | | | |

_____continuation sheets attached     Total ▶     $ _____

(Include amounts from any continuation
sheets attached.  Report total also on
Summary of Schedules.)

*This page intentionally blank.*

Form B6C
(10/05)

In re _____,     Case No. _____
              **Debtor**                                                    **(If known)**

# SCHEDULE C - PROPERTY CLAIMED AS EXEMPT

Debtor claims the exemptions to which debtor is entitled under:    ☐ Check if debtor claims a homestead exemption that exceeds
(Check one box)                                                        $125,000.
  ☐   11 U.S.C. § 522(b)(2)
  ☐   11 U.S.C. § 522(b)(3)

| DESCRIPTION OF PROPERTY | SPECIFY LAW PROVIDING EACH EXEMPTION | VALUE OF CLAIMED EXEMPTION | CURRENT VALUE OF PROPERTY WITHOUT DEDUCTING EXEMPTION |
|---|---|---|---|
| | | | |

*This page intentionally blank.*

Form B6D

(10/05)        **In re** _____ ,      **Case No.** _____
                        **Debtor**                                                **(If known)**

# SCHEDULE D – CREDITORS HOLDING SECURED CLAIMS

State the name, mailing address, including zip code, and last four digits of any account number of all entities holding claims secured by property of the debtor as of the date of filing of the petition. The complete account number of any account the debtor has with the creditor is useful to the trustee and the creditor and may be provided if the debtor chooses to do so. List creditors holding all types of secured interests such as judgment liens, garnishments, statutory liens, mortgages, deeds of trust, and other security interests.

List creditors in alphabetical order to the extent practicable. If a minor child is a creditor, indicate that by stating "a minor child" and do not disclose the child's name. See 11 U.S.C. § 112; Fed. R. Bankr. P. 1007(m). If all secured creditors will not fit on this page, use the continuation sheet provided.

If any entity other than a spouse in a joint case may be jointly liable on a claim, place an "X" in the column labeled "Codebtor," include the entity on the appropriate schedule of creditors, and complete Schedule H – Codebtors. If a joint petition is filed, state whether husband, wife, both of them, or the marital community may be liable on each claim by placing an "H," "W," "J," or "C" in the column labeled "Husband, Wife, Joint, or Community."

If the claim is contingent, place an "X" in the column labeled "Contingent." If the claim is unliquidated, place an "X" in the column labeled "Unliquidated." If the claim is disputed, place an "X" in the column labeled "Disputed." (You may need to place an "X" in more than one of these three columns.)

Report the total of all claims listed on this schedule in the box labeled "Total" on the last sheet of the completed schedule. Report this total also on the Summary of Schedules.

☐      Check this box if debtor has no creditors holding secured claims to report on this Schedule D.

| CREDITOR'S NAME AND MAILING ADDRESS INCLUDING ZIP CODE AND AN ACCOUNT NUMBER *(See Instructions Above)* | CODEBTOR | HUSBAND, WIFE, JOINT, OR COMMUNITY | DATE CLAIM WAS INCURRED, NATURE OF LIEN , AND DESCRIPTION AND VALUE OF PROPERTY SUBJECT TO LIEN | CONTINGENT | UNLIQUIDATED | DISPUTED | AMOUNT OF CLAIM WITHOUT DEDUCTING VALUE OF COLLATERAL | UNSECURED PORTION, IF ANY |
|---|---|---|---|---|---|---|---|---|
| **ACCOUNT NO.** | | | | | | | | |
| | | | VALUE $ | | | | | |
| **ACCOUNT NO.** | | | | | | | | |
| | | | VALUE $ | | | | | |
| **ACCOUNT NO.** | | | | | | | | |
| | | | VALUE $ | | | | | |
| **ACCOUNT NO.** | | | | | | | | |
| | | | VALUE $ | | | | | |

_____ continuation sheets attached

Subtotal ▶    $
(Total of this page)

Total ▶    $
(Use only on last page)

(Report total also on Summary of Schedules)

Form B6D – Cont.
(10/05)

**In re** _____,  **Case No.** _____
          **Debtor**                                                    **(If known)**

## SCHEDULE D – CREDITORS HOLDING SECURED CLAIMS
(Continuation Sheet)

| CREDITOR'S NAME AND MAILING ADDRESS INCLUDING ZIP CODE AND AN ACCOUNT NUMBER (*See Instructions Above*) | CODEBTOR | HUSBAND, WIFE, JOINT, OR COMMUNITY | DATE CLAIM WAS INCURRED, NATURE OF LIEN , AND DESCRIPTION AND VALUE OF PROPERTY SUBJECT TO LIEN | CONTINGENT | UNLIQUIDATED | DISPUTED | AMOUNT OF CLAIM WITHOUT DEDUCTING VALUE OF COLLATERAL | UNSECURED PORTION, IF ANY |
|---|---|---|---|---|---|---|---|---|
| ACCOUNT NO. | | | | | | | | |
| | | | VALUE $ | | | | | |
| ACCOUNT NO. | | | | | | | | |
| | | | VALUE $ | | | | | |
| ACCOUNT NO. | | | | | | | | |
| | | | VALUE $ | | | | | |
| ACCOUNT NO. | | | | | | | | |
| | | | VALUE $ | | | | | |
| ACCOUNT NO. | | | | | | | | |
| | | | VALUE $ | | | | | |

Sheet no.___of___continuation sheets attached to Schedule of Creditors Holding Secured Claims

Subtotal ▶
(Total of this page)

$

Total ▶
(Use only on last page)

$

Form B6E
(10/05)

In re _____ ,          Case No._____
                          Debtor                                                    (if known)

# SCHEDULE E - CREDITORS HOLDING UNSECURED PRIORITY CLAIMS

A complete list of claims entitled to priority, listed separately by type of priority, is to be set forth on the sheets provided. Only holders of unsecured claims entitled to priority should be listed in this schedule. In the boxes provided on the attached sheets, state the name, mailing address, including zip code, and last four digits of the account number, if any, of all entities holding priority claims against the debtor or the property of the debtor, as of the date of the filing of the petition. Use a separate continuation sheet for each type of priority and label each with the type of priority.

The complete account number of any account the debtor has with the creditor is useful to the trustee and the creditor and may be provided if the debtor chooses to do so. If a minor child is a creditor, indicate that by stating "a minor child" and do not disclose the child's name. See 11 U.S.C. § 112; Fed.R.Bankr.P. 1007(m).

If any entity other than a spouse in a joint case may be jointly liable on a claim, place an "X" in the column labeled "Codebtor," include the entity on the appropriate schedule of creditors, and complete Schedule H-Codebtors. If a joint petition is filed, state whether husband, wife, both of them or the marital community may be liable on each claim by placing an "H,""W,""J," or "C" in the column labeled "Husband, Wife, Joint, or Community."       If the claim is contingent, place an "X" in the column labeled "Contingent." If the claim is unliquidated, place an "X" in the column labeled "Unliquidated." If the claim is disputed, place an "X" in the column labeled "Disputed." (You may need to place an "X" in more than one of these three columns.)

Report the total of claims listed on each sheet in the box labeled "Subtotal" on each sheet. Report the total of all claims listed on this Schedule E in the box labeled "Total" on the last sheet of the completed schedule. Report this total also on the Summary of Schedules.

Report the total of amounts entitled to priority listed on each sheet in the box labeled "Subtotal" on each sheet. Report the total of all amounts entitled to priority listed on this Schedule E in the box labeled "Total" on the last sheet of the completed schedule. If applicable, also report this total on the Means Test form.

☐  Check this box if debtor has no creditors holding unsecured priority claims to report on this Schedule E.

**TYPES OF PRIORITY CLAIMS** (Check the appropriate box(es) below if claims in that category are listed on the attached sheets)

☐ **Domestic Support Obligations**

Claims for domestic support that are owed to or recoverable by a spouse, former spouse, or child of the debtor, or the parent, legal guardian, or responsible relative of such a child, or a governmental unit to whom such a domestic support claim has been assigned to the extent provided in 11 U.S.C. § 507(a)(1).

☐ **Extensions of credit in an involuntary case**

Claims arising in the ordinary course of the debtor's business or financial affairs after the commencement of the case but before the earlier of the appointment of a trustee or the order for relief. 11 U.S.C. § 507(a)(3).

☐ **Wages, salaries, and commissions**

Wages, salaries, and commissions, including vacation, severance, and sick leave pay owing to employees and commissions owing to qualifying independent sales representatives up to $10,000* per person earned within 180 days immediately preceding the filing of the original petition, or the cessation of business, whichever occurred first, to the extent provided in 11 U.S.C. § 507(a)(4).

☐ **Contributions to employee benefit plans**

Money owed to employee benefit plans for services rendered within 180 days immediately preceding the filing of the original petition, or the cessation of business, whichever occurred first, to the extent provided in 11 U.S.C. § 507(a)(5).

Form B6E Contd.
(10/05)

In re _____ ,          Case No._____
                    Debtor                                                          (if known)

☐ **Certain farmers and fishermen**

Claims of certain farmers and fishermen, up to $4,925* per farmer or fisherman, against the debtor, as provided in 11 U.S.C. § 507(a)(6).

☐ **Deposits by individuals**

Claims of individuals up to $2,225* for deposits for the purchase, lease, or rental of property or services for personal, family, or household use, that were not delivered or provided. 11 U.S.C. § 507(a)(7).

☐ **Taxes and Certain Other Debts Owed to Governmental Units**

Taxes, customs duties, and penalties owing to federal, state, and local governmental units as set forth in 11 U.S.C. § 507(a)(8).

☐ **Commitments to Maintain the Capital of an Insured Depository Institution**

Claims based on commitments to the FDIC, RTC, Director of the Office of Thrift Supervision, Comptroller of the Currency, or Board of Governors of the Federal Reserve System, or their predecessors or successors, to maintain the capital of an insured depository institution. 11 U.S.C. § 507 (a)(9).

☐ **Claims for Death or Personal Injury While Debtor Was Intoxicated**

Claims for death or personal injury resulting from the operation of a motor vehicle or vessel while the debtor was intoxicated from using alcohol, a drug, or another substance. 11 U.S.C. § 507(a)(10).

* Amounts are subject to adjustment on April 1, 2007, and every three years thereafter with respect to cases commenced on or after the date of adjustment.

_____ continuation sheets attached

Form B6E - Cont.
(10/05)

In re _____ ,  Case No. _____
           **Debtor**                                                    **(If known)**

# SCHEDULE E - CREDITORS HOLDING UNSECURED PRIORITY CLAIMS
(Continuation Sheet)

TYPE OF PRIORITY
_____

| CREDITOR'S NAME, MAILING ADDRESS INCLUDING ZIP CODE, AND ACCOUNT NUMBER (See instructions.) | CODEBTOR | HUSBAND, WIFE, JOINT, OR COMMUNITY | DATE CLAIM WAS INCURRED AND CONSIDERATION FOR CLAIM | CONTINGENT | UNLIQUIDATED | DISPUTED | AMOUNT OF CLAIM | AMOUNT ENTITLED TO PRIORITY |
|---|---|---|---|---|---|---|---|---|
| Account No. | | | | | | | | |
| Account No. | | | | | | | | |
| Account No. | | | | | | | | |
| Account No. | | | | | | | | |
| Account No. | | | | | | | | |
| Sheet no. ___ of ___ sheets attached to Schedule of Creditors Holding Priority Claims | | | Subtotal➤ (Total of this page) | | | | $ | $ |
| | | | Total➤ (Use only on last page of the completed Schedule E. (Report total also on Summary of Schedules) | | | | $ | $ |

*This page intentionally blank.*

Form B6F (10/05)

**In re** _____ ,    **Case No.** _____

Debtor                                              **(If known)**

# SCHEDULE F- CREDITORS HOLDING UNSECURED NONPRIORITY CLAIMS

State the name, mailing address, including zip code, and last four digits of any account number, of all entities holding unsecured claims without priority against the debtor or the property of the debtor, as of the date of filing of the petition. The complete account number of any account the debtor has with the creditor is useful to the trustee and the creditor and may be provided if the debtor chooses to do so. If a minor child is a creditor, indicate that by stating "a minor child" and do not disclose the child's name. See 11 U.S.C. § 112; Fed.R.Bankr.P. 1007(m). Do not include claims listed in Schedules D and E. If all creditors will not fit on this page, use the continuation sheet provided.

If any entity other than a spouse in a joint case may be jointly liable on a claim, place an "X" in the column labeled "Codebtor," include the entity on the appropriate schedule of creditors, and complete Schedule H - Codebtors. If a joint petition is filed, state whether husband, wife, both of them, or the marital community maybe liable on each claim by placing an "H," "W," "J," or "C" in the column labeled "Husband, Wife, Joint, or Community."

If the claim is contingent, place an "X" in the column labeled "Contingent." If the claim is unliquidated, place an "X" in the column labeled "Unliquidated." If the claim is disputed, place an "X" in the column labeled "Disputed." (You may need to place an "X" in more than one of these three columns.)

Report the total of all claims listed on this schedule in the box labeled "Total" on the last sheet of the completed schedule. Report this total also on the Summary of Schedules.

☐ Check this box if debtor has no creditors holding unsecured claims to report on this Schedule F.

| CREDITOR'S NAME, MAILING ADDRESS INCLUDING ZIP CODE, AND ACCOUNT NUMBER (See instructions above.) | CODEBTOR | HUSBAND, WIFE, JOINT, OR COMMUNITY | DATE CLAIM WAS INCURRED AND CONSIDERATION FOR CLAIM. IF CLAIM IS SUBJECT TO SETOFF, SO STATE. | CONTINGENT | UNLIQUIDATED | DISPUTED | AMOUNT OF CLAIM |
|---|---|---|---|---|---|---|---|
| ACCOUNT NO. | | | | | | | |
| ACCOUNT NO. | | | | | | | |
| ACCOUNT NO. | | | | | | | |
| ACCOUNT NO. | | | | | | | |
| | | | | Subtotal ➤ | | | $ |
| | | | | Total ➤ | | | $ |

_____ continuation sheets attached

Total ➤
(Use only on last page of the completed Schedule F.)
( Report also on Summary of Schedules.)

In re _____,    Case No. _____
                    **Debtor**                                              **(If known)**

# SCHEDULE F - CREDITORS HOLDING UNSECURED NONPRIORITY CLAIMS
(Continuation Sheet)

| CREDITOR'S NAME, MAILING ADDRESS INCLUDING ZIP CODE, AND ACCOUNT NUMBER (See instructions above.) | CODEBTOR | HUSBAND, WIFE, JOINT, OR COMMUNITY | DATE CLAIM WAS INCURRED AND CONSIDERATION FOR CLAIM. IF CLAIM IS SUBJECT TO SETOFF, SO STATE. | CONTINGENT | UNLIQUIDATED | DISPUTED | AMOUNT OF CLAIM |
|---|---|---|---|---|---|---|---|
| ACCOUNT NO. | | | | | | | |
| ACCOUNT NO. | | | | | | | |
| ACCOUNT NO. | | | | | | | |
| ACCOUNT NO. | | | | | | | |
| ACCOUNT NO. | | | | | | | |

Sheet no.____of____sheets attached to Schedule of
Creditors Holding Unsecured Nonpriority Claims

Subtotal➤  $

Total➤  $
(Use only on last page of the completed Schedule F.)
( Report also on Summary of Schedules.)

Form B6G
(10/05)

In re _____ ,    Case No._____
        **Debtor**                                        **(if known)**

## SCHEDULE G - EXECUTORY CONTRACTS AND UNEXPIRED LEASES

Describe all executory contracts of any nature and all unexpired leases of real or personal property.  Include any timeshare interests.  State nature of debtor's interest in contract, i.e., "Purchaser," "Agent," etc.  State whether debtor is the lessor or lessee of a lease.  Provide the names and complete mailing addresses of all other parties to each lease or contract described.  If a minor child is a party to one of the leases or contracts, indicate that by stating "a minor child" and do not disclose the child's name.  See 11 U.S.C. § 112;  Fed.R. Bankr. P. 1007(m).

☐ Check this box if debtor has no executory contracts or unexpired leases.

| NAME AND MAILING ADDRESS, INCLUDING ZIP CODE, OF OTHER PARTIES TO LEASE OR CONTRACT. | DESCRIPTION OF CONTRACT OR LEASE AND NATURE OF DEBTOR'S INTEREST.  STATE WHETHER LEASE IS FOR NONRESIDENTIAL REAL PROPERTY.  STATE CONTRACT NUMBER OF ANY GOVERNMENT CONTRACT. |
|---|---|
|  |  |
|  |  |
|  |  |
|  |  |
|  |  |
|  |  |
|  |  |

*This page intentionally blank.*

Form B6H
(10/05)

In re _____ ,          Case No. _____
          **Debtor**                                                    **(if known)**

## SCHEDULE H - CODEBTORS

    Provide the information requested concerning any person or entity, other than a spouse in a joint case, that is also liable on any debts listed by debtor in the schedules of creditors. Include all guarantors and co-signers. If the debtor resides or resided in a community property state, commonwealth, or territory (including Alaska, Arizona, California, Idaho, Louisiana, Nevada, New Mexico, Puerto Rico, Texas, Washington, or Wisconsin) within the eight year period immediately preceding the commencement of the case, identify the name of the debtor's spouse and of any former spouse who resides or resided with the debtor in the community property state, commonwealth, or territory. Include all names used by the nondebtor spouse during the eight years immediately preceding the commencement of this case. If a minor child is a codebtor or a creditor, indicate that by stating "a minor child" and do not disclose the child's name. See 11 U.S.C. § 112; Fed. Bankr. P. 1007(m).

☐  Check this box if debtor has no codebtors.

| NAME AND ADDRESS OF CODEBTOR | NAME AND ADDRESS OF CREDITOR |
|---|---|
|  |  |

*This page intentionally blank.*

Form B6I
(10/05)

In re _____ ,        Case No._____
              **Debtor**                                                    **(if known)**

# SCHEDULE I - CURRENT INCOME OF INDIVIDUAL DEBTOR(S)

The column labeled "Spouse" must be completed in all cases filed by joint debtors and by a married debtor in a chapter 7, 11, 12, or 13 case whether or not a joint petition is filed, unless the spouses are separated and a joint petition is not filed.  Do not state the name of any minor child.

| Debtor's Marital Status: | DEPENDENTS OF DEBTOR AND SPOUSE | |
|---|---|---|
| | RELATIONSHIP: | AGE: |

| **Employment:** | DEBTOR | SPOUSE |
|---|---|---|
| Occupation | | |
| Name of Employer | | |
| How long employed | | |
| Address of Employer | | |
| | | |

INCOME: (Estimate of average monthly income)          DEBTOR          SPOUSE

1.  Current monthly gross wages, salary, and commissions          $_____          $_____
       (Prorate if not paid monthly.)
2.  Estimate monthly overtime          $_____          $_____

3.  SUBTOTAL          $_____          $_____

4.  LESS PAYROLL DEDUCTIONS
      a.  Payroll taxes and social security          $_____          $_____
      b.  Insurance          $_____          $_____
      c.  Union dues          $_____          $_____
      d.  Other (Specify): _____          $_____          $_____

5.  SUBTOTAL OF PAYROLL DEDUCTIONS          $_____          $_____

6.  TOTAL NET MONTHLY TAKE HOME PAY          $_____          $_____

7.  Regular income from operation of business or profession or farm.          $_____          $_____
       (Attach detailed statement)
8.  Income from real property          $_____          $_____
9.  Interest and dividends          $_____          $_____
10. Alimony, maintenance or support payments payable to the debtor for          $_____          $_____
       the debtor's use or that of dependents listed above.
11. Social security or government assistance
       (Specify):_____          $_____          $_____
12. Pension or retirement income          $_____          $_____
13. Other monthly income
       (Specify):_____          $_____          $_____

14. SUBTOTAL OF LINES 7 THROUGH 13
15. TOTAL MONTHLY INCOME (Add amounts shown on lines 6 and 14)          $_____          $_____

16. TOTAL COMBINED MONTHLY INCOME:          $ _____
                                                        (Report also on Summary of Schedules.)

17. Describe any increase or decrease in income reasonably anticipated to occur within the year following the filing of this document:

_____

_____

*This page intentionally blank.*

Form B6J
(10/05)

In re _____ ,        Case No._____
                    **Debtor**                                                    **(if known)**

# SCHEDULE J - CURRENT EXPENDITURES OF INDIVIDUAL DEBTOR(S)

Complete this schedule by estimating the average monthly expenses of the debtor and the debtor's family.  Pro rate any payments made bi-weekly, quarterly, semi-annually, or annually to show monthly rate.

☐        Check this box if a joint petition is filed and debtor's spouse maintains a separate household.  Complete a separate schedule of expenditures labeled "Spouse."

1. Rent or home mortgage payment (include lot rented for mobile home)                                    $ _____

    a. Are real estate taxes included?                Yes _____   No _____

    b. Is property insurance included?                Yes _____   No _____

2. Utilities: a. Electricity and heating fuel                                                                                $ _____

        b. Water and sewer                                                                                            $ _____

        c. Telephone                                                                                                      $ _____

        d. Other _____                  $ _____

3. Home maintenance (repairs and upkeep)                                                                              $ _____

4. Food                                                                                                                                      $ _____

5. Clothing                                                                                                                                $ _____

6. Laundry and dry cleaning                                                                                                     $ _____

7. Medical and dental expenses                                                                                               $ _____

8. Transportation (not including car payments)                                                                       $ _____

9. Recreation, clubs and entertainment, newspapers, magazines, etc.                                     $ _____

10.Charitable contributions                                                                                                     $ _____

11.Insurance (not deducted from wages or included in home mortgage payments)

        a. Homeowner's or renter's                                                                                 $ _____

        b. Life                                                                                                                  $ _____

        c. Health                                                                                                             $ _____

        d. Auto                                                                                                               $ _____

        e. Other _____                    $ _____

12.Taxes (not deducted from wages or included in home mortgage payments)
(Specify) _____                          $ _____

13. Installment payments: (In chapter 11, 12, and 13 cases, do not list payments to be included in the plan)

        a. Auto                                                                                                               $
                                                                                                                                            _____

        b. Other _____                      $ _____

        c. Other _____                          $ _____

14. Alimony, maintenance, and support paid to others                                                           $ _____

15. Payments for support of additional dependents not living at your home                           $ _____

16. Regular expenses from operation of business, profession, or farm (attach detailed statement)   $ _____

17. Other _____                              $_____

18. TOTAL MONTHLY EXPENSES (Report also on Summary of Schedules)                           $_____

19. Describe any increase or decrease in expenditures reasonably anticipated to occur within the year following the filing of

this document:

_____

20. STATEMENT OF MONTHLY NET INCOME

    a. Total monthly income from Line 16 of Schedule I                                                    $ _____

    b. Total monthly expenses from Line 18 above                                                             $ _____

    c. Monthly net income (a. minus b.)                                                                          $ _____

*This page intentionally blank.*

Official Form 6-Decl.
(10/05)

In re _____ ,    Case No. _____
        Debtor                                        _____
                                                      (If known)

# DECLARATION CONCERNING DEBTOR'S SCHEDULES

### DECLARATION UNDER PENALTY OF PERJURY BY INDIVIDUAL DEBTOR

I declare under penalty of perjury that I have read the foregoing summary and schedules, consisting of _____
                                                                    *(Total shown on summary page plus 1.)*
sheets, and that they are true and correct to the best of my knowledge, information, and belief.

Date _____    Signature: _____
                                                            Debtor

Date _____    Signature: _____
                                                        *(Joint Debtor, if any)*

                                     [If joint case, both spouses must sign.]

-------------------------------------------------------------------------------

### DECLARATION AND SIGNATURE OF NON-ATTORNEY BANKRUPTCY PETITION PREPARER (See 11 U.S.C. § 110)

I declare under penalty of perjury that: (1) I am a bankruptcy petition preparer as defined in 11 U.S.C. § 110; (2) I prepared this document for compensation and have provided the debtor with a copy of this document and the notices and information required under 11 U.S.C. §§ 110(b), 110(h) and 342(b); and, (3) if rules or guidelines have been promulgated pursuant to 11 U.S.C. § 110(h) setting a maximum fee for services chargeable by bankruptcy petition preparers, I have given the debtor notice of the maximum amount before preparing any document for filing for a debtor or accepting any fee from the debtor, as required by that section.

_____    _____
Printed or Typed Name of Bankruptcy Petition Preparer    Social Security No.
                                                  *(Required by 11 U.S.C. § 110.)*
*If the bankruptcy petition preparer is not an individual, state the name, title (if any), address, and social security number of the officer, principal, responsible person, or partner who signs this document.*

_____

_____
Address

X _____    _____
Signature of Bankruptcy Petition Preparer    Date

Names and Social Security numbers of all other individuals who prepared or assisted in preparing this document, unless the bankruptcy petition preparer is not an individual:

*If more than one person prepared this document, attach additional signed sheets conforming to the appropriate Official Form for each person.*

*A bankruptcy petition preparer's failure to comply with the provisions of title 11 and the Federal Rules of Bankruptcy Procedure may result in fines or imprisonment or both. 11 U.S.C. § 110; 18 U.S.C. § 156.*

-------------------------------------------------------------------------------

### DECLARATION UNDER PENALTY OF PERJURY ON BEHALF OF A CORPORATION OR PARTNERSHIP

I, the _____ [the president or other officer or an authorized agent of the corporation or a member or an authorized agent of the partnership ] of the _____ [corporation or partnership] named as debtor in this case, declare under penalty of perjury that I have read the foregoing summary and schedules, consisting of _____ sheets, and that they are true and correct to the best of my knowledge, information, and belief.    *(Total shown on summary page plus 1.)*

Date _____

                    Signature: _____

                               _____
                               [Print or type name of individual signing on behalf of debtor.]

*[An individual signing on behalf of a partnership or corporation must indicate position or relationship to debtor.]*

-------------------------------------------------------------------------------

--------*Penalty for making a false statement or concealing property:* Fine of up to $500,000 or imprisonment for up to 5 years or both. 18 U.S.C. §§ 152 and 3571.

*This page intentionally blank.*

Official Form 7
(10/05)

# UNITED STATES BANKRUPTCY COURT

_____ DISTRICT OF _____

In re: _____,    Case No. _____
              Debtor                                                           (if known)

# STATEMENT OF FINANCIAL AFFAIRS

This statement is to be completed by every debtor. Spouses filing a joint petition may file a single statement on which the information for both spouses is combined. If the case is filed under chapter 12 or chapter 13, a married debtor must furnish information for both spouses whether or not a joint petition is filed, unless the spouses are separated and a joint petition is not filed. An individual debtor engaged in business as a sole proprietor, partner, family farmer, or self-employed professional, should provide the information requested on this statement concerning all such activities as well as the individual's personal affairs. Do not include the name or address of a minor child in this statement. Indicate payments, transfers and the like to minor children by stating "a minor child." See 11 U.S.C. § 112; Fed. R. Bankr. P. 1007(m).

Questions 1 - 18 are to be completed by all debtors. Debtors that are or have been in business, as defined below, also must complete Questions 19 - 25. **If the answer to an applicable question is "None," mark the box labeled "None."** If additional space is needed for the answer to any question, use and attach a separate sheet properly identified with the case name, case number (if known), and the number of the question.

## DEFINITIONS

"*In business.*" A debtor is "in business" for the purpose of this form if the debtor is a corporation or partnership. An individual debtor is "in business" for the purpose of this form if the debtor is or has been, within six years immediately preceding the filing of this bankruptcy case, any of the following: an officer, director, managing executive, or owner of 5 percent or more of the voting or equity securities of a corporation; a partner, other than a limited partner, of a partnership; a sole proprietor or self-employed full-time or part-time. An individual debtor also may be "in business" for the purpose of this form if the debtor engages in a trade, business, or other activity, other than as an employee, to supplement income from the debtor's primary employment.

"*Insider.*" The term "insider" includes but is not limited to: relatives of the debtor; general partners of the debtor and their relatives; corporations of which the debtor is an officer, director, or person in control; officers, directors, and any owner of 5 percent or more of the voting or equity securities of a corporate debtor and their relatives; affiliates of the debtor and insiders of such affiliates; any managing agent of the debtor. 11 U.S.C. § 101.

---

1. **Income from employment or operation of business**

None
☐

State the gross amount of income the debtor has received from employment, trade, or profession, or from operation of the debtor's business, including part-time activities either as an employee or in independent trade or business, from the beginning of this calendar year to the date this case was commenced. State also the gross amounts received during the **two years** immediately preceding this calendar year. (A debtor that maintains, or has maintained, financial records on the basis of a fiscal rather than a calendar year may report fiscal year income. Identify the beginning and ending dates of the debtor's fiscal year.) If a joint petition is filed, state income for each spouse separately. (Married debtors filing under chapter 12 or chapter 13 must state income of both spouses whether or not a joint petition is filed, unless the spouses are separated and a joint petition is not filed.)

AMOUNT                                        SOURCE

**2. Income other than from employment or operation of business**

None
☐

State the amount of income received by the debtor other than from employment, trade, profession, operation of the debtor's business during the **two years** immediately preceding the commencement of this case. Give particulars. If a joint petition is filed, state income for each spouse separately. (Married debtors filing under chapter 12 or chapter 13 must state income for each spouse whether or not a joint petition is filed, unless the spouses are separated and a joint petition is not filed.)

AMOUNT                                                                       SOURCE

---

**3. Payments to creditors**

*Complete a. or b., as appropriate, and c.*

None
☐

a. *Individual or joint debtor(s) with primarily consumer debts:*  List all payments on loans, installment purchases of goods or services, and other debts to any creditor made within **90 days** immediately preceding the commencement of this case if the aggregate value of all property that constitutes or is affected by such transfer is not less than $600. Indicate with an asterisk (*) any payments that were made to a creditor on account of a domestic support obligation or as  part of an alternative repayment schedule under a plan by an approved nonprofit budgeting and creditor counseling agency.  (Married debtors filing under chapter 12 or chapter 13 must include payments by either or both spouses whether or not a joint petition is filed, unless the spouses are separated and a joint petition is not filed.)

| NAME AND ADDRESS OF CREDITOR | DATES OF PAYMENTS | AMOUNT PAID | AMOUNT STILL OWING |
| --- | --- | --- | --- |

---

None
☐

b. *Debtor whose debts are not primarily consumer debts:* List each payment or other transfer to any creditor made within **90** days immediately preceding the commencement of the case if the aggregate value of all property that constitutes or is affected by such transfer is not less than $5,000.  (Married debtors filing under chapter 12 or chapter 13 must include payments and other transfers by either or both spouses whether or not a joint petition is filed, unless the spouses are separated and a joint petition is not filed.)

| NAME AND ADDRESS OF CREDITOR | DATES OF PAYMENTS/ TRANSFERS | AMOUNT PAID OR VALUE OF TRANSFERS | AMOUNT STILL OWING |
| --- | --- | --- | --- |

---

None
☐

c. *All debtors:*  List all payments made within **one year** immediately preceding the commencement of this case to or for the benefit of creditors who are or were insiders.  (Married debtors filing under chapter 12 or chapter 13 must include payments by either or both spouses whether or not a joint petition is filed, unless the spouses are separated and a joint petition is not filed.)

| NAME AND ADDRESS OF CREDITOR AND RELATIONSHIP TO DEBTOR | DATE OF PAYMENT | AMOUNT PAID | AMOUNT STILL OWING |
| --- | --- | --- | --- |

---

**4. Suits and administrative proceedings, executions, garnishments and attachments**

None ☐ a. List all suits and administrative proceedings to which the debtor is or was a party within **one year** immediately preceding the filing of this bankruptcy case. (Married debtors filing under chapter 12 or chapter 13 must include information concerning either or both spouses whether or not a joint petition is filed, unless the spouses are separated and a joint petition is not filed.)

| CAPTION OF SUIT AND CASE NUMBER | NATURE OF PROCEEDING | COURT OR AGENCY AND LOCATION | STATUS OR DISPOSITION |
|---|---|---|---|
| | | | |

None ☐ b. Describe all property that has been attached, garnished or seized under any legal or equitable process within **one year** immediately preceding the commencement of this case. (Married debtors filing under chapter 12 or chapter 13 must include information concerning property of either or both spouses whether or not a joint petition is filed, unless the spouses are separated and a joint petition is not filed.)

| NAME AND ADDRESS OF PERSON FOR WHOSE BENEFIT PROPERTY WAS SEIZED | DATE OF SEIZURE | DESCRIPTION AND VALUE OF PROPERTY |
|---|---|---|
| | | |

## 5. Repossessions, foreclosures and returns

None ☐ List all property that has been repossessed by a creditor, sold at a foreclosure sale, transferred through a deed in lieu of foreclosure or returned to the seller, within **one year** immediately preceding the commencement of this case. (Married debtors filing under chapter 12 or chapter 13 must include information concerning property of either or both spouses whether or not a joint petition is filed, unless the spouses are separated and a joint petition is not filed.)

| NAME AND ADDRESS OF CREDITOR OR SELLER | DATE OF REPOSSESSION, FORECLOSURE SALE, TRANSFER OR RETURN | DESCRIPTION AND VALUE OF PROPERTY |
|---|---|---|
| | | |

## 6. Assignments and receiverships

None ☐ a. Describe any assignment of property for the benefit of creditors made within **120 days** immediately preceding the commencement of this case. (Married debtors filing under chapter 12 or chapter 13 must include any assignment by either or both spouses whether or not a joint petition is filed, unless the spouses are separated and a joint petition is not filed.)

| NAME AND ADDRESS OF ASSIGNEE | DATE OF ASSIGNMENT | TERMS OF ASSIGNMENT OR SETTLEMENT |
|---|---|---|
| | | |

None ☐ b. List all property which has been in the hands of a custodian, receiver, or court-appointed official within **one year** immediately preceding the commencement of this case. (Married debtors filing under chapter 12 or chapter 13 must include information concerning property of either or both spouses whether or not a joint petition is filed, unless the spouses are separated and a joint petition is not filed.)

| NAME AND ADDRESS OF CUSTODIAN | NAME AND LOCATION OF COURT CASE TITLE & NUMBER | DATE OF ORDER | DESCRIPTION AND VALUE Of PROPERTY |
|---|---|---|---|

### 7. Gifts

None ☐ List all gifts or charitable contributions made within **one year** immediately preceding the commencement of this case except ordinary and usual gifts to family members aggregating less than $200 in value per individual family member and charitable contributions aggregating less than $100 per recipient. (Married debtors filing under chapter 12 or chapter 13 must include gifts or contributions by either or both spouses whether or not a joint petition is filed, unless the spouses are separated and a joint petition is not filed.)

| NAME AND ADDRESS OF PERSON OR ORGANIZATION | RELATIONSHIP TO DEBTOR, IF ANY | DATE OF GIFT | DESCRIPTION AND VALUE OF GIFT |
|---|---|---|---|

### 8. Losses

None ☐ List all losses from fire, theft, other casualty or gambling within **one year** immediately preceding the commencement of this case **or since the commencement of this case**. (Married debtors filing under chapter 12 or chapter 13 must include losses by either or both spouses whether or not a joint petition is filed, unless the spouses are separated and a joint petition is not filed.)

| DESCRIPTION AND VALUE OF PROPERTY | DESCRIPTION OF CIRCUMSTANCES AND, IF LOSS WAS COVERED IN WHOLE OR IN PART BY INSURANCE, GIVE PARTICULARS | DATE OF LOSS |
|---|---|---|

### 9. Payments related to debt counseling or bankruptcy

None ☐ List all payments made or property transferred by or on behalf of the debtor to any persons, including attorneys, for consultation concerning debt consolidation, relief under the bankruptcy law or preparation of a petition in bankruptcy within **one year** immediately preceding the commencement of this case.

| NAME AND ADDRESS OF PAYEE | DATE OF PAYMENT, NAME OF PAYER IF OTHER THAN DEBTOR | AMOUNT OF MONEY OR DESCRIPTION AND VALUE OF PROPERTY |
|---|---|---|

### 10. Other transfers

None

☐

a. List all other property, other than property transferred in the ordinary course of the business or financial affairs of the debtor, transferred either absolutely or as security within **two years** immediately preceding the commencement of this case. (Married debtors filing under chapter 12 or chapter 13 must include transfers by either or both spouses whether or not a joint petition is filed, unless the spouses are separated and a joint petition is not filed.)

|  | | DESCRIBE PROPERTY |
| NAME AND ADDRESS OF TRANSFEREE, | | TRANSFERRED AND |
| RELATIONSHIP TO DEBTOR | DATE | VALUE RECEIVED |

None

☐

b. List all property transferred by the debtor within **ten years** immediately preceding the commencement of this case to a self-settled trust or similar device of which the debtor is a beneficiary.

| NAME OF TRUST OR OTHER | DATE(S) OF | AMOUNT OF MONEY OR DESCRIPTION |
| DEVICE | TRANSFER(S) | AND VALUE OF PROPERTY OR DEBTOR'S |
|  | | INTEREST IN PROPERTY |

### 11. Closed financial accounts

None

☐

List all financial accounts and instruments held in the name of the debtor or for the benefit of the debtor which were closed, sold, or otherwise transferred within **one year** immediately preceding the commencement of this case. Include checking, savings, or other financial accounts, certificates of deposit, or other instruments; shares and share accounts held in banks, credit unions, pension funds, cooperatives, associations, brokerage houses and other financial institutions. (Married debtors filing under chapter 12 or chapter 13 must include information concerning accounts or instruments held by or for either or both spouses whether or not a joint petition is filed, unless the spouses are separated and a joint petition is not filed.)

|  | TYPE OF ACCOUNT, LAST FOUR | AMOUNT AND |
| NAME AND ADDRESS | DIGITS OF ACCOUNT NUMBER, | DATE OF SALE |
| OF INSTITUTION | AND AMOUNT OF FINAL BALANCE | OR CLOSING |

### 12. Safe deposit boxes

None

☐

List each safe deposit or other box or depository in which the debtor has or had securities, cash, or other valuables within **one year** immediately preceding the commencement of this case. (Married debtors filing under chapter 12 or chapter 13 must include boxes or depositories of either or both spouses whether or not a joint petition is filed, unless the spouses are separated and a joint petition is not filed.)

| NAME AND ADDRESS | NAMES AND ADDRESSES | DESCRIPTION | DATE OF TRANSFER |
| OF BANK OR | OF THOSE WITH ACCESS | OF | OR SURRENDER, |
| OTHER DEPOSITORY | TO BOX OR DEPOSITORY | CONTENTS | IF ANY |

### 13. Setoffs

None
☐ List all setoffs made by any creditor, including a bank, against a debt or deposit of the debtor within **90 days** preceding the commencement of this case. (Married debtors filing under chapter 12 or chapter 13 must include information concerning either or both spouses whether or not a joint petition is filed, unless the spouses are separated and a joint petition is not filed.)

|  | DATE OF | AMOUNT |
| NAME AND ADDRESS OF CREDITOR | SETOFF | OF SETOFF |

---

### 14. Property held for another person

None
☐ List all property owned by another person that the debtor holds or controls.

| NAME AND ADDRESS OF OWNER | DESCRIPTION AND VALUE OF PROPERTY | LOCATION OF PROPERTY |

---

### 15. Prior address of debtor

None
☐ If debtor has moved within **three years** immediately preceding the commencement of this case, list all premises which the debtor occupied during that period and vacated prior to the commencement of this case. If a joint petition is filed, report also any separate address of either spouse.

| ADDRESS | NAME USED | DATES OF OCCUPANCY |

---

### 16. Spouses and Former Spouses

None
☐ If the debtor resides or resided in a community property state, commonwealth, or territory (including Alaska, Arizona, California, Idaho, Louisiana, Nevada, New Mexico, Puerto Rico, Texas, Washington, or Wisconsin) within **eight years** immediately preceding the commencement of the case, identify the name of the debtor's spouse and of any former spouse who resides or resided with the debtor in the community property state.

NAME

**17. Environmental Information.**

For the purpose of this question, the following definitions apply:

"Environmental Law" means any federal, state, or local statute or regulation regulating pollution, contamination, releases of hazardous or toxic substances, wastes or material into the air, land, soil, surface water, groundwater, or other medium, including, but not limited to, statutes or regulations regulating the cleanup of these substances, wastes, or material.

"Site" means any location, facility, or property as defined under any Environmental Law, whether or not presently or formerly owned or operated by the debtor, including, but not limited to, disposal sites.

"Hazardous Material" means anything defined as a hazardous waste, hazardous substance, toxic substance, hazardous material, pollutant, or contaminant or similar term under an Environmental Law.

None ☐   a. List the name and address of every site for which the debtor has received notice in writing by a governmental unit that it may be liable or potentially liable under or in violation of an Environmental Law. Indicate the governmental unit, the date of the notice, and, if known, the Environmental Law:

| SITE NAME AND ADDRESS | NAME AND ADDRESS OF GOVERNMENTAL UNIT | DATE OF NOTICE | ENVIRONMENTAL LAW |
|---|---|---|---|

None ☐   b. List the name and address of every site for which the debtor provided notice to a governmental unit of a release of Hazardous Material. Indicate the governmental unit to which the notice was sent and the date of the notice.

| SITE NAME AND ADDRESS | NAME AND ADDRESS OF GOVERNMENTAL UNIT | DATE OF NOTICE | ENVIRONMENTAL LAW |
|---|---|---|---|

None ☐   c. List all judicial or administrative proceedings, including settlements or orders, under any Environmental Law with respect to which the debtor is or was a party. Indicate the name and address of the governmental unit that is or was a part to the proceeding, and the docket number.

| NAME AND ADDRESS OF GOVERNMENTAL UNIT | DOCKET NUMBER | STATUS OR DISPOSITION |
|---|---|---|

**18 . Nature, location and name of business**

None ☐   a. *If the debtor is an individual*, list the names, addresses, taxpayer identification numbers, nature of the businesses, and beginning and ending dates of all businesses in which the debtor was an officer, director, partner, or managing executive of a corporation, partner in a partnership, sole proprietor, or was self-employed in a trade, profession, or other activity either full- or part-time within **six years** immediately preceding the commencement of this case, or in which the debtor owned 5 percent or more of the voting or equity securities within **six years** immediately preceding the commencement of this case.

*If the debtor is a partnership*, list the names, addresses, taxpayer identification numbers, nature of the businesses, and beginning and ending dates of all businesses in which the debtor was a partner or owned 5 percent or more of the voting or equity securities, within **six years** immediately preceding the commencement of this case.

*If the debtor is a corporation*, list the names, addresses, taxpayer identification numbers, nature of the businesses, and beginning and ending dates of all businesses in which the debtor was a partner or owned 5 percent or more of the voting or equity securities within **six years** immediately preceding the commencement of this case.

| NAME | LAST FOUR DIGITS OF SOC. SEC. NO./ COMPLETE EIN OR OTHER TAXPAYER I.D. NO. | ADDRESS | NATURE OF BUSINESS | BEGINNING AND ENDING DATES |
|------|------|------|------|------|

None ☐  b. Identify any business listed in response to subdivision a., above, that is "single asset real estate" as defined in 11 U.S.C. § 101.

    NAME                          ADDRESS

The following questions are to be completed by every debtor that is a corporation or partnership and by any individual debtor who is or has been, within **six years** immediately preceding the commencement of this case, any of the following: an officer, director, managing executive, or owner of more than 5 percent of the voting or equity securities of a corporation; a partner, other than a limited partner, of a partnership, a sole proprietor, or self-employed in a trade, profession, or other activity, either full- or part-time.

*(An individual or joint debtor should complete this portion of the statement **only** if the debtor is or has been in business, as defined above, within six years immediately preceding the commencement of this case. A debtor who has not been in business within those six years should go directly to the signature page.)*

### 19. Books, records and financial statements

None ☐  a. List all bookkeepers and accountants who within **two years** immediately preceding the filing of this bankruptcy case kept or supervised the keeping of books of account and records of the debtor.

    NAME AND ADDRESS                                  DATES SERVICES RENDERED

None ☐  b. List all firms or individuals who within **two years** immediately preceding the filing of this bankruptcy case have audited the books of account and records, or prepared a financial statement of the debtor.

    NAME                          ADDRESS                  DATES SERVICES RENDERED

None ☐  c. List all firms or individuals who at the time of the commencement of this case were in possession of the books of account and records of the debtor. If any of the books of account and records are not available, explain.

    NAME                                          ADDRESS

None ☐    d. List all financial institutions, creditors and other parties, including mercantile and trade agencies, to whom a financial statement was issued by the debtor within **two years** immediately preceding the commencement of this case.

        NAME AND ADDRESS                          DATE ISSUED

### 20. Inventories

None ☐    a. List the dates of the last two inventories taken of your property, the name of the person who supervised the taking of each inventory, and the dollar amount and basis of each inventory.

| | | DOLLAR AMOUNT OF INVENTORY |
|---|---|---|
| DATE OF INVENTORY | INVENTORY SUPERVISOR | (Specify cost, market or other basis) |

None ☐    b. List the name and address of the person having possession of the records of each of the inventories reported in a., above.

| | NAME AND ADDRESSES OF CUSTODIAN |
|---|---|
| DATE OF INVENTORY | OF INVENTORY RECORDS |

### 21 . Current Partners, Officers, Directors and Shareholders

None ☐    a. If the debtor is a partnership, list the nature and percentage of partnership interest of each member of the partnership.

| NAME AND ADDRESS | NATURE OF INTEREST | PERCENTAGE OF INTEREST |
|---|---|---|

None ☐    b. If the debtor is a corporation, list all officers and directors of the corporation, and each stockholder who directly or indirectly owns, controls, or holds 5 percent or more of the voting or equity securities of the corporation.

| | | NATURE AND PERCENTAGE OF STOCK OWNERSHIP |
|---|---|---|
| NAME AND ADDRESS | TITLE | |

### 22 . Former partners, officers, directors and shareholders

None ☐    a. If the debtor is a partnership, list each member who withdrew from the partnership within **one year** immediately preceding the commencement of this case.

| NAME | ADDRESS | DATE OF WITHDRAWAL |
|---|---|---|

None ☐ b. If the debtor is a corporation, list all officers, or directors whose relationship with the corporation terminated within **one year** immediately preceding the commencement of this case.

| NAME AND ADDRESS | TITLE | DATE OF TERMINATION |
|---|---|---|

## 23 . Withdrawals from a partnership or distributions by a corporation

None ☐ If the debtor is a partnership or corporation, list all withdrawals or distributions credited or given to an insider, including compensation in any form, bonuses, loans, stock redemptions, options exercised and any other perquisite during **one year** immediately preceding the commencement of this case.

| NAME & ADDRESS OF RECIPIENT, RELATIONSHIP TO DEBTOR | DATE AND PURPOSE OF WITHDRAWAL | AMOUNT OF MONEY OR DESCRIPTION AND VALUE OF PROPERTY |
|---|---|---|

## 24. Tax Consolidation Group.

None ☐ If the debtor is a corporation, list the name and federal taxpayer identification number of the parent corporation of any consolidated group for tax purposes of which the debtor has been a member at any time within **six years** immediately preceding the commencement of the case.

| NAME OF PARENT CORPORATION | TAXPAYER IDENTIFICATION NUMBER (EIN) |
|---|---|

## 25. Pension Funds.

None ☐ If the debtor is not an individual, list the name and federal taxpayer identification number of any pension fund to which the debtor, as an employer, has been responsible for contributing at any time within **six years** immediately preceding the commencement of the case.

| NAME OF PENSION FUND | TAXPAYER IDENTIFICATION NUMBER (EIN) |
|---|---|

\* \* \* \* \* \*

*[If completed by an individual or individual and spouse]*

I declare under penalty of perjury that I have read the answers contained in the foregoing statement of financial affairs and any attachments thereto and that they are true and correct.

Date _____     Signature _____
                                    of Debtor

Date _____     Signature_____
                                    of Joint Debtor
                                    (if any)

_____

*[If completed on behalf of a partnership or corporation]*

I, declare under penalty of perjury that I have read the answers contained in the foregoing statement of financial affairs and any attachments thereto and that they are true and correct to the best of my knowledge, information and belief.

Date _____     Signature _____

                                              _____
                                              Print Name and Title

[An individual signing on behalf of a partnership or corporation must indicate position or relationship to debtor.]

_____ continuation sheets attached

*Penalty for making a false statement: Fine of up to $500,000 or imprisonment for up to 5 years, or both. 18 U.S.C. §§ 152 and 3571*

---

### DECLARATION AND SIGNATURE OF NON-ATTORNEY BANKRUPTCY PETITION PREPARER (See 11 U.S.C. § 110)

I declare under penalty of perjury that: (1) I am a bankruptcy petition preparer as defined in 11 U.S.C. § 110; (2) I prepared this document for compensation and have provided the debtor with a copy of this document and the notices and information required under 11 U.S.C. §§ 110(b), 110(h), and 342(b); and, (3) if rules or guidelines have been promulgated pursuant to 11 U.S.C. § 110(h) setting a maximum fee for services chargeable by bankruptcy petition preparers, I have given the debtor notice of the maximum amount before preparing any document for filing for a debtor or accepting any fee from the debtor, as required by that section.

_____          _____
Printed or Typed Name and Title, if any, of Bankruptcy Petition Preparer     Social Security No.(Required by 11 U.S.C. § 110.)

*If the bankruptcy petition preparer is not an individual, state the name, title (if any), address, and social security number of the officer, principal, responsible person, or partner who signs this document.*

_____

_____
Address

X _____          _____
   Signature of Bankruptcy Petition Preparer                              Date

Names and Social Security numbers of all other individuals who prepared or assisted in preparing this document unless the bankruptcy petition preparer is not an individual:

If more than one person prepared this document, attach additional signed sheets conforming to the appropriate Official Form for each person.

*A bankruptcy petition preparer's failure to comply with the provisions of title 11 and the Federal Rules of Bankruptcy Procedure may result in fines or imprisonment or both. 18 U.S.C. § 156.*

*This page intentionally blank.*

Form 8
(10/05)

# United States Bankruptcy Court
_____ District Of _____

In re _____,                    Case No. _____

Debtor                                          Chapter 7

## CHAPTER 7 INDIVIDUAL DEBTOR'S STATEMENT OF INTENTION

☐ I have filed a schedule of assets and liabilities which includes debts secured by property of the estate.
☐ I have filed a schedule of executory contracts and unexpired leases which includes personal property subject to an unexpired lease.
☐ I intend to do the following with respect to the property of the estate which secures those debts or is subject to a lease:

| Description of Secured Property | Creditor's Name | Property will be Surrendered | Property is claimed as exempt | Property will be redeemed pursuant to 11 U.S.C. § 722 | Debt will be reaffirmed pursuant to 11 U.S.C. § 524(c) |
|---|---|---|---|---|---|
| | | | | | |

| Description of Leased Property | Lessor's Name | Lease will be assumed pursuant to 11 U.S.C. § 362(h)(1)(A) |
|---|---|---|
| | | |

Date: _____

_____
Signature of Debtor

------------------------------------------------------------------------------------------

### DECLARATION OF NON-ATTORNEY BANKRUPTCY PETITION PREPARER (See 11 U.S.C. § 110)

I declare under penalty of perjury that: (1) I am a bankruptcy petition preparer as defined in 11 U.S.C. § 110; (2) I prepared this document for compensation and have provided the debtor with a copy of this document and the notices and information required under 11 U.S.C. §§ 110(b), 110(h), and 342(b); and, (3) if rules or guidelines have been promulgated pursuant to 11 U.S.C. § 110(h) setting a maximum fee for services chargeable by bankruptcy petition preparers, I have given the debtor notice of the maximum amount before preparing any document for filing for a debtor or accepting any fee from the debtor, as required in that section.

_____          _____
Printed or Typed Name of Bankruptcy Petition Preparer      Social Security No. (Required under 11 U.S.C. § 110.)
_If the bankruptcy petition preparer is not an individual, state the name, title (if any), address, and social security number of the officer, principal, responsible person or partner who signs this document._
_____

_____
Address

X_____          _____
Signature of Bankruptcy Petition Preparer          Date

Names and Social Security Numbers of all other individuals who prepared or assisted in preparing this document unless the bankruptcy petition preparer is not an individual:

If more than one person prepared this document, attach additional signed sheets conforming to the appropriate Official Form for each person.

_A bankruptcy petition preparer's failure to comply with the provisions of title 11 and the Federal Rules of Bankruptcy Procedure may result in fines or imprisonment or both. 11 U.S.C. § 110; 18 U.S.C. § 156._

*This page intentionally blank.*

**Form B22A (Chapter 7) (10/05)**

In re _____
                    Debtor(s)

Case Number: _____
                    (If known)

# STATEMENT OF CURRENT MONTHLY INCOME AND MEANS TEST CALCULATION
### FOR USE IN CHAPTER 7 ONLY

In addition to Schedule I and J, this statement must be completed by every individual Chapter 7 debtor, whether or not filing jointly, whose debts are primarily consumer debts. Joint debtors may complete one statement only.

## Part I. EXCLUSION FOR DISABLED VETERANS

| | |
|---|---|
| 1 | If you are a disabled veteran described in the Veteran's Declaration in this Part I, (1) check the box at the beginning of the Veteran's Declaration, (2) check the box for "The presumption does not arise" at the top of this statement, and (3) complete the verification in Part VIII. Do not complete any of the remaining parts of this statement. <br><br> ☐ **Veteran's Declaration.** By checking this box, I declare under penalty of perjury that I am a disabled veteran (as defined in 38 U.S.C. § 3741(1)) whose indebtedness occurred primarily during a period in which I was on active duty (as defined in 10 U.S.C. § 101(d)(1)) or while I was performing a homeland defense activity (as defined in 32 U.S.C. §901(1)). |

## Part II. CALCULATION OF MONTHLY INCOME FOR § 707(b)(7) EXCLUSION

| | | Column A<br>Debtor's<br>Income | Column B<br>Spouse's<br>Income |
|---|---|---|---|
| 2 | **Marital/filing status.** Check the box that applies and complete the balance of this part of this statement as directed. <br><br> a. ☐ Unmarried. **Complete only Column A ("Debtor's Income") for Lines 3-11.** <br><br> b. ☐ Married, not filing jointly, with declaration of separate households. By checking this box, debtor declares under penalty of perjury: "My spouse and I are legally separated under applicable non-bankruptcy law or my spouse and I are living apart other than for the purpose of evading the requirements of § 707(b)(2)(A) of the Bankruptcy Code." **Complete only Column A ("Debtor's Income") for Lines 3-11.** <br><br> c. ☐ Married, not filing jointly, without the declaration of separate households set out in Line 2.b above. **Complete both Column A ("Debtor's Income") and Column B (Spouse's Income) for Lines 3-11.** <br><br> d. ☐ Married, filing jointly. **Complete both Column A ("Debtor's Income") and Column B ("Spouse's Income") for Lines 3-11.** | | |
| | All figures must reflect average monthly income for the six calendar months prior to filing the bankruptcy case, ending on the last day of the month before the filing. If you received different amounts of income during these six months, you must total the amounts received during the six months, divide this total by six, and enter the result on the appropriate line. | | |
| 3 | Gross wages, salary, tips, bonuses, overtime, commissions. | $ | $ |

| 4 | Income from the operation of a business, profession or farm. Subtract Line b from Line a and enter the difference on Line 4. Do not enter a number less than zero. **Do not include any part of the business expenses entered on Line b as a deduction in Part V.** | | | |
|---|---|---|---|---|
| | a. | Gross receipts | $ | |
| | b. | Ordinary and necessary business expenses | $ | |
| | c. | Business income | Subtract Line b from Line a | $      $ |

| 5 | Rent and other real property income. Subtract Line b from Line a and enter the difference on Line 5. Do not enter a number less than zero. **Do not include any part of the operating expenses entered on Line b as a deduction in Part V.** | | | |
|---|---|---|---|---|
| | a. | Gross receipts | $ | |
| | b. | Ordinary and necessary operating expenses | $ | |
| | c. | Rental income | Subtract Line b from Line a | $      $ |

| 6 | Interest, dividends and royalties. | $ | $ |
|---|---|---|---|
| 7 | Pension and retirement income. | $ | $ |
| 8 | Regular contributions to the household expenses of the debtor or the debtor's dependents, including child or spousal support. Do not include contributions from the debtor's spouse if Column B is completed. | $ | $ |

| | | | |
|---|---|---|---|
| 9 | Unemployment compensation. Enter the amount in Column A and, if applicable, Column B. However, if you contend that unemployment compensation received by you or your spouse was a benefit under the Social Security Act, do not list the amount of such compensation in Column A or B, but instead state the amount in the space below:<br><br>Unemployment compensation claimed to be a benefit under the Social Security Act  Debtor $ _____  Spouse $ _____ | $ | $ |
| 10 | Income from all other sources. If necessary, list additional sources on a separate page. **Do not include** any benefits received under the Social Security Act or payments received as a victim of a war crime, crime against humanity, or as a victim of international or domestic terrorism. Specify source and amount.<br>a. _____ $ _____<br>b. _____ $ _____<br>Total and enter on Line 10 | $ | $ |
| 11 | **Subtotal of Current Monthly Income for § 707(b)(7).** Add Lines 3 thru 10 in Column A, and, if Column B is completed, add Lines 3 through 10 in Column B. Enter the total(s). | $ | $ |
| 12 | **Total Current Monthly Income for § 707(b)(7).** If Column B has been completed, add Line 11, Column A to Line 11, Column B, and enter the total. If Column B has not been completed, enter the amount from Line 11, Column A. | $ | |

### Part III. APPLICATION OF § 707(b)(7) EXCLUSION

| | | |
|---|---|---|
| 13 | **Annualized Current Monthly Income for § 707(b)(7).** Multiply the amount from Line 12 by the number 12 and enter the result. | $ |
| 14 | **Applicable median family income.** Enter the median family income for the applicable state and household size. (This information is available by family size at www.usdoj.gov/ust/ or from the clerk of the bankruptcy court.)<br>a. Enter debtor's state of residence: _____  b. Enter debtor's household size: _____ | $ |
| 15 | **Application of Section 707(b)(7).** Check the applicable box and proceed as directed.<br><br>☐ **The amount on Line 13 is less than or equal to the amount on Line 14.** Check the box for "The presumption does not arise" at the top of page 1 of this statement, and complete Part VIII; do not complete Parts IV, V, VI or VII.<br><br>☐ **The amount on Line 13 is more than the amount on Line 14.** Complete the remaining parts of this statement. | |

**Complete Parts IV, V, VI, and VII of this statement only if required. (See Line 15.)**

### Part IV. CALCULATION OF CURRENT MONTHLY INCOME FOR § 707(b)(2)

| | | |
|---|---|---|
| 16 | **Enter the amount from Line 12.** | $ |
| 17 | **Marital adjustment.** If you checked the box at Line 2.c, enter the amount of the income listed in Line 11, Column B that was NOT regularly contributed to the household expenses of the debtor or the debtor's dependents. If you did not check box at Line 2.c, enter zero. | $ |
| 18 | **Current monthly income for § 707(b)(2).** Subtract Line 17 from Line 16 and enter the result. | $ |

### Part V. CALCULATION OF DEDUCTIONS ALLOWED UNDER § 707(b)(2)

#### Subpart A: Deductions under Standards of the Internal Revenue Service (IRS)

| | | |
|---|---|---|
| 19 | **National Standards: food, clothing, household supplies, personal care, and miscellaneous.** Enter "Total" amount from IRS National Standards for Allowable Living Expenses for the applicable family size and income level. (This information is available at www.usdoj.gov/ust/ or from the clerk of the bankruptcy court.) | $ |
| 20A | **Local Standards: housing and utilities; non-mortgage expenses.** Enter the amount of the IRS Housing and Utilities Standards; non-mortgage expenses for the applicable county and family size. | $ |

**Form B 22A (Chapter 7) (10/05)** 3

| | (This information is available at www.usdoj.gov/ust/ or from the clerk of the bankruptcy court). | | |
|---|---|---|---|
| 20B | **Local Standards: housing and utilities; mortgage/rent expense.** Enter, in Line a below, the amount of the IRS Housing and Utilities Standards; mortgage/rent expense for your county and family size (this information is available at www.usdoj.gov/ust/ or from the clerk of the bankruptcy court); enter on Line b the total of the Average Monthly Payments for any debts secured by your home, as stated in Line 42; subtract Line b from Line a and enter the result in Line 20B. **Do not enter an amount less than zero.** | | |
| | a. IRS Housing and Utilities Standards; mortgage/rental expense | $ | |
| | b. Average Monthly Payment for any debts secured by your home, if any, as stated in Line 42 | $ | |
| | c. Net mortgage/rental expense | Subtract Line b from Line a. | $ |
| 21 | **Local Standards: housing and utilities; adjustment.** if you contend that the process set out in Lines 20A and 20B does not accurately compute the allowance to which you are entitled under the IRS Housing and Utilities Standards, enter any additional amount to which you contend you are entitled, and state the basis for your contention in the space below: _____ _____ | | $ |
| 22 | **Local Standards: transportation; vehicle operation/public transportation expense.** You are entitled to an expense allowance in this category regardless of whether you pay the expenses of operating a vehicle and regardless of whether you use public transportation. Check the number of vehicles for which you pay the operating expenses or for which the operating expenses are included as a contribution to your household expenses in Line 8. ☐ 0  ☐ 1  ☐ 2 or more. Enter the amount from IRS Transportation Standards, Operating Costs & Public Transportation Costs for the applicable number of vehicles in the applicable Metropolitan Statistical Area or Census Region. (This information is available at www.usdoj.gov/ust/ or from the clerk of the bankruptcy court.) | | $ |
| 23 | **Local Standards: transportation ownership/lease expense; Vehicle 1.** Check the number of vehicles for which you claim an ownership/lease expense. (You may not claim an ownership/lease expense for more than two vehicles.) ☐ 1  ☐ 2 or more. Enter, in Line a below, the amount of the IRS Transportation Standards, Ownership Costs, First Car (available at www.usdoj.gov/ust/ or from the clerk of the bankruptcy court); enter in Line b the total of the Average Monthly Payments for any debts secured by Vehicle 1, as stated in Line 42; subtract Line b from Line a and enter the result in Line 23. **Do not enter an amount less than zero.** | | |
| | a. IRS Transportation Standards, Ownership Costs, First Car | $ | |
| | b. Average Monthly Payment for any debts secured by Vehicle 1, as stated in Line 42 | $ | |
| | c. Net ownership/lease expense for Vehicle 1 | Subtract Line b from Line a. | $ |
| 24 | **Local Standards: transportation ownership/lease expense; Vehicle 2.** Complete this Line only if you checked the "2 or more" Box in Line 23. Enter, in Line a below, the amount of the IRS Transportation Standards, Ownership Costs, Second Car (available at www.usdoj.gov/ust/ or from the clerk of the bankruptcy court); enter in Line b the total of the Average Monthly Payments for any debts secured by Vehicle 2, as stated in Line 42; subtract Line b from Line a and enter the result in Line 24. **Do not enter an amount less than zero.** | | |
| | a. IRS Transportation Standards, Ownership Costs, Second Car | $ | |
| | b. Average Monthly Payment for any debts secured by Vehicle 2, as stated in Line 42 | $ | |
| | c. Net ownership/lease expense for Vehicle 2 | Subtract Line b from Line a. | $ |
| 25 | **Other Necessary Expenses: taxes.** Enter the total average monthly expense that you actually incur for all federal, state and local taxes, other than real estate and sales taxes, such as income taxes, self employment taxes, social security taxes, and Medicare taxes. **Do not include real estate or sales taxes.** | | |
| 26 | **Other Necessary Expenses: mandatory payroll deductions.** Enter the total average monthly payroll deductions that are required for your employment, such as mandatory retirement contributions, union dues, and uniform costs. **Do not include discretionary amounts, such as non-mandatory 401(k) contributions.** | | $ |

**Form B 22A (Chapter 7) (10/05)** 4

| 27 | **Other Necessary Expenses: life insurance.** Enter average monthly premiums that you actually pay for term life insurance for yourself. **Do not include premiums for insurance on your dependents, for whole life or for any other form of insurance.** | $ |
|---|---|---|
| 28 | **Other Necessary Expenses: court-ordered payments.** Enter the total monthly amount that you are required to pay pursuant to court order, such as spousal or child support payments. **Do not include payments on past due support obligations included in Line 44.** | $ |
| 29 | **Other Necessary Expenses: education for employment or for a physically or mentally challenged child.** Enter the total monthly amount that you actually expend for education that is a condition of employment and for education that is required for a physically or mentally challenged dependent child for whom no public education providing similar services is available. | $ |
| 30 | **Other Necessary Expenses: childcare.** Enter the average monthly amount that you actually expend on childcare. **Do not include payments made for children's education.** | $ |
| 31 | **Other Necessary Expenses: health care.** Enter the average monthly amount that you actually expend on health care expenses that are not reimbursed by insurance or paid by a health savings account. **Do not include payments for health insurance listed in Line 34.** | $ |
| 32 | **Other Necessary Expenses: telecommunication services.** Enter the average monthly expenses that you actually pay for cell phones, pagers, call waiting, caller identification, special long distance or internet services necessary for the health and welfare of you or your dependents. **Do not include any amount previously deducted.** | $ |
| 33 | **Total Expenses Allowed under IRS Standards.** Enter the total of Lines 19 through 32. | $ |

### Subpart B: Additional Expense Deductions under § 707(b)
#### Note: Do not include any expenses that you have listed in Lines 19-32

| 34 | **Health Insurance, Disability Insurance and Health Savings Account Expenses.** List the average monthly amounts that you actually expend in each of the following categories and enter the total. | |
|---|---|---|
| | a. | Health Insurance | $ | |
| | b. | Disability Insurance | $ | |
| | c. | Health Savings Account | $ | |
| | | | Total: Add Lines a, b and c | $ |
| 35 | **Continued contributions to the care of household or family members.** Enter the actual monthly expenses that you will continue to pay for the reasonable and necessary care and support of an elderly, chronically ill, or disabled member of your household or member of your immediate family who is unable to pay for such expenses. | $ |
| 36 | **Protection against family violence.** Enter any average monthly expenses that you actually incurred to maintain the safety of your family under the Family Violence Prevention and Services Act or other applicable federal law. | $ |
| 37 | **Home energy costs in excess of the allowance specified by the IRS Local Standards.** Enter the average monthly amount by which your home energy costs exceed the allowance in the IRS Local Standards for Housing and Utilities. **You must provide your case trustee with documentation demonstrating that the additional amount claimed is reasonable and necessary.** | $ |
| 38 | **Education expenses for dependent children less than 18.** Enter the average monthly expenses that you actually incur, not to exceed $125 per child, in providing elementary and secondary education for your dependent children less than 18 years of age. **You must provide your case trustee with documentation demonstrating that the amount claimed is reasonable and necessary and not already accounted for in the IRS Standards.** | $ |
| 39 | **Additional food and clothing expense.** Enter the average monthly amount by which your food and clothing expenses exceed the combined allowances for food and apparel in the IRS National Standards, not to exceed five percent of those combined allowances. (This information is available at www.usdoj.gov/ust/ or from the clerk of the bankruptcy court.) **You must provide your case trustee with documentation demonstrating that the additional amount claimed is reasonable and necessary.** | $ |
| 40 | **Continued charitable contributions.** Enter the amount that you will continue to contribute in the form of cash or financial instruments to a charitable organization as defined in 26 U.S.C. § 170(c)(1)-(2). | $ |
| 41 | **Total Additional Expense Deductions under § 707(b).** Enter the total of Lines 34 through 40 | $ |

**Form B 22A (Chapter 7) (10/05)**                                                    5

| | Subpart C: Deductions for Debt Payment | |
|---|---|---|
| 42 | **Future payments on secured claims.** For each of your debts that is secured by an interest in property that you own, list the name of the creditor, identify the property securing the debt, and state the Average Monthly Payment. The Average Monthly Payment is the total of all amounts contractually due to each Secured Creditor in the 60 months following the filing of the bankruptcy case, divided by 60. Mortgage debts should include payments of taxes and insurance required by the mortgage. If necessary, list additional entries on a separate page. | |

| | | Name of Creditor | Property Securing the Debt | 60-month Average Payment | |
|---|---|---|---|---|---|
| 42 | a. | | | $ | |
| | b. | | | $ | |
| | c. | | | $ | |
| | | | | Total: Add Lines a, b and c. | $ |

| 43 | **Past due payments on secured claims.** If any of the debts listed in Line 42 are in default, and the property securing the debt is necessary for your support or the support of your dependents, you may include in your deductions 1/60th of the amount that you must pay the creditor as a result of the default (the "cure amount") in order to maintain possession of the property. List any such amounts in the following chart and enter the total. If necessary, list additional entries on a separate page. | |
|---|---|---|

| | | Name of Creditor | Property Securing the Debt in Default | 1/60th of the Cure Amount | |
|---|---|---|---|---|---|
| 43 | a. | | | $ | |
| | b. | | | $ | |
| | c. | | | $ | |
| | | | | Total: Add Lines a, b and c | $ |

| 44 | **Payments on priority claims.** Enter the total amount of all priority claims (including priority child support and alimony claims), divided by 60. | $ |
|---|---|---|

| 45 | **Chapter 13 administrative expenses.** If you are eligible to file a case under Chapter 13, complete the following chart, multiply the amount in line a by the amount in line b, and enter the resulting administrative expense. | |
|---|---|---|

| | a. | Projected average monthly Chapter 13 plan payment. | $ | |
|---|---|---|---|---|
| 45 | b. | Current multiplier for your district as determined under schedules issued by the Executive Office for United States Trustees. (This information is available at www.usdoj.gov/ust/ or from the clerk of the bankruptcy court.) | x | |
| | c. | Average monthly administrative expense of Chapter 13 case | Total: Multiply Lines a and b | $ |

| 46 | **Total Deductions for Debt Payment.** Enter the total of Lines 42 through 45. | $ |
|---|---|---|

| | Subpart D: Total Deductions Allowed under § 707(b)(2) | |
|---|---|---|
| 47 | **Total of all deductions allowed under § 707(b)(2).** Enter the total of Lines 33, 41, and 46. | $ |

## Part VI. DETERMINATION OF § 707(b)(2) PRESUMPTION

| 48 | **Enter the amount from Line 18 (Current monthly income for § 707(b)(2))** | $ |
|---|---|---|
| 49 | **Enter the amount from Line 47 (Total of all deductions allowed under § 707(b)(2))** | $ |
| 50 | **Monthly disposable income under § 707(b)(2).** Subtract Line 49 from Line 48 and enter the result | $ |
| 51 | **60-month disposable income under § 707(b)(2).** Multiply the amount in Line 50 by the number 60 and enter the result. | $ |

| 52 | **Initial presumption determination.** Check the applicable box and proceed as directed. |
|---|---|
| | ☐ **The amount on Line 51 is less than $6,000** Check the box for "The presumption does not arise" at the top of page 1 of this statement, and complete the verification in Part VIII. Do not complete the remainder of Part VI. |
| | ☐ **The amount set forth on Line 51 is more than $10,000.** Check the box for "The presumption arises" at the top of page 1 of this statement, and complete the verification in Part VIII. You may also complete Part VII. Do not complete the remainder of Part VI. |
| | ☐ **The amount on Line 51 is at least $6,000, but not more than $10,000.** Complete the remainder of Part VI (Lines 53 through 55). |

| 53 | Enter the amount of your total non-priority unsecured debt | $ |
|---|---|---|

| 54 | **Threshold debt payment amount.** Multiply the amount in Line 53 by the number 0.25 and enter the result. | $ |
|---|---|---|

| 55 | **Secondary presumption determination.** Check the applicable box and proceed as directed. |
|---|---|
| | ☐ **The amount on Line 51 is less than the amount on Line 54.** Check the box for "The presumption does not arise" at the top of page 1 of this statement, and complete the verification in Part VIII. |
| | ☐ **The amount on Line 51 is equal to or greater than the amount on Line 54.** Check the box for "The presumption arises" at the top of page 1 of this statement, and complete the verification in Part VIII. You may also complete Part VII. |

## Part VII: ADDITIONAL EXPENSE CLAIMS

| 56 | **Other Expenses.** List and describe any monthly expenses, not otherwise stated in this form, that are required for the health and welfare of you and your family and that you contend should be an additional deduction from your current monthly income under § 707(b)(2)(A)(ii)(I). If necessary, list additional sources on a separate page. All figures should reflect your average monthly expense for each item. Total the expenses. |
|---|---|

| | Expense Description | Monthly Amount |
|---|---|---|
| a. | | $ |
| b. | | $ |
| c. | | $ |
| | Total: Add Lines a, b and c | $ |

## Part VIII: VERIFICATION

| 57 | I declare under penalty of perjury that the information provided in this statement is true and correct. *(If this a joint case, both debtors must sign.)* |
|---|---|
| | Date: _____ Signature: _____ <br> (Debtor) |
| | Date: _____ Signature: _____ <br> (Joint Debtor, if any) |

**Form B22C (Chapter 13)  (10/05)**

In re _____
　　　　　　　　Debtor(s)

Case Number: _____
　　　　　　　　(If known)

# STATEMENT OF CURRENT MONTHLY INCOME
# AND CALCULATION OF COMMITMENT PERIOD AND DISPOSABLE INCOME
### FOR USE IN CHAPTER 13

In addition to Schedules I and J, this statement must be completed by every individual Chapter 13 debtor, whether or not filing jointly. Joint debtors may complete one statement only.

| | Part I. REPORT OF INCOME | | |
|---|---|---|---|
| 1 | **Marital/filing status.** Check the box that applies and complete the balance of this part of this statement as directed.<br>a. ☐ Unmarried. **Complete only Column A ("Debtor's Income") for Lines 2-10.**<br>b. ☐ Married. **Complete both Column A ("Debtor's Income") and Column B ("Spouse's Income") for Lines 2-10.** | | |
| | All figures must reflect average monthly income for the six calendar months prior to filing the bankruptcy case, ending on the last day of the month before the filing. If you received different amounts of income during these six months, you must total the amounts received during the six months, divide this total by six, and enter the result on the appropriate line. | **Column A**<br>Debtor's<br>Income | **Column B**<br>Spouse's<br>Income |
| 2 | **Gross wages, salary, tips, bonuses, overtime, commissions.** | $ | $ |
| 3 | **Income from the operation of a business, profession, or farm.** Subtract Line b from Line a and enter the difference on Line 3. Do not enter a number less than zero. **Do not include any part of the business expenses entered on Line b as a deduction in Part IV.**<br>a. Gross receipts ... $<br>b. Ordinary and necessary business expenses ... $<br>c. Business income ... Subtract Line b from Line a | $ | $ |
| 4 | **Rent and other real property income.** Subtract Line b from Line a and enter the difference on Line 4. Do not enter a number less than zero. **Do not include any part of the operating expenses entered on Line b as a deduction in Part IV.**<br>a. Gross receipts ... $<br>b. Ordinary and necessary operating expenses ... $<br>c. Rental income ... Subtract Line b from Line a | $ | $ |
| 5 | **Interest, dividends, and royalties.** | $ | $ |
| 6 | **Pension and retirement income.** | $ | $ |
| 7 | **Regular contributions to the household expenses of the debtor or the debtor's dependents, including child or spousal support.** Do not include contributions from the debtor's spouse. | $ | $ |
| 8 | **Unemployment compensation.** Enter the amount in the appropriate column(s) of Line 8. However, if you contend that unemployment compensation received by you or your spouse was a benefit under the Social Security Act, do not list the amount of such compensation in Column A or B, but instead state the amount in the space below:<br>Unemployment compensation claimed to be a benefit under the Social Security Act  Debtor $ _____  Spouse $ _____ | $ | $ |
| 9 | **Income from all other sources.** Specify source and amount. If necessary, list additional sources on a separate page. Total and enter on Line 9. **Do not include** any benefits received under the Social Security Act or payments received as a victim of a war crime, crime against humanity, or as a victim of international or domestic terrorism.<br>a. _____ $<br>b. _____ $ | $ | $ |
| 10 | **Subtotal.** Add Lines 2 thru 9 in Column A, and, if Column B is completed, add Lines 2 through 9 in Column B. Enter the total(s). | $ | $ |
| 11 | **Total.** If Column B has been completed, add Line 10, Column A to Line 10, Column B, and enter the total. If Column B has not been completed, enter the amount from Line 10, Column A. | $ | |

## Part II. CALCULATION OF § 1325(b)(4) COMMITMENT PERIOD

| 12 | **Enter the amount from Line 11.** | |
|----|----|----|
| 13 | **Marital adjustment.** If you are married, but are not filing jointly with your spouse, AND if you contend that calculation of the commitment period under § 1325(b)(4) does not require inclusion of the income of your spouse, enter the amount of the income listed in Line 10, Column B that was NOT regularly contributed to the household expenses of you or your dependents.  Otherwise, enter zero. | |
| 14 | **Subtract Line 13 from Line 12 and enter the result.** | |
| 15 | **Annualized current monthly income for § 1325(b)(4).** Multiply the amount from Line 14 by the number 12 and enter the result. | $ |
| 16 | **Applicable median family income.** Enter the median family income for applicable state and house-hold size.  (This information is available by family size at www.usdoj.gov/ust/ or from the clerk of the bankruptcy court.)  <br><br>a. Enter debtor's state of residence: _____     b. Enter debtor's household size: _____ | $ |
| 17 | **Application of § 1325(b)(4).** Check the applicable box and proceed as directed.  <br><br>☐ **The amount on Line 15 is less than the amount on Line 16.**  Check the box for "The applicable commit-ment period is 3 years" at the top of page 1 of this statement and complete Part VII of this statement.  **Do not com-plete Parts III, IV, V or VI.**  <br><br>☐ **The amount on Line 15 is not less than the amount on Line 16.** Check the box for "The applicable com-mitment period is 5 years" at the top of page 1 of this statement and continue with Part III of this statement. | |

## Part III. APPLICATION OF § 1325(b)(3) FOR DETERMINING DISPOSABLE INCOME

| 18 | **Enter the amount from Line 11.** | $ |
|----|----|----|
| 19 | **Marital adjustment.** If you are married, but are not filing jointly with your spouse, enter the amount of the income listed in Line 10, Column B that was NOT regularly contributed to the household expenses of you or your dependents.  If you are unmarried or married and filing jointly with your spouse, enter zero. | $ |
| 20 | **Current monthly income for § 1325(b)(3).** Subtract Line 19 from Line 18 and enter the result. | |
| 21 | **Annualized current monthly income for § 1325(b)(3).** Multiply the amount from Line 20 by the number 12 and enter the result. | $ |
| 22 | **Applicable median family income.** Enter the amount from Line 16. | $ |
| 23 | **Application of § 1325(b)(3).** Check the applicable box and proceed as directed.  <br><br>☐ **The amount on Line 21 is more than the amount on Line 22.** Check the box for "Disposable income is de-termined under § 1325(b)(3)" at the top of page 1 of this statement and complete the remaining parts of this state-ment.  <br><br>☐ **The amount on Line 21 is not more than the amount on Line 22.**  Check the box for "Disposable income is not determined under § 1325(b)(3)" at the top of page 1 of this statement and complete Part VII of this statement.  **Do not complete Parts IV, V, or VI.** | |

## Part IV. CALCULATION OF DEDUCTIONS ALLOWED UNDER § 707(b)(2)

### Subpart A: Deductions under Standards of the Internal Revenue Service (IRS)

| 24 | **National Standards: food, clothing, household supplies, personal care, and miscella-neous.** Enter the "Total" amount from IRS National Standards for Allowable Living Expenses for the appli-cable family size and income level.  (This information is available at www.usdoj.gov/ust/ or from the clerk of the bankruptcy court.) | $ |
|----|----|----|
| 25A | **Local Standards: housing and utilities; non-mortgage expenses.** Enter the amount of the IRS Housing and Utilities Standards; non-mortgage expenses for the applicable county and family size. (This information is available at www.usdoj.gov/ust/ or from the clerk of the bankruptcy court). | $ |

**Form B 22C (Chapter 13) (10/05)**                                                    3

| | | |
|---|---|---|
| 25B | **Local Standards: housing and utilities; mortgage/rent expense.** Enter, in Line a below, the amount of the IRS Housing and Utilities Standards; mortgage/rent expense for your county and family size (this information is available at www.usdoj.gov/ust/ or from the clerk of the bankruptcy court); enter on Line b the total of the Average Monthly Payments for any debts secured by your home, as stated in Line 47; subtract Line b from Line a and enter the result in Line 25B. **Do not enter an amount less than zero.** | |

| | | | |
|---|---|---|---|
| | a. | IRS Housing and Utilities Standards; mortgage/rent Expense | $ |
| | b. | Average Monthly Payment for any debts secured by your home, if any, as stated in Line 47 | $ |
| | c. | Net mortgage/rental expense | Subtract Line b from Line a. |

$

| | |
|---|---|
| 26 | **Local Standards: housing and utilities; adjustment.** if you contend that the process set out in Lines 25A and 25B does not accurately compute the allowance to which you are entitled under the IRS Housing and Utilities Standards, enter any additional amount to which you contend you are entitled, and state the basis for your contention in the space below: |

_____

_____

$

| | |
|---|---|
| 27 | **Local Standards: transportation; vehicle operation/public transportation expense.** You are entitled to an expense allowance in this category regardless of whether you pay the expenses of operating a vehicle and regardless of whether you use public transportation. |

Check the number of vehicles for which you pay the operating expenses or for which the operating expenses are included as a contribution to your household expenses in Line 7. ☐ 0  ☐ 1  ☐ 2 or more.

Enter the amount from IRS Transportation Standards, Operating Costs & Public Transportation Costs for the applicable number of vehicles in the applicable Metropolitan Statistical Area or Census Region. (This information is available at www.usdoj.gov/ust/ or from the clerk of the bankruptcy court.)

$

| | |
|---|---|
| 28 | **Local Standards: transportation ownership/lease expense; Vehicle 1.** Check the number of vehicles for which you claim an ownership/lease expense. (You may not claim an ownership/lease expense for more than two vehicles.)  ☐ 1  ☐ 2 or more. |

Enter, in Line a below, the amount of the IRS Transportation Standards, Ownership Costs, First Car (available at www.usdoj.gov/ust/ or from the clerk of the bankruptcy court); enter in Line b the total of the Average Monthly Payments for any debts secured by Vehicle 1, as stated in Line 47; subtract Line b from Line a and enter the result in Line 28. **Do not enter an amount less than zero.**

| | | | |
|---|---|---|---|
| | a. | IRS Transportation Standards, Ownership Costs, First Car | $ |
| | b. | Average Monthly Payment for any debts secured by Vehicle 1, as stated in Line 47 | $ |
| | c. | Net ownership/lease expense for Vehicle 1 | Subtract Line b from Line a. |

$

| | |
|---|---|
| 29 | **Local Standards: transportation ownership/lease expense; Vehicle 2.** Complete this Line only if you checked the "2 or more" Box in Line 28. |

Enter, in Line a below, the amount of the IRS Transportation Standards, Ownership Costs, Second Car (available at www.usdoj.gov/ust/ or from the clerk of the bankruptcy court); enter in Line b the total of the Average Monthly Payments for any debts secured by Vehicle 2, as stated in Line 47; subtract Line b from Line a and enter the result in Line 29. **Do not enter an amount less than zero.**

| | | | |
|---|---|---|---|
| | a. | IRS Transportation Standards, Ownership Costs, Second Car | $ |
| | b. | Average Monthly Payment for any debts secured by Vehicle 2, as stated in Line 47 | $ |
| | c. | Net ownership/lease expense for Vehicle 2 | Subtract Line b from Line a. |

$

| | | |
|---|---|---|
| 30 | **Other Necessary Expenses: taxes.** Enter the total average monthly expense that you actually incur for all federal, state, and local taxes, other than real estate and sales taxes, such as income taxes, self employment taxes, social security taxes, and Medicare taxes. **Do not include real estate or sales taxes.** | $ |
| 31 | **Other Necessary Expenses: mandatory payroll deductions.** Enter the total average monthly payroll deductions that are required for your employment, such as mandatory retirement contributions, union dues, and uniform costs. **Do not include discretionary amounts, such as non-mandatory 401(k) contributions.** | $ |

**Form B 22C (Chapter 13) (10/05)** 4

| 32 | **Other Necessary Expenses: life insurance.** Enter average monthly premiums that you actually pay for term life insurance for yourself. **Do not include premiums for insurance on your dependents, for whole life or for any other form of insurance.** | $ |
|---|---|---|
| 33 | **Other Necessary Expenses: court-ordered payments.** Enter the total monthly amount that you are required to pay pursuant to court order, such as spousal or child support payments. **Do not include payments on past due support obligations included in Line 49.** | $ |
| 34 | **Other Necessary Expenses: education for employment or for a physically or mentally challenged child.** Enter the total monthly amount that you actually expend for education that is a condition of employment and for education that is required for a physically or mentally challenged dependent child for whom no public education providing similar services is available. | |
| 35 | **Other Necessary Expenses: childcare.** Enter the average monthly amount that you actually expend on childcare. **Do not include payments made for children's education.** | $ |
| 36 | **Other Necessary Expenses: health care.** Enter the average monthly amount that you actually expend on health care expenses that are not reimbursed by insurance or paid by a health savings account. **Do not include payments for health insurance listed in Line 39.** | $ |
| 37 | **Other Necessary Expenses: telecommunication services.** Enter the average monthly expenses that you actually pay for cell phones, pagers, call waiting, caller identification, special long distance, or internet services necessary for the health and welfare of you or your dependents. **Do not include any amount previously deducted.** | $ |
| 38 | **Total Expenses Allowed under IRS Standards.** Enter the total of Lines 24 through 37. | $ |

| **Subpart B: Additional Expense Deductions under § 707(b)** |
|---|
| **Note: Do not include any expenses that you have listed in Lines 24-37** |

| 39 | **Health Insurance, Disability Insurance, and Health Savings Account Expenses.** List the average monthly amounts that you actually expend in each of the following categories and enter the total. | |
|---|---|---|
| | a. Health Insurance $ | |
| | b. Disability Insurance $ | |
| | c. Health Savings Account $ | |
| | Total: Add Lines a, b, and c | $ |
| 40 | **Continued contributions to the care of household or family members.** Enter the actual monthly expenses that you will continue to pay for the reasonable and necessary care and support of an elderly, chronically ill, or disabled member of your household or member of your immediate family who is unable to pay for such expenses. **Do not include payments listed in Line 34.** | $ |
| 41 | **Protection against family violence.** Enter any average monthly expenses that you actually incurred to maintain the safety of your family under the Family Violence Prevention and Services Act or other applicable federal law. | $ |
| 42 | **Home energy costs in excess of the allowance specified by the IRS Local Standards.** Enter the average monthly amount by which your home energy costs exceed the allowance in the IRS Local Standards for Housing and Utilities. **You must provide your case trustee with documentation demonstrating that the additional amount claimed is reasonable and necessary.** | $ |
| 43 | **Education expenses for dependent children under 18.** Enter the average monthly expenses that you actually incur, not to exceed $125 per child, in providing elementary and secondary education for your dependent children less than 18 years of age. **You must provide your case trustee with documentation demonstrating that the amount claimed is reasonable and necessary and not already accounted for in the IRS Standards.** | $ |
| 44 | **Additional food and clothing expense.** Enter the average monthly amount by which your food and clothing expenses exceed the combined allowances for food and apparel in the IRS National Standards, not to exceed five percent of those combined allowances. (This information is available at www.usdoj.gov/ust/ or from the clerk of the bankruptcy court.) **You must provide your case trustee with documentation demonstrating that the additional amount claimed is reasonable and necessary.** | $ |
| 45 | **Continued charitable contributions.** Enter the amount that you will continue to contribute in the form of cash or financial instruments to a charitable organization as defined in 26 U.S.C. § 170(c)(1)-(2). | $ |
| 46 | **Total Additional Expense Deductions under § 707(b).** Enter the total of Lines 39 through 45. | $ |

| | Subpart C: Deductions for Debt Payment | | |
|---|---|---|---|
| 47 | **Future payments on secured claims.** For each of your debts that is secured by an interest in property that you own, list the name of the creditor, identify the property securing the debt, and state the Average Monthly Payment. The Average Monthly Payment is the total of all amounts contractually due to each Secured Creditor in the 60 months following the filing of the bankruptcy case, divided by 60. Mortgage debts should include payments of taxes and insurance required by the mortgage. If necessary, list additional entries on a separate page. | | |

| | | Name of Creditor | Property Securing the Debt | 60-month Average Payment |
|---|---|---|---|---|
| | a. | | | $ |
| | b. | | | $ |
| | c. | | | $ |
| | | | | Total: Add Lines a, b, and c | $ |

| 48 | **Past due payments on secured claims.** If any of the debts listed in Line 47 are in default, and the property securing the debt is necessary for your support or the support of your dependents, you may include in your deductions 1/60th of the amount that you must pay the creditor as a result of the default (the "cure amount") in order to maintain possession of the property. List any such amounts in the following chart and enter the total. If necessary, list additional entries on a separate page. | | |
|---|---|---|---|

| | | Name of Creditor | Property Securing the Debt in Default | 1/60th of the Cure Amount |
|---|---|---|---|---|
| | a. | | | $ |
| | b. | | | $ |
| | c. | | | $ |
| | | | | Total: Add Lines a, b, and c | $ |

| 49 | **Payments on priority claims.** Enter the total amount of all priority claims (including priority child support and alimony claims), divided by 60. | $ |
|---|---|---|

| 50 | **Chapter 13 administrative expenses.** Multiply the amount in Line a by the amount in Line b, and enter the resulting administrative expense. | |
|---|---|---|

| | a. | Projected average monthly Chapter 13 plan payment. | $ |
|---|---|---|---|
| | b. | Current multiplier for your district as determined under schedules issued by the Executive Office for United States Trustees. (This information is available at www.usdoj.gov/ust/ or from the clerk of the bankruptcy court.) | x |
| | c. | Average monthly administrative expense of Chapter 13 case | Total: Multiply Lines a and b | $ |

| 51 | **Total Deductions for Debt Payment.** Enter the total of Lines 47 through 50. | $ |
|---|---|---|

| | Subpart D: Total Deductions Allowed under § 707(b)(2) | |
|---|---|---|
| 52 | **Total of all deductions allowed under § 707(b)(2).** Enter the total of Lines 38, 46, and 51. | $ |

# Part V. DETERMINATION OF DISPOSABLE INCOME UNDER § 1325(b)(2)

| 53 | **Total current monthly income.** Enter the amount from Line 20. | $ |
|---|---|---|
| 54 | **Support income.** Enter the monthly average of any child support payments, foster care payments, or disability payments for a dependent child, included in Line 7, that you received in accordance with applicable nonbankruptcy law, to the extent reasonably necessary to be expended for such child. | $ |
| 55 | **Qualified retirement deductions.** Enter the monthly average of (a) all contributions or wage deductions made to qualified retirement plans, as specified in § 541(b)(7) and (b) all repayments of loans from retirement plans, as specified in § 362(b)(19). | $ |
| 56 | **Total of all deductions allowed under § 707(b)(2).** Enter the amount from Line 52. | $ |
| 57 | **Total adjustments to determine disposable income.** Add the amounts on Lines 54, 55, and 56 and enter the result. | $ |
| 58 | **Monthly Disposable Income Under § 1325(b)(2).** Subtract Line 57 from Line 53 and enter the | $ |

| | result. | |
|---|---|---|

## Part VI: ADDITIONAL EXPENSE CLAIMS

59

**Other Expenses.** List and describe any monthly expenses, not otherwise stated in this form, that are required for the health and welfare of you and your family and that you contend should be an additional deduction from your current monthly income under § 707(b)(2)(A)(ii)(I). If necessary, list additional sources on a separate page. All figures should reflect your average monthly expense for each item. Total the expenses.

| | Expense Description | Monthly Amount |
|---|---|---|
| a. | | $ |
| b. | | $ |
| c. | | $ |
| | Total: Add Lines a, b, and c | $ |

## Part VII: VERIFICATION

60

I declare under penalty of perjury that the information provided in this statement is true and correct. *(If this a joint case, both debtors must sign.)*

Date: _____     Signature: _____
                                                       (Debtor)

Date: _____     Signature: _____
                                                   (Joint Debtor, if any)

UNITED STATES BANKRUPTCY COURT
_____ DISTRICT OF _____

In re _____    Case No. _____
   Debtor        (if known)

CHAPTER 13 PLAN

The debtor shall pay to the trustee out of the debtor's future earnings or other income the sum of $_____ (weekly) (semi-monthly) (monthly). From the funds received the trustee shall make distribution as follows:

 1. Expenses of administration and debts entitled to priority under 11 U.S.C. Section 507.

 2. Payments to secured creditors whose claims are duly filed and allowed as follows:

 3. From the balance remaining after the above payments, dividends to unsecured creditors whose claims are duly filed and allowed as follows:

 4. Except as provided in this plan or in the order confirming this plan, upon confirmation of this plan, all property of the estate shall vest in the debtor free and clear of any claim or interest of any creditor provided for by this plan pursuant to 11 U.S.C. Section 1327.

 5. [ ] See attached addendum for additional terms.

Dated: _____    _____
           Petitioner

           _____
           Petitioner

*This page intentionally blank.*

Form 23
(10/05)

# United States Bankruptcy Court

_____ District Of _____

In re _____,          Case No. _____
                    Debtor
                                                 Chapter _____

### DEBTOR'S CERTIFICATION OF COMPLETION OF INSTRUCTIONAL COURSE
### CONCERNING PERSONAL FINANCIAL MANAGEMENT

*[Complete one of the following statements.]*

☐  I/We, _____. the debtor(s) in the above-
                (Printed Name(s) of Debtor and Joint Debtor, if any)
styled case hereby certify that on _____ I/we completed an instructional
                                        (Date)
course in personal financial management provided by _____,
                                                            (Name of Provider)
an approved personal financial management instruction provider.  If the provider furnished a
document attesting to the completion of the personal financial management instructional
course, a copy of that document is attached.

☐  I/We, _____, the debtor(s) in the above-
styled
                (Printed Names of Debtor and Joint Debtor, if any)
case, hereby certify that no personal financial management course is required because:
*[Check the appropriate box.]*
☐  I am/We are incapacitated or disabled, as defined in 11 U.S.C. § 109(h);
☐  I am/We are on active military duty in a military combat zone; or
☐  I/We reside in a district in which the United States trustee (or bankruptcy administrator) has
determined that the approved instructional courses are not adequate at this time to serve the
additional individuals who would otherwise be required to complete such courses.

Signature of Debtor: _____

Date: _____

Signature of Joint Debtor: _____

Date: _____

*This page intentionally blank.*

*This page intentionally blank.*

)
)
)
)
vs.    )   Case No. _____
)
)
)
)

## SUGGESTION OF BANKRUPTCY

The Defendant(s), _____ hereby notifies this Court that said defendant(s) filed a Petition for Bankruptcy in the United States District Court on _____. A copy of said petition is attached hereto.

Dated: _____  Signed  :  _____

                  Defendant

                  _____

                  Defendant

## CERTIFICATE OF SERVICE

I hereby certify that a copy of the foregoing was sent by first class, U.S. Mail on _____, to the following parties:

_____

*This page intentionally blank.*

UNITED STATES BANKRUPTCY COURT
_____ DISTRICT OF _____

In re _____          Case No. _____
          Debtor                                    (if known)

**PROOF OF SERVICE BY MAIL**

I, _____ {name}, declare that:

I am over the age of 18 years and am not a party to the within bankruptcy.

I reside, or am employed, in the County of _____ {name of county}, _____ {state}.

My residence/business address is _____
_____.

On _____, 20___, I served the within _____
_____ {title of document(s) served} by placing a true
and correct copy of it (them) in a sealed envelope with first-class postage fully prepaid, in the
United States mail at _____ {post office location}, addressed
as follows:


I declare under penalty of perjury that the foregoing is true and correct. Executed on
_____, 20_____, at _____ {city}, _____ {state}.


_____
Signature

*This page intentionally blank.*

UNITED STATES BANKRUPTCY COURT
_____ DISTRICT OF _____

In re _____          Case No. _____
      Debtor                                    (if known)


## AMENDMENT COVER SHEET


The Debtor hereby files the attached amendment documents, consisting of:

[   ] Voluntary Petition

[   ] Summary of Schedules

[   ] Schedule(s) _____

[   ] Statement of Financial Affairs

[   ] Chapter 7 Individual Debtor's Statement of Intention

[   ] Chapter 13 Plan

[   ] Other _____


## UNSWORN DECLARATION UNDER PENALTY OF PERJURY


I, _____, and I, _____, declare under penalty of perjury that the information set forth above, and contained in the attached amendment documents, consisting of ___ pages, is true and correct to the best of my (our) information and belief.


Dated: _____          _____
                                Debtor


                                _____
                                Debtor's Spouse

*This page intentionally blank.*

UNITED STATES BANKRUPTCY COURT

_____ DISTRICT OF _____

In re _____     Case No. _____
       Debtor                             (if known)

**MOTION TO CONVERT TO CHAPTER 7**

The Debtor, having originally filed this action pursuant to Chapter 13 of the U.S. Bankruptcy Code, hereby moves this court to convert this action to a proceeding pursuant to Chapter 7 of the U.S. Bankruptcy Code. In furtherance of this motion the Debtor has attached a Chapter 7 Individual Debtor's Statement of Intention.

Dated: _____     _____
                            Petitioner


                            _____
                            Petitioner


**ORDER**

IN CONSIDERATION of the foregoing motion of the Debtor,

IT IS HEREBY ORDERED, that this action is converted to a proceeding pursuant to Chapter 7 of the U.S. Bankruptcy Code.

Dated: _____     _____
                            Judge

# Index

# C

California, 69, 72, 106

cars, 7, 9, 24, 28, 29, 30, 34, 35, 36, 39, 47, 48, 49, 53, 54, 61, 73, 75, 77, 78, 85, 93, 98, 110, 112, 115, 129, 135, 141

case number, 66, 67, 70, 71, 74, 77, 78, 79, 80, 81, 82, 83, 86, 89, 92, 103, 104, 107, 108, 110, 113, 115, 116, 118, 119, 120, 121, 123, 125, 128

cash, 29, 30, 31, 32, 37, 48, 50, 54, 141

certificates of deposit, 26, 29, 54

Chapter 7 Debtor's Statement of Intention, 84, 135

Chapter 11, 3, 8, 63, 101

Chapter 12, 3

Chapter 13 Plan, 38, 121

child support, 7, 11, 26, 34, 95

claiming property, 33, 71, 72, 75, 77, 78, 107, 109, 111, 115

clerk, 4, 6, 46, 55, 61, 62, 66, 67, 70, 71, 74, 77, 78, 79, 80, 81, 82, 83, 86, 87, 89, 90, 91, 92, 94, 99, 100, 103, 104, 107, 108, 110, 113, 115, 116, 118, 119, 120, 121, 123, 124, 125, 126, 127, 128, 130, 133, 134, 137

clothing, 9, 28, 31, 32, 47, 54

codebtors, 74, 80, 110, 116, 117

codes. *See statutes*

collateral, 75, 78, 111, 115

collectibles, 31, 54

Collier Bankruptcy Manual, 56

Collier Forms Manual, 56

commissions, 76, 113

community property, 69, 71, 74, 106, 108, 111

Congress, 2, 45, 62, 100

Connecticut, 29, 30, 72, 135

consideration, 18, 78, 115

consumer debt, 136

contingent debt, 74, 111

continuation sheets, 75, 77, 79, 82, 83, 112, 114, 115, 118, 120

contracts, 68, 79, 84, 105, 116

corporation, 15, 82, 83, 119, 120

costs of bankruptcy, 10, 16, 17, 18, 19, 36, 38, 43, 54, 66, 95, 103, 133

court, 1, 2, 3, 4, 5, 6, 7, 8, 10, 11, 20, 34, 38, 46, 47, 48, 49, 50, 56, 57, 60, 61, 62, 63, 64, 65, 66, 81, 87, 89, 90, 91, 94, 95, 98, 99, 100, 101, 102, 103, 104, 112, 118, 124, 125, 126, 127, 130, 131, 133, 135, 136, 137, 138

credit, 2, 7, 9, 10, 18, 24, 27, 34, 35, 37, 38, 39, 40, 43, 46, 49, 50, 53, 54, 55, 73, 76, 77, 78, 110, 113, 114, 115, 139, 140, 141, 142

credit cards, 2, 9, 10, 27, 34, 35, 38, 39, 40, 53, 54, 73, 77, 78, 110, 114, 115, 140, 141

credit counseling, 37, 38, 43, 46, 78, 114

creditors, 1, 2, 6, 7, 8, 10, 11, 12, 13, 15, 17, 23, 24, 25, 33, 34, 36, 37, 38, 39, 40, 41, 43, 46, 47, 49, 50, 51, 60, 71, 72, 73, 74, 76, 77, 78, 80, 81, 83, 84, 85, 86, 88, 90, 91, 93, 94, 95, 98, 101, 108, 109, 110, 112, 114, 115, 117, 118, 120, 121, 122, 123, 126, 127, 129, 130, 131, 134, 135, 136, 137

# D

debt consolidation loans, 37

Debt Worksheet, 35, 73, 110

Debtor's Certification of Completion of Instructional Course Concerning Personal Financial Management, 89, 125

# M

# N

# O

# P

# R

# S

# T

# U

# V

# W

# Y

# About the Author

**Edward A. Haman** received his law degree from the University of Toledo College of Law. As a student, he served as coordinator of the law school's Client Counseling Competition team, and as editor of the law school's legal journal *Discovery*. He also has a Bachelor of Arts degree from Western Michigan University, with a major in communication, and minors in accounting and general business.

Since graduating from law school, he has practiced law in three states. In Hawaii, Mr. Haman was engaged in general private practice, initially as a sole practitioner, then with a small law firm emphasizing family law, real estate, and business law. This included trial practice, as well as criminal appellate work before the Supreme Court of Hawaii and the U.S. Court of Appeals in San Francisco. In Michigan, he served as a Circuit Court domestic relations hearing officer. After moving to Florida, he spent several years as an attorney for the Florida social services agency, handling a variety of legal matters, including cases involving the abuse and neglect of children, the elderly, and the disabled; public health matters; child support enforcement; welfare fraud; and, the licensing of assisted living facilities, nursing homes, and other health care facilities. Mr. Haman has also engaged in private practice in the areas of real estate, family law, and probate.

Mr. Haman has authored and co-authored numerous self-help law books, including *The Complete Bankruptcy Guide*, *File Your Own Divorce*, and *How to Write Your Own Living Will*. In connection with the self-help law books, he has been a guest on numerous radio programs, and has appeared on the Fox News Channel. He has also written several articles for *The Florida Keystone Series*, a legal publication for attorneys. Currently residing in Tampa, Florida, Mr. Haman continues to write books, and also volunteers as a support group facilitator for the Alzheimer's Association. In his spare time, he enjoys travel, kayaking, snow skiing, hiking, and mountaineering.

# SPHINX® PUBLISHING'S STATE TITLES

*Up-to-Date for Your State*

**California Titles**

| | |
|---|---|
| How to File for Divorce in CA (5E) | $26.95 |
| How to Settle & Probate an Estate in CA (2E) | $28.95 |
| How to Start a Business in CA (2E) | $21.95 |
| How to Win in Small Claims Court in CA (2E) | $18.95 |
| Landlords' Legal Guide in CA (2E) | $24.95 |
| Make Your Own CA Will | $18.95 |
| Tenants' Rights in CA (2E) | $24.95 |

**Florida Titles**

| | |
|---|---|
| How to File for Divorce in FL (8E) | $28.95 |
| How to Form a Limited Liability Co. in FL (3E) | $24.95 |
| How to Form a Partnership in FL | $22.95 |
| How to Make a FL Will (7E) | $16.95 |
| How to Start a Business in FL (7E) | $21.95 |
| How to Win in Small Claims Court in FL (7E) | $18.95 |
| Incorporate in FL (7E) | $29.95 |
| Land Trusts in Florida (6E) | $29.95 |
| Landlords' Rights and Duties in FL (10E) | $24.95 |
| Probate and Settle an Estate in FL (6E) | $29.95 |

**Georgia Titles**

| | |
|---|---|
| How to File for Divorce in GA (5E) | $21.95 |
| How to Start a Business in GA (4E) | $21.95 |

**Illinois Titles**

| | |
|---|---|
| Child Custody, Visitation and Support in IL | $24.95 |
| File for Divorce in IL (4E) | $26.95 |
| How to Make an IL Will (3E) | $16.95 |
| How to Start a Business in IL (4E) | $21.95 |
| Landlords' Legal Guide in IL | $24.95 |

**Maryland, Virginia and the District of Columbia Titles**

| | |
|---|---|
| How to File for Divorce in MD, VA, and DC | $28.95 |
| How to Start a Business in MD, VA, or DC | $21.95 |

**Massachusetts Titles**

| | |
|---|---|
| How to Form a Corporation in MA | $24.95 |
| How to Start a Business in MA (4E) | $21.95 |
| Landlords' Legal Guide in MA (2E) | $24.95 |

**Michigan Titles**

| | |
|---|---|
| How to File for Divorce in MI (4E) | $24.95 |
| How to Make a MI Will (3E) | $16.95 |
| How to Start a Business in MI (4E) | $24.95 |

**Minnesota Titles**

| | |
|---|---|
| How to File for Divorce in MN | $21.95 |
| How to Form a Corporation in MN | $24.95 |
| How to Make a MN Will (2E) | $16.95 |

**New Jersey Titles**

| | |
|---|---|
| File for Divorce in NJ | $24.95 |
| How to Start a Business in NJ | $21.95 |

**New York Titles**

| | |
|---|---|
| Child Custody, Visitation and Support in NY | $26.95 |
| File for Divorce in NY | $26.95 |
| How to Form a Corporation in NY (2E) | $21.95 |
| How to Make a NY Will (3E) | $16.95 |
| How to Start a Business in NY (2E) | $18.95 |
| How to Win in Small Claims Court in NY (3E) | $18.95 |
| Tenants' Rights in NY | $21.95 |

**North Carolina and South Carolina Titles**

| | |
|---|---|
| How to File for Divorce in NC (4E) | $26.95 |
| How to Make a NC Will (3E) | $16.95 |
| How to Start a Business in NC or SC | $24.95 |
| Landlords' Rights & Duties in NC | $21.95 |

**Ohio Titles**

| | |
|---|---|
| How to File for Divorce in OH (3E) | $24.95 |
| How to Form a Corporation in OH | $24.95 |
| How to Make an OH Will | $16.95 |

**Pennsylvania Titles**

| | |
|---|---|
| Child Custody, Visitation and Support in PA | $26.95 |
| How to File for Divorce in PA (4E) | $24.95 |
| How to Form a Corporation in PA | $24.95 |
| How to Make a PA Will (2E) | $16.95 |
| How to Start a Business in PA (3E) | $21.95 |
| Landlords' Legal Guide in PA | $24.95 |

**Texas Titles**

| | |
|---|---|
| Child Custody, Visitation and Support in TX | $22.95 |
| How to File for Divorce in TX (4E) | $24.95 |
| How to Form a Corporation in TX (3E) | $24.95 |
| How to Probate and Settle an Estate in TX (4E) | $26.95 |
| How to Start a Business in TX (4E) | $21.95 |
| How to Win in Small Claims Court in TX (2E) | $16.95 |
| Landlords' Legal Guide in TX | $24.95 |
| Write Your Own TX Will (4E) | $16.95 |

**Washington Titles**

| | |
|---|---|
| File for Divorce in Washington | $24.95 |

# Sphinx® Publishing's National Titles
*Valid in All 50 States*

### LEGAL SURVIVAL IN BUSINESS

| | |
|---|---|
| The Complete Book of Corporate Forms (2E) | $29.95 |
| The Complete Hiring and Firing Handbook | $19.95 |
| The Complete Limited Liability Kit | $24.95 |
| The Complete Partnership Book | $24.95 |
| The Complete Patent Book | $26.95 |
| The Complete Patent Kit | $39.95 |
| The Entrepreneur's Internet Handbook | $21.95 |
| The Entrepreneur's Legal Guide | $26.95 |
| Financing Your Small Business | $16.95 |
| Fired, Laid-Off or Forced Out | $14.95 |
| Form Your Own Corporation (5E) | $29.95 |
| The Home-Based Business Kit | $14.95 |
| How to Buy a Franchise | $19.95 |
| How to Form a Nonprofit Corporation (3E) | $24.95 |
| How to Register Your Own Copyright (5E) | $24.95 |
| HR for Small Business | $14..95 |
| Incorporate in Delaware from Any State | $26.95 |
| Incorporate in Nevada from Any State | $24.95 |
| The Law (In Plain English)® for Restaurants | $16.95 |
| The Law (In Plain English)® for Small Business | $19.95 |
| The Law (In Plain English)® for Writers | $14.95 |
| Making Music Your Business | $18.95 |
| Minding Her Own Business (4E) | $14.95 |
| Most Valuable Business Legal Forms You'll Ever Need (3E) | $21.95 |
| Profit from Intellectual Property | $28.95 |
| Protect Your Patent | $24.95 |
| The Small Business Owner's Guide to Bankruptcy | $21.95 |
| Start Your Own Law Practice | $16.95 |
| Tax Power for the Self-Eemployed | $17.95 |
| Tax Smarts for Small Business | $21.95 |
| Your Rights at Work | $14.95 |

### LEGAL SURVIVAL IN COURT

| | |
|---|---|
| Attorney Responsibilities & Client Rights | $19.95 |
| Crime Victim's Guide to Justice (2E) | $21.95 |
| Legal Research Made Easy (4E) | $24.95 |
| Winning Your Personal Injury Claim (3E) | $24.95 |

### LEGAL SURVIVAL IN REAL ESTATE

| | |
|---|---|
| The Complete Kit to Selling Your Own Home | $18.95 |
| The Complete Book of Real Estate Contracts | $18.95 |
| Essential Guide to Real Estate Leases | $18.95 |
| Homeowner's Rights | $19.95 |
| How to Buy a Condominium or Townhome (2E) | $19.95 |
| How to Buy Your First Home (2E) | $14.95 |
| How to Make Money on Foreclosures | $16.95 |
| The Mortgage Answer Book | $14.95 |
| Sell Your Own Home Without a Broker | $14.95 |
| The Weekend Landlord | $16.95 |
| The Weekend Real Estate Investor | $14.95 |
| Working with Your Homeowners Association | $19.95 |

### LEGAL SURVIVAL IN SPANISH

| | |
|---|---|
| Cómo Comprar su Primera Casa | $8.95 |
| Cómo Conseguir Trabajo en los Estados Unidos | $8.95 |
| Cómo Hacer su Propio Testamento | $16.95 |
| Cómo Iniciar su Propio Negocio | $8.95 |
| Cómo Negociar su Crédito | $8.95 |
| Cómo Organizar un Presupuesto | $8.95 |
| Cómo Solicitar su Propio Divorcio | $24.95 |
| Guía de Inmigración a Estados Unidos (4E) | $24.95 |

| | |
|---|---|
| Guía de Justicia para Víctimas del Crimen | $21.95 |
| Guía Esencial para los Contratos de Arrendamiento de Bienes Raices | $22.95 |
| Inmigración y Ciudadanía en los EE.UU. Preguntas y Respuestas | $16.95 |
| Inmigración a los EE.UU. Paso a Paso (2E) | $24.95 |
| Manual de Beneficios del Seguro Social | $18.95 |
| El Seguro Social Preguntas y Respuestas | $16.95 |
| ¡Visas! ¡Visas! ¡Visas! | $9.95 |

### LEGAL SURVIVAL IN PERSONAL AFFAIRS

| | |
|---|---|
| 101 Complaint Letters That Get Results | $18.95 |
| The 529 College Savings Plan (2E) | $18.95 |
| The 529 College Savings Plan Made Simple | $7.95 |
| The Alternative Minimum Tax | $14.95 |
| The Antique and Art Collector's Legal Guide | $24.95 |
| The Childcare Answer Book | $12.95 |
| Child Support | $18.95 |
| The Complete Book of Insurance | $18.95 |
| The Complete Book of Personal Legal Forms | $24.95 |
| The Complete Credit Repair Kit | $19.95 |
| The Complete Legal Guide to Senior Care | $21.95 |
| The Complete Personal Bankruptcy Guide | $21.95 |
| Credit Smart | $18.95 |
| The Easy Will and Living Will Kit | $16.95 |
| Fathers' Rights | $19.95 |
| File Your Own Divorce (6E) | $24.95 |
| The Frequent Traveler's Guide | $14.95 |
| Gay & Lesbian Rights | $26.95 |
| Grandparents' Rights (4E) | $24.95 |
| How to Parent with Your Ex | $12.95 |
| How to Write Your Own Living Will (4E) | $18.95 |
| How to Write Your Own Premarital Agreement (3E) | $24.95 |
| The Infertility Answer Book | $16.95 |
| Law 101 | $16.95 |
| Law School 101 | $16.95 |
| The Living Trust Kit | $21.95 |
| Living Trusts and Other Ways to Avoid Probate (3E) | $24.95 |
| Make Your Own Simple Will (4E) | $26.95 |
| Mastering the MBE | $16.95 |
| Nursing Homes and Assisted Living Facilities | $19.95 |
| The Power of Attorney Handbook (5E) | $22.95 |
| Quick Cash | $14.95 |
| Seniors' Rights | $19.95 |
| Sexual Harassment in the Workplace | $18.95 |
| Sexual Harassment: Your Guide to Legal Action | $18.95 |
| Sisters-in-Law | $16.95 |
| The Social Security Benefits Handbook (4E) | $18.95 |
| Social Security Q&A | $12.95 |
| Starting Out or Starting Over | $14.95 |
| Teen Rights (and Responsibilities) (2E) | $14.95 |
| Unmarried Parents' Rights (and Responsibilities)(3E) | $16.95 |
| U.S. Immigration and Citizenship Q&A | $18.95 |
| U.S. Immigration Step by Step (2E) | $24.95 |
| U.S.A. Immigration Guide (5E) | $26.95 |
| What They Don't Teach You in College | $12.95 |
| What to Do—Before "I DO" | $14.95 |
| The Wills and Trusts Kit (2E) | $29.95 |
| Win Your Unemployment Compensation Claim (2E) | $21.95 |
| Your Right to Child Custody, Visitation and Support (3E) | $24.95 |

# SPHINX® PUBLISHING ORDER FORM

| BILL TO: | | SHIP TO: | |
|---|---|---|---|
| | | | |
| | | | |
| Phone # | Terms | F.O.B. Chicago, IL | Ship Date |

**Charge my:** ☐ VISA ☐ MasterCard ☐ American Express

☐ Money Order or Personal Check

Credit Card Number

Expiration Date

| Qty | ISBN | Title | Retail | Ext. |
|---|---|---|---|---|
| | | **SPHINX PUBLISHING NATIONAL TITLES** | | |
| ____ | 1-57248-363-6 | 101 Complaint Letters That Get Results | $18.95 | ____ |
| ____ | 1-57248-361-X | The 529 College Savings Plan (2E) | $18.95 | ____ |
| ____ | 1-57248-483-7 | The 529 College Savings Plan Made Simple | $7.95 | ____ |
| ____ | 1-57248-460-8 | The Alternative Minimum Tax | $14.95 | ____ |
| ____ | 1-57248-349-0 | The Antique and Art Collector's Legal Guide | $24.95 | ____ |
| ____ | 1-57248-347-4 | Attorney Responsibilities & Client Rights | $19.95 | ____ |
| ____ | 1-57248-482-9 | The Childcare Answer Book | $12.95 | ____ |
| ____ | 1-57248-382-2 | Child Support | $18.95 | ____ |
| ____ | 1-57248-487-X | Cómo Comprar su Primera Casa | $8.95 | ____ |
| ____ | 1-57248-488-8 | Cómo Conseguir Trabajo en los Estados Unidos | $8.95 | ____ |
| ____ | 1-57248-148-X | Cómo Hacer su Propio Testamento | $16.95 | ____ |
| ____ | 1-57248-532-9 | Cómo Iniciar su Propio Negocio | $8.95 | ____ |
| ____ | 1-57248-462-4 | Cómo Negociar su Crédito | $8.95 | ____ |
| ____ | 1-57248-463-2 | Cómo Organizar un Presupuesto | $8.95 | ____ |
| ____ | 1-57248-147-1 | Cómo Solicitar su Propio Divorcio | $24.95 | ____ |
| ____ | 1-57248-507-8 | The Complete Book of Corporate Forms (2E) | $29.95 | ____ |
| ____ | 1-57248-383-0 | The Complete Book of Insurance | $18.95 | ____ |
| ____ | 1-57248499-3 | The Complete Book of Personal Legal Forms | $24.95 | ____ |
| ____ | 1-57248-528-0 | The Complete Book of Real Estate Contracts | $18.95 | ____ |
| ____ | 1-57248-500-0 | The Complete Credit Repair Kit | $19.95 | ____ |
| ____ | 1-57248-458-6 | The Complete Hiring and Firing Handbook | $18.95 | ____ |
| ____ | 1-57248-484-5 | The Complete Home-Based Business Kit | $16.95 | ____ |
| ____ | 1-57248-353-9 | The Complete Kit to Selling Your Own Home | $18.95 | ____ |
| ____ | 1-57248-229-X | The Complete Legal Guide to Senior Care | $21.95 | ____ |
| ____ | 1-57248-498-5 | The Complete Limited Liability Company Kit | $24.95 | ____ |
| ____ | 1-57248-391-1 | The Complete Partnership Book | $24.95 | ____ |
| ____ | 1-57248-201-X | The Complete Patent Book | $26.95 | ____ |
| ____ | 1-57248-514-0 | The Complete Patent Kit | $39.95 | ____ |
| ____ | 1-57248-545-0 | The Complete Personal Bankruptcy Guide | $21.95 | ____ |
| ____ | 1-57248-480-2 | The Mortgage Answer Book | $14.95 | ____ |
| ____ | 1-57248-369-5 | Credit Smart | $18.95 | ____ |
| ____ | 1-57248-163-3 | Crime Victim's Guide to Justice (2E) | $21.95 | ____ |
| ____ | 1-57248-481-0 | The Easy Will and Living Will Kit | $16.95 | ____ |
| ____ | 1-57248-251-6 | The Entrepreneur's Internet Handbook | $21.95 | ____ |
| ____ | 1-57248-235-4 | The Entrepreneur's Legal Guide | $26.95 | ____ |
| ____ | 1-57248-160-9 | Essential Guide to Real Estate Leases | $18.95 | ____ |
| ____ | 1-57248-375-X | Fathers' Rights | $19.95 | ____ |
| ____ | 1-57248-517-5 | File Your Own Divorce (6E) | $24.95 | ____ |
| ____ | 1-57248-553-1 | Financing Your Small Business | $16.95 | ____ |
| ____ | 1-57248-459-4 | Fired, Laid Off or Forced Out | $14.95 | ____ |
| ____ | 1-57248-516-7 | Form Your Own Corporation (4E) | $29.95 | ____ |
| ____ | 1-57248-502-7 | The Frequent Traveler's Guide | $14.95 | ____ |
| ____ | 1-57248-331-8 | Gay & Lesbian Rights | $26.95 | ____ |
| ____ | 1-57248-526-4 | Grandparents' Rights (4E) | $24.95 | ____ |
| ____ | 1-57248-475-6 | Guía de Inmigración a Estados Unidos (4E) | $24.95 | ____ |
| ____ | 1-57248-187-0 | Guía de Justicia para Víctimas del Crimen | $21.95 | ____ |
| ____ | 1-57248-253-2 | Guía Esencial para los Contratos de Arrendamiento de Bienes Raíces | $22.95 | ____ |
| ____ | 1-57248-334-2 | Homeowner's Rights | $19.95 | ____ |
| ____ | 1-57248-164-1 | How to Buy a Condominium or Townhome (2E) | $19.95 | ____ |
| ____ | 1-57248-197-7 | How to Buy Your First Home (2E) | $14.95 | ____ |
| ____ | 1-57248-384-9 | How to Buy a Franchise | $19.95 | ____ |
| ____ | 1-57248-390-3 | How to Form a Nonprofit Corporation (3E) | $24.95 | ____ |
| ____ | 1-57248-520-5 | How to Make Money on Foreclosures | $16.95 | ____ |
| ____ | 1-57248-479-9 | How to Parent with Your Ex | $12.95 | ____ |
| ____ | 1-57248-379-2 | How to Register Your Own Copyright (5E) | $24.95 | ____ |
| ____ | 1-57248-394-6 | How to Write Your Own Living Will (4E) | $18.95 | ____ |
| ____ | 1-57248-156-0 | How to Write Your Own Premarital Agreement (3E) | $24.95 | ____ |
| ____ | 1-57248-504-3 | HR for Small Business | $14.95 | ____ |
| ____ | 1-57248-230-3 | Incorporate in Delaware from Any State | $26.95 | ____ |
| ____ | 1-57248-158-7 | Incorporate in Nevada from Any State | $24.95 | ____ |
| ____ | 1-57248-531-0 | The Infertility Answer Book | $16.95 | ____ |
| ____ | 1-57248-474-8 | Inmigración a los EE.UU. Paso a Paso (2E) | $24.95 | ____ |
| ____ | 1-57248-400-4 | Inmigración y Ciudadanía en los EE.UU. Preguntas y Respuestas | $16.95 | ____ |
| ____ | 1-57248-453-5 | Law 101 | $16.95 | ____ |
| ____ | 1-57248-374-1 | Law School 101 | $16.95 | ____ |
| ____ | 1-57248-523-X | The Law (In Plain English)® for Restaurants | $16.95 | ____ |
| ____ | 1-57248-377-6 | The Law (In Plain English)® for Small Business | $19.95 | ____ |
| ____ | 1-57248-476-4 | The Law (In Plain English)® for Writers | $14.95 | ____ |
| ____ | 1-57248-509-4 | Legal Research Made Easy (4E) | $24.95 | ____ |
| ____ | 1-57248-449-7 | The Living Trust Kit | $21.95 | ____ |
| ____ | 1-57248-165-X | Living Trusts and Other Ways to Avoid Probate (3E) | $24.95 | ____ |
| ____ | 1-57248-511-6 | Make Your Own Simple Will (4E) | $26.95 | ____ |
| ____ | 1-57248-486-1 | Making Music Your Business | $18.95 | ____ |
| ____ | 1-57248-186-2 | Manual de Beneficios para el Seguro Social | $18.95 | ____ |
| ____ | 1-57248-220-6 | Mastering the MBE | $16.95 | ____ |
| ____ | 1-57248-455-1 | Minding Her Own Business, 4E | $14.95 | ____ |
| ____ | 1-57248-480-2 | The Mortgage Answer Book | $14.95 | ____ |
| ____ | 1-57248-167-6 | Most Val. Business Legal Forms You'll Ever Need (3E) | $21.95 | ____ |
| ____ | 1-57248-388-1 | The Power of Attorney Handbook (5E) | $22.95 | ____ |
| ____ | 1-57248-332-6 | Profit from Intellectual Property | $28.95 | ____ |
| ____ | 1-57248-329-4 | Protect Your Patent | $24.95 | ____ |
| ____ | 1-57248-376-8 | Nursing Homes and Assisted Living Facilities | $19.95 | ____ |
| ____ | 1-57248-385-7 | Quick Cash | $14.95 | ____ |
| ____ | 1-57248-350-4 | El Seguro Social Preguntas y Respuestas | $16.95 | ____ |
| ____ | 1-57248-529-9 | Sell Your Home Without a Broker | $14.95 | ____ |
| ____ | 1-57248386-5 | Seniors' Rights | $19.95 | ____ |
| ____ | 1-57248-527-2 | Sexual Harassment in the Workplace | $18.95 | ____ |
| ____ | 1-57248-217-6 | Sexual Harassment: Your Guide to Legal Action | $18.95 | ____ |
| ____ | 1-57248-378-4 | Sisters-in-Law | $16.95 | ____ |
| ____ | 1-57248-219-2 | The Small Business Owner's Guide to Bankruptcy | $21.95 | ____ |
| ____ | 1-57248-395-4 | The Social Security Benefits Handbook (4E) | $18.95 | ____ |
| ____ | 1-57248-216-8 | Social Security Q&A | $12.95 | ____ |
| ____ | 1-57248-521-3 | Start Your Own Law Practice | $16.95 | ____ |
| ____ | 1-57248-328-8 | Starting Out or Starting Over | $14.95 | ____ |
| ____ | 1-57248-525-6 | Teen Rights (and Responsibilities) (2E) | $14.95 | ____ |
| ____ | 1-57248-457-8 | Tax Power for the Self-Employed | $17.95 | ____ |
| ____ | 1-57248-366-0 | Tax Smarts for Small Business | $21.95 | ____ |
| ____ | 1-57248-530-2 | Unmarried Parents' Rights (3E) | $16.95 | ____ |
| ____ | 1-57248-362-8 | U.S. Immigration and Citizenship Q&A | $18.95 | ____ |
| ____ | 1-57248-387-3 | U.S. Immigration Step by Step (2E) | $24.95 | ____ |
| ____ | 1-57248-392-X | U.S.A. Immigration Guide (5E) | $26.95 | ____ |
| ____ | 1-57248-178-0 | ¡Visas! ¡Visas! ¡Visas! | $9.95 | ____ |
| ____ | 1-57248-554-X | What They Don't Teach You in College | $12.95 | ____ |

**(Form Continued on Following Page)**　　　　**Subtotal** ____

To order, call Sourcebooks at 1-800-432-7444 or FAX (630) 961-2168 (Bookstores, libraries, wholesalers—please call for discount)
*Prices are subject to change without notice.*
Find more legal information at: **www.SphinxLegal.com**

# SPHINX® PUBLISHING ORDER FORM

| Qty | ISBN | Title | Retail | Ext. |
|---|---|---|---|---|
| ____ | 1-57248-177-2 | The Weekend Landlord | $16.95 | ____ |
| ____ | 1-57248-557-4 | The Weekend Real Estate Investor | $14.95 | ____ |
| ____ | 1-57248-451-9 | What to Do — Before "I DO" | $14.95 | ____ |
| ____ | 1-57248-225-7 | Win Your Unemployment Compensation Claim (2E) | $21.95 | ____ |
| ____ | 1-57248-518-3 | The Wills and Trusts Kit | $29.95 | ____ |
| ____ | 1-57248-473-X | Winning Your Personal Injury Claim (3E) | $24.95 | ____ |
| ____ | 1-57248-333-4 | Working with Your Homeowners Association | $19.95 | ____ |
| ____ | 1-57248-380-6 | Your Right to Child Custody, Visitation and Support (3E) | $24.95 | ____ |
| ____ | 1-57248-505-1 | Your Rights at Work | $14.95 | ____ |
| | | **CALIFORNIA TITLES** | | |
| ____ | 1-57248-489-6 | How to File for Divorce in CA (5E) | $26.95 | ____ |
| ____ | 1-57248-464-0 | How to Settle and Probate an Estate in CA (2E) | $28.95 | ____ |
| ____ | 1-57248-336-9 | How to Start a Business in CA (2E) | $21.95 | ____ |
| ____ | 1-57248-194-3 | How to Win in Small Claims Court in CA (2E) | $18.95 | ____ |
| ____ | 1-57248-246-X | Make Your Own CA Will | $18.95 | ____ |
| ____ | 1-57248-397-0 | Landlords' Legal Guide in CA (2E) | $24.95 | ____ |
| ____ | 1-57248-515-9 | Tenants' Rights in CA (2E) | $24.95 | ____ |
| | | **FLORIDA TITLES** | | |
| ____ | 1-57248-396-2 | How to File for Divorce in FL (8E) | $28.95 | ____ |
| ____ | 1-57248-490-X | How to Form a Limited Liability Co. in FL (4E) | $24.95 | ____ |
| ____ | 1-57071-401-0 | How to Form a Partnership in FL | $22.95 | ____ |
| ____ | 1-57248-456-X | How to Make a FL Will (7E) | $16.95 | ____ |
| ____ | 1-57248-339-3 | How to Start a Business in FL (7E) | $21.95 | ____ |
| ____ | 1-57248-204-4 | How to Win in Small Claims Court in FL (7E) | $18.95 | ____ |
| ____ | 1-57248-540-X | Incorporate in FL (7E) | $29.95 | ____ |
| ____ | 1-57248-381-4 | Land Trusts in Florida (7E) | $29.95 | ____ |
| ____ | 1-57248-491-8 | Landlords' Rights and Duties in FL (10E) | $24.95 | ____ |
| ____ | 1-57248-558-2 | Probate and Settle an Estate in FL (6E) | $29.95 | ____ |
| | | **GEORGIA TITLES** | | |
| ____ | 1-57248-340-7 | How to File for Divorce in GA (5E) | $21.95 | ____ |
| ____ | 1-57248-493-4 | How to Start a Business in GA (4E) | $21.95 | ____ |
| | | **ILLINOIS TITLES** | | |
| ____ | 1-57248-244-3 | Child Custody, Visitation, and Support in IL | $24.95 | ____ |
| ____ | 1-57248-510-8 | File for Divorce in IL (4E) | $26.95 | ____ |
| ____ | 1-57248-170-6 | How to Make an IL Will (3E) | $16.95 | ____ |
| ____ | 1-57248-265-9 | How to Start a Business in IL (4E) | $21.95 | ____ |
| ____ | 1-57248-252-4 | Landlords' Legal Guide in IL | $24.95 | ____ |
| | | **MARYLAND, VIRGINIA AND THE DISTRICT OF COLUMBIA** | | |
| ____ | 1-57248-240-0 | How to File for Divorce in MD, VA, and DC | $28.95 | ____ |
| ____ | 1-57248-359-8 | How to Start a Business in MD, VA, or DC | $21.95 | ____ |
| | | **MASSACHUSETTS TITLES** | | |
| ____ | 1-57248-115-3 | How to Form a Corporation in MA | $24.95 | ____ |
| ____ | 1-57248-466-7 | How to Start a Business in MA (4E) | $21.95 | ____ |
| ____ | 1-57248-398-9 | Landlords' Legal Guide in MA (2E) | $24.95 | ____ |
| | | **MICHIGAN TITLES** | | |
| ____ | 1-57248-467-5 | How to File for Divorce in MI (4E) | $24.95 | ____ |
| ____ | 1-57248-182-X | How to Make a MI Will (3E) | $16.95 | ____ |
| ____ | 1-57248-468-3 | How to Start a Business in MI (4E) | $18.95 | ____ |
| | | **MINNESOTA TITLES** | | |
| ____ | 1-57248-142-0 | How to File for Divorce in MN | $21.95 | ____ |
| ____ | 1-57248-179-X | How to Form a Corporation in MN | $24.95 | ____ |
| ____ | 1-57248-178-1 | How to Make a MN Will (2E) | $16.95 | ____ |
| | | **NEW JERSEY TITLES** | | |
| ____ | 1-57248-512-4 | File for Divorce in NJ (2E) | $24.95 | ____ |

| Qty | ISBN | Title | Retail | Ext. |
|---|---|---|---|---|
| ____ | 1-57248-448-9 | How to Start a Business in NJ | $21.95 | ____ |
| | | **NEW YORK TITLES** | | |
| ____ | 1-57248-193-5 | Child Custody, Visitation and Support in NY | $26.95 | ____ |
| ____ | 1-57248-351-2 | File for Divorce in NY | $26.95 | ____ |
| ____ | 1-57248-249-4 | How to Form a Corporation in NY (2E) | $24.95 | ____ |
| ____ | 1-57248-401-2 | How to Make a NY Will (3E) | $16.95 | ____ |
| ____ | 1-57248-469-1 | How to Start a Business in NY (3E) | $21.95 | ____ |
| ____ | 1-57248-198-6 | How to Win in Small Claims Court in NY (2E) | $18.95 | ____ |
| ____ | 1-57248-122-6 | Tenants' Rights in NY | $21.95 | ____ |
| | | **NORTH CAROLINA AND SOUTH CAROLINA TITLES** | | |
| ____ | 1-57248-508-6 | How to File for Divorce in NC (4E) | $26.95 | ____ |
| ____ | 1-57248-371-7 | How to Start a Business in NC or SC | $24.95 | ____ |
| ____ | 1-57248-091-2 | Landlords' Rights & Duties in NC | $21.95 | ____ |
| | | **OHIO TITLES** | | |
| ____ | 1-57248-503-5 | How to File for Divorce in OH (3E) | $24.95 | ____ |
| ____ | 1-57248-174-9 | How to Form a Corporation in OH | $24.95 | ____ |
| ____ | 1-57248-173-0 | How to Make an OH Will | $16.95 | ____ |
| | | **PENNSYLVANIA TITLES** | | |
| ____ | 1-57248-242-7 | Child Custody, Visitation and Support in PA | $26.95 | ____ |
| ____ | 1-57248-495-0 | How to File for Divorce in PA (4E) | $24.95 | ____ |
| ____ | 1-57248-358-X | How to Form a Corporation in PA | $24.95 | ____ |
| ____ | 1-57248-094-7 | How to Make a PA Will (2E) | $16.95 | ____ |
| ____ | 1-57248-357-1 | How to Start a Business in PA (3E) | $21.95 | ____ |
| ____ | 1-57248-245-1 | Landlords' Legal Guide in PA | $24.95 | ____ |
| | | **TEXAS TITLES** | | |
| ____ | 1-57248-171-4 | Child Custody, Visitation, and Support in TX | $22.95 | ____ |
| ____ | 1-57248-399-7 | How to File for Divorce in TX (4E) | $24.95 | ____ |
| ____ | 1-57248-470-5 | How to Form a Corporation in TX (3E) | $24.95 | ____ |
| ____ | 1-57248-496-9 | How to Probate and Settle an Estate in TX (4E) | $26.95 | ____ |
| ____ | 1-57248-471-3 | How to Start a Business in TX (4E) | $21.95 | ____ |
| ____ | 1-57248-111-0 | How to Win in Small Claims Court in TX (2E) | $16.95 | ____ |
| ____ | 1-57248-355-5 | Landlords' Legal Guide in TX | $24.95 | ____ |
| ____ | 1-57248-513-2 | Write Your Own TX Will (4E) | $16.95 | ____ |
| | | **WASHINGTON TITLES** | | |
| ____ | 1-57248-522-1 | File for Divorce in WA | $24.95 | ____ |

SubTotal This page ____
SubTotal previous page ____
Shipping — $5.00 for 1st book, $1.00 each additional ____
Illinois residents add 6.75% sales tax ____
Connecticut residents add 6.00% sales tax ____

**Total** ____

WITHDRAWN

To order, call Sourcebooks at 1-800-432-7444 or FAX (630) 961-2168 (Bookstores, libraries, wholesalers—please call for discount)
*Prices are subject to change without notice.*
Find more legal information at: **www.SphinxLegal.com**